D1612754

NEW DIRECTIONS IN EUROPEAN PUBLIC LAW

New Directions in
European Public Law

Edited by
JACK BEATSON and TAKIS TRIDIMAS

·HART·
PUBLISHING
OXFORD
1998

Hart Publishing
Oxford
UK

Distributed in North America
by Northwestern University Press
625 Colfax, Evanston,
Illinois 60208-4210 USA

Distributed in Australia and New Zealand
by Federation Press Pty
PO Box 45, Annandale,
2038 NSW, Australia

Hart Publishing is a specialist legal publisher based in Oxford, England.
To order further copies of this book or to request a list of other
publications please write to:

Hart Publishing, 19 Whitehouse Road, Oxford, OX1 4PA
Telephone: +44 (0) 1865 434459 or Fax (0) 1865 794882
e-mail: hartpub@janep.demon.co.uk

British Library Cataloguing in Publication Data
Data Available

ISBN: 1-901362-24-8 (cloth)

Typeset in 10pt Sabon
by SetAll, Abingdon
Printed in Great Britain on acid-free paper
by Bookcraft Ltd., Midsomer Norton, Somerset

Foreword

The origins of this book lie in two one day conferences held at St John's College, Cambridge, in 1997 under the auspices of the Cambridge Centre for European Legal Studies and its Centre for Public Law. Our aims in organising the conferences are stated in Chapter 1 and Chapter 13 deals with a number of important developments in the law concerning State Liability which occurred after the submission of the manuscript, and also deals with the judgment of the Divisional Court on 31 July 1997 in the *Factortame* saga.

We are grateful to those who attended and commented on the papers, in particular Lord Slynn of Hadley, Sir Anthony Mason AC, KBE, and Professor Sir David Williams QC, who chaired sessions, Professor Alan Dashwood, Director of the Centre for European Legal Studies, Vlad Constantinesco, Dr Yvonne Cripps, Dr Christopher Forsyth, Nicholas Forwood QC, and Professor Carol Harlow QC. Caroline Forsell, Veronica Kendall, Susan Mansfield, and Dr Angela Ward, Assistant Director of the Centre for European Legal Studies provided invaluable administrative assistance, and Peter Zawada of the Squire Law Library went far beyond the call of duty in helping to track down elusive decisions.

We are also grateful for generous support for the conferences from St John's College, Cambridge, which made it all possible, and from the partners of Herbert Smith and the Centre for European Legal Studies. Our publisher Richard Hart has been a steadfast friend of the project.

Jack Beatson
Takis Tridimas

November 1997

Contents

Contributors

John W. F. Allison is a Fellow of Queens' College, Cambridge, and Lecturer in Law, University of Cambridge.

Jack Beatson is a Fellow of St John's College, Cambridge, and Rouse Ball Professor of English Law, and Director of the Centre for Public Law, University of Cambridge.

John Bell is Professor and Dean of the Law Faculty, University of Leeds.

Paul Craig is Fellow of Worcester College, Oxford, and Professor of Law, University of Oxford.

Piet Eeckhout is Herbert Smith Professor of European Law, King's College, London.

Ivan Hare is a Fellow of Trinity College, Cambridge, and Lecturer in Law, and Assistant Director of the Centre for Public Law, University of Cambridge.

Mark Hoskins is a Barrister, Brick Court Chambers, London.

Peter Oliver is a Member of the Legal Service, Commission of the European Community.

Eivind Smith is Professor of Public Law, University of Oslo and Director of Research (Norwegian Research Council) at the Institute of Social Sciences (Oslo).

Luisa Torchia is Professor of Law, University of Urbino.

Takis Tridimas is Professor of European Law, University of Southampton, and was formerly Fellow of St. John's College, Cambridge.

Walter van Gerven is Professor of Law, Universities of Leuven and Maastricht, and was formerly Advocate General, European Court of Justice.

Table of Cases

1

Introduction

JACK BEATSON AND TAKIS TRIDIMAS

(A) FERTILISATION, CROSS-FERTILISATION AND TRANSPLANTATION

The contributions contained in this volume are based on the papers delivered at two conferences, the first on "The Liability of Public Authorities in Damages", and the second on the "Cross-Fertilisation of Concepts in European Public Law". One of our aims was to discuss the fundamentally important development in which the European Court of Justice established the liability in damages of Member States for breach of Community law, and the implications for Member States, particularly those in which, as in the United Kingdom, there has been no similar liability in national law for loss caused by *ultra vires* administrative action. More broadly, we wished to consider whether the traditional nervousness of those who endeavour to engage in comparative constitutional and administrative law is no longer so necessary, at least in a European context, and to consider the circumstances in which influence (whether by fertilisation and cross-fertilisation or transplantation) is legitimate in this context. Fertilisation and cross-fertilisation, unlike transplantation,[1] involve an external stimulus promoting a careful internal evolution within the receiving legal system, an evolution in which the receiving system may accommodate the external concept or principle to local conditions to a greater or lesser extent depending on its domestic tradition. If we are seeing a slow process of "Europeanisation" of public law, a regional version of the "globalisation" so often talked about, it becomes important to know which principles, doctrines and structures are properly susceptible to the process and which are not.

Traditional nervousness concerning comparative public law lies in a well founded perception of the typically national character of constitutional and administrative laws and the more limited number of points of comparison than in private law, particularly as between the common law systems of the British Commonwealth, which, under the influence of Dicey, denied and suppressed a distinction between public law and private law, and civil law systems for which this distinction was central. As Professor Chiti has noted, with the exception of administrative justice:

---

[1] The difference is considered by Professor Bell and Dr Allison in Chs. 11–12 *infra*.

"at the beginning of the second half of this century there were still very large gulfs separating the various legal systems   due to the almost unanimously held view that any . . . comparison was impossible, because of a lack of corresponding institutions and principles, and at times even the absence of a similar branch of the legal system".[2]

There is no doubt that as a result of European Community law and the European Convention of Human Rights public lawyers in the United Kingdom are becoming more familiar with concepts from countries with a civil law tradition and a more systematic (and separate) body of public law. And in certain areas this influence has clearly been significant, not only where Community law applies, but also by a carry-over into contexts which solely concern national law. The best known examples are the availability of interim relief against the Crown in *M v. Home Office*,[3] as a result of the decisions of the ECJ and the House of Lords in *Factortame*, and the right to restitution of *ultra vires* receipts by public authorities.[4] In both these areas, it must be said, there had been powerful critiques of the position in English law which did not rely on Community law and virtually no support for the previous position in the commentaries or in the responses to Law Commission Consultation Papers on these topics.[5] In these circumstances the effect of Community law was probably as a catalyst to assist a change for which there was much support, for reasons quite apart from Community law, both from judges and from commentators. It would be possible to envisage a similar process in the development of a general duty to give reasons, towards which English administrative law has been edging in a very cautious, and somewhat crab-like manner.[6]

But in the case of the liability of the State in damages, the position may be more complicated. In Chapter 10 Professor Torchia points to the reluctance of Italian law to take on compensation in respect of disappointed legitimate expectations. In the United Kingdom, although there is, and has been for some time, a body of opinion which has argued that it is possible to ground such liability based on common law principles favouring such liability, at least where the authority knew that it did not have the power to take the action in question,[7] there are also those who do not favour such liability as a method

---

[2] Chiti, "Administrative Comparative Law" (1989) 4 *ERPL* 11, 20. On the problems of comparison between common law and civil law in this context, see Kahn-Freund, in Cappelletti (ed.), *Nouvelles Perspectives d'un Droit Commune de L'Europe* (1978).

[3] [1994] 1 AC 377.

[4] *Woolwich Building Society* v. *Inland Revenue Commissioners* [1994] AC 70.

[5] Law Com. CP No. 120 (1991), *Restitution of Payments made Under a Mistake of Law*; Law Com. CP No. 126 (1993), *Administrative Law: Judicial Review and Statutory Appeals*. The Reports are Law Com. 227 (1994) and Law Com. 226 (1994).

[6] On the need for caution when considering convergence of procedural requirements, see Harlow, "Codification of EC Procedures: Fitting the Foot to the Shoe or the Shoe to the Foot" (1996) 2 *Eur. LJ* 3.

[7] *David v. Abdul Cader* [1963] 1 WLR 834, 840; *Farrington v. Thomson & Bridgland* [1959] VR 286; *Bourgoin SA v. Ministry of Agriculture, Fisheries & Food* [1986] QB 591. Suggestions in other decisions, which went further, have not been taken up: see the discussion in Wade & Forsyth, *Administrative Law* (7th edn., Oxford, Clarendon Press, 1994), Ch. 20.

of controlling unlawful administrative action. First, our law of tort is firmly based on the fault principle, but a finding that a public authority has acted *ultra vires* does not necessarily mean that it has been negligent. Secondly, the width of the concepts of jurisdictional error and excess of discretion, and the complex and contestable issues of statutory construction involved in determining whether a decision is *ultra vires*, point against liability.[8] Thirdly, there is concern about the potential impact of compensation on the administrative system as a whole. Professor Harlow asks whether the cost would be too great, whether unmeritorious claimants would succeed in speculative claims, and whether our public servants would be deterred from enforcing the law.[9] Behind this there may lurk a fear that such liability might have the effect that courts would, in effect, be dictating the financial priorities of government.[10] It is possible that, despite the undoubted pressure to "carry over" the principle of state liability and the arguments Professor Craig makes in Chapter 6, as he also recognises, courts in this country may be less inclined to "carry over" this body of Community law into a purely national context.[11] We have seen reluctance to "import" the principle of proportionality into the English law of judicial review partly because it is considered to involve an undue interference with the merits of decisions rather than the more limited supervisory jurisdiction,[12] and partly (and rather inconsistently) because it is thought that all that might be achieved by a concept of proportionality might be achieved by review on the ground of *Wednesbury* unreasonableness. It is for these reasons that it is important to be able to develop a principled approach to the question of influence and transplantation of doctrine in constitutional and administrative law.

We were also motivated by a third factor. While the external influences on the constitutional and administrative law of the United Kingdom are keenly felt by practitioners and commentators in this country, it is of interest to know whether the movement has all been one way, or whether English law has been able to make a contribution to other, non-common law, systems. Others have pointed to the influence of United Kingdom law in establishing

---

[8] Craig, *Administrative Law* (3rd edn., London, Sweet & Maxwell, 1994), 648–9, and see pp. 83 et seq.

[9] See Harlow, *Compensation and Government Torts* (1982), 100. See also her "Francovich and the Problem of the Disobedient State" (1996) 2 *Eur. LJ* 199.

[10] See the decisions cited at 179 n. 71 below, and, albeit in the context of judicial review, *R. v. Secretary of State for the Environment, ex parte Nottinghamshire CC* [1986] AC 240, 247; *R. v. Secretary of State for the Environment, ex parte Hammersmith & Fulham LBC* [1991] 1 AC 521, 593, 601; *R. v. Cambridge District Health Authority, ex parte B* [1995] 1 WLR 898.

[11] We are grateful to Carol Harlow and Clive Lewis who raised this point in discussion at the "cross-fertilisation" conference, although Harlow has argued that "infection" of national liability systems by the new principle is both inevitable and problematic: (1996) 2 *Eur. LJ* 199, 201.

[12] *R. v. Secretary of State for the Home Department, ex parte Brind* [1991] 1 AC 696, although note the distinction now made between the review of central government decisions and that of local government decisions, which may be subject to a requirement of proportionality: *R. v. Secretary of State for the Environment, ex parte NALGO* (1992) 5 Admin. LR 785, 799–801.

the principles of natural justice as principles of Community law[13] and the influence of "the common law approach" in matters of technique and procedure in the Community legal system.[14] In short, is there a potential market for exports as well as for imports? It would not be surprising if, given the relatively recent emergence of administrative law in the United Kingdom, there is a greater potential for the export of systems, for example, those concerning privatised utilities, than doctrines.

The liability of the state in damages, where, as noted, from a United Kingdom perspective, the process is likely to be almost exclusively one of import, is addressed in Chapters 2 to 7 and 13 (an epilogue dealing with the most recent developments). Chapters 8 to 12 are concerned with the more general question of fertilisation, cross-fertilisation and transplantation of concepts, principles, doctrines and structures in European public law.

(B) THE LIABILITY OF THE STATE IN DAMAGES

There can be little doubt that the judgments of the European Court of Justice establishing Member State liability for breach of Community law are among the most important that the Court has ever delivered. They open a new chapter in the law of remedies, they have potentially enormous economic repercussions, and they are "constitutional" in character in that they affect the core of the relationship between the Community and the Member States. In short, they belong to the same class as *Van Gend en Loos*[15] and *Costa* v. *ENEL*.[16] The next six Chapters examine various aspects of Member State liability in damages and of the cognate right to reparation of injured parties. In Chapter 2 one of us traces the development of the law and discusses in some detail the conditions of liability. The national reaction to *Brasserie du Pêcheur*[17] is considered by reference to the judgment of the Bundesgerichtshof of 24 October 1996. The judgment of the European Court of Justice in *Sutton*[18] is also examined. All in all, despite certain shortcomings in the reasoning of the Court and fact that certain areas of law remain problematic, the case law on state liability is assessed favourably.

How does the liability of Member States differ from the liability of Community institutions? In *Brasserie du Pêcheur* the Court declared that the conditions under which a Member State may incur liability for damage caused

---

[13] Brown and Jacobs, *The Court of Justice of the European Communities* (London, Sweet & Maxwell, 1989), 302, citing Case 17/74 *Transocean Marine Paint Association* [1974] ECR 1063.

[14] Wyatt, in Markesinis (ed.), *The Gradual Convergence* (Oxford, Clarendon Press, 1994), 191.

[15] Case 26/62 *Van Gend en Loos* v. *Nederlandse Administratie der Belastingen* [1963] ECR 1.

[16] Case 6/64 *Costa* v. *ENEL* [1964] ECR 585.

[17] Joined Cases C-46 and 48/93 *Brasserie du Pêcheur* v. *Germany* and *The Queen* v. *Secretary of State for Transport, ex parte Factortame* [1996] ECR I-1029.

[18] Case C-66/95 *R.* v. *Secretary of State for Social Security, ex parte Sutton*, judgment of 22 Apr. 1997.

to individuals by a breach of Community law may not, in the absence of particular justification, differ from those governing the liability of the Community in like circumstances. In the course of its reasoning the Court drew parallels between the liability of Member States and the liability of Community institutions and referred to Article 215(2) as a model for defining the liability of Member States. In Chapter 3, Professor van Gerven makes a critique of that analogy. He points out that the Court's reference to Article 215(2) in *Brasserie* is rather selective and limited in scope. The Court refers to the *Schöppenstedt* formula[19] in order to define some of the conditions of state liability but makes no reference to Article 215(2) as to the conditions and the extend of the remedy of compensation. The result is that ample discretion is left to national courts to define the conditions further, with the ensuing danger of lack of uniformity. He takes the view that the Court should work out common rules of state liability applicable throughout the Community so as to ensure uniformity in the enforcement of Community law. Such common rules must be the result of a genuine search for common general principles extrapolated from the laws of the Member States, an exercise in comparative law which so far is lacking in the case law. Professor van Gerven considers that instead of the criterion of "serious breach" adopted in *Brasserie*, it is better to adopt a more flexible standard, namely that of how a reasonably diligent authority would have acted under the circumstances. That standard would be easier for national courts to apply and would bring the extra-contractual liability of Member States and that of Community institutions closer together.

In Chapters 4 and 5, Dr Oliver and Professor Eeckhout, respectively, place state liability in the context of the various remedies available for breach of Community law. The case law of the Court of Justice on remedies seeks to strike a balance between two competing interests, namely, the need to ensure the effective protection of Community rights and the need to safeguard the procedural autonomy of Member States. There is no doubt that in recent years the scales have tilted firmly in favour of the first. The case law has gradually derived from the constitutional principles of primacy and direct effect a specific obligation on national courts to provide full and effective remedies for the protection of Community rights, if necessary by setting aside national procedural obstacles.[20] The recognition of a right of reparation for loss suffered as a result of State failure to comply with Community law is perhaps the culmination of that trend in the case law.

Dr Oliver examines a host of important, and as yet unresolved, issues. He identifies *locus standi* as one area in the law concerning the protection of Community rights in national courts in which no concrete guidelines have been formulated by the case law. He argues that the enforcement of Community rights before national courts should not be fettered by restrictive

---

[19] Case 571 *Zuckerfabrik Schöppenstedt* v. *Council* [1971] ECR 975.
[20] See e.g. Case 106/77 *Simmenthal* [1978] ECR 629; Case C–213/89 *The Queen* v. *Secretary of State for Transport, ex parte Factortame* [1990] ECR I–2433.

locus standi requirements imposed by national law. The fundamental issue of whether national law may make the action for damages subsidiary to other remedies is discussed. The liability of a Member State in damages where the wrongful act consists in the faithful implementation of a Community act which subsequently turns out to be unlawful is also examined. Dr Oliver further examines whether there is a right to interim damages in national proceedings and whether interest must be awarded as of right in an action for damages. He is critical of the judgment in *Sutton* in which the Court drew a distinction between the payment of interest on damages and the payment of interest on a social security allowance.

Professor Eeckhout's analysis concentrates on the relationship between liability in damages and other remedies before national courts for breach of Community law. The case law seems to suggest that liability in damages is an autonomous remedy. It does not operate, however, in a legal vacuum and the relationship between Community law and national law remains problematic. In *Brasserie* the Court referred to the duty of the injured party to mitigate the loss suffered. But what is the exact scope of that duty? Does it require the timely use of available remedies? May it affect the restitutionary part of a claim? As the law stands at present, the scope of the duty to mitigate is all but certain. Professor Eeckhout also refers to the need for uniformity and points out that uniformity may be achieved either through the judicial or through the legislative route.

Professor Craig and Mr Hoskins address the implications of *Brasserie* for English law. What is the appropriate cause of action for a claim based on state liability for breach of Community law? Following *Brasserie*, in its judgment of 31 July 1997 in *R. v. Secretary of State for Transport, ex parte Factortame*[21] (also considered in Chapter 13), the Divisional Court understood such liability as a breach of statutory duty. Mr Hoskins challenges that assumption. He points out that breach of statutory duty is not a tort designed specifically to deal with unlawful State acts, much less to encompass state liability arising from legislative action, an idea wholly alien to English law. A breach of Community law, he argues, does not give rise to damages in English courts because there has been a breach of the European Communities Act 1972. Rather, the duty to pay damages arises from Community law. He considers that a more orthodox approach would be to recognise the existence of a new cause of action, the tort of state liability for breach of Community law.

Similarly, Professor Craig argues that the action for breach of statutory duty could be modified to give effect to the new remedy but that the creation of a new, autonomous, cause of action would be preferable. Professor Craig's contribution also deals with whether the principles of Community law on the liability of the State in damages will influence the development of national law concerning the liability of public authorities in areas unrelated to Community law. Although

[21] The Times, 11 September 1997.

national courts are under no obligation to apply *Brasserie* in cases with no Community law component, the potential spillover effect of Community law ought not to be ignored. Professor Craig believes that lessons may be learned from the jurisprudence of the Court of Justice with regard to the development of United Kingdom law both in relation to the action for breach of statutory duty and in relation to the action for negligence. He guides us through the reasoning of the House of Lords in *X (Minors)* v. *Bedfordshire CC*[22] and compares it with the test used by the Court of Justice in *Brasserie*. The two may not be as far apart as might appear at first sight. Craig suggests, however, that the concept of serious breach, established in *Brasserie*, is richer and better worked out than its English law counterpart and ventures to outline a possible development of domestic law on liability along the lines charted by the Court of Justice.[23]

(C) CONSTITUTIONAL LAW

Turning to the more general question of fertilisation, cross-fertilisation and transplantation, in Chapters 8 and 9, Professor Smith and Mr Hare concentrate on constitutional law and the judicial review of legislation. Professor Smith reminds us that constitutions primarily depend on national phenomena and culture, and that judicial borrowings from other systems may upset the delicate balance of a particular national constitution. Although certain fundamental values of human rights have a transnational influence in democracies, external influences are always tempered by a process of acclimatisation to local conditions and the dynamism in the concepts of "fertilisation" and "cross-fertilisation" may not always be a positive influence. He notes that the influence of the United States system with its Supreme Court has led to a negative attitude to judicial review and fears of "*gouvernement des juges*". He comments that in countries which have either not suffered from dictatorship or in which dictatorship was the result of subjugation to a foreign power there is greater scepticism about the imposition of effective constitutional limits to the majority's freedom of action and more sympathy for what Professor Griffith, in his Chorley lecture, described as a "political constitution".[24]

Having dealt with the dangers, Professor Smith turns to an examination of the proper role of judicial review in a democratic society. He accepts the argument that judicial review flows as of necessity from the existence of a constitution with the status of law, noting that, although it may sometimes be difficult to distinguish an "interpretative" approach (such as that in the United Kingdom) from full blooded constitutional review with its "setting aside" of legislation, the former is not necessarily enough to protect minorities. Mr Hare points out that the argument from necessity has never been regarded as

[22] [1995] 2 AC 633.
[23] But cf Dr Allison's critique at 176–182 *infra* and our summary of it at 10 below.
[24] "The Political Constitution" (1979) 42 *MLR* 1.

sufficient, even in the United States, and that it does not always follow that where a constitution has the status of law it is the courts that ensure the constitutionality, and that there are other controls on unconstitutional legislation.

Professor Smith then considers the areas in which it is proper for there to be a limit on majoritarianism, and in which the independence of the judiciary and the strength of the judicial system in providing a procedure for contradiction and formal justification can be deployed beneficially. While the judicial method is not necessarily appropriate for broad policy issues, it is useful in ensuring that equality, tolerance and respect for individuals and minorities are considered without the compromises that are a feature of the political system. He sees judicial review and legislation not as conflicting, but rather as useful, complementary means of achieving better societies. Mr Hare, while noting that, like all catalogues of protected interests, Professor Smith's is not uncontroversial or incontestable, broadly agrees with the interests so identified, but notes that even judges are not immune from the temporary pressures of extreme circumstances. He then analyses a number of arguments for and against judicial review, including the right to participate fully in the democratic running of the country. He concludes by questioning whether a society is really more democratic and a better respecter of all rights if it places no limits on the power of its legislative majority, and rejecting the extremism of both British legislative and United States judicial supremacy.

The last part of Professor Smith's chapter discusses the importance for the legitimacy of judicial review of the extent of power to correct constitutional choices made by the judges. So he argues that, if change is in practice never open, even for qualified political majorities, judicial review becomes more difficult to defend. At a time when constitutional reform is on the agenda in the United Kingdom, this point is of fundamental importance, particularly in the context of the debate about how to incorporate the European Convention of Human Rights into our law. For if the judges have a common law right to protect fundamental rights, as some have come close to suggesting, how, given our unwritten constitution,[25] can a qualified political majority change a judicial choice that has been made?

(D) ADMINISTRATIVE LAW

Turning to administrative law and systems, we have noted some of the currents in the first part of this chapter. In Chapter 10 Professor Torchia considers both the direct and the indirect influence of Community law on

---

[25] See Sir John Laws, "Is the High Court the Guardian of Fundamental Constitutional Rights?" [1993] *PL* 59 and "The Constitution: Morals and Rights" [1997] *PL* 622; Sir Stephen Sedley, "The Sound of Silence: Constitutional Law Without a Constitution (1994) 110 *LQR* 270. Cf. Lord Irvine of Lairg QC, "Judges and Decision-Makers: The Theory and Practice of *Wednesbury* Review [1996] *PL* 59, [1997] *PL* 636.

Italian administrative law. She notes conspicuous developments in the concepts of State and public administration, where functionality is replacing the traditional Italian structural approach. She also points out that the new concern with the nature of the activity tends to break down the separation of the "public" from the "private", a process also fostered by the liberalisation and privatisation of markets. Professor Torchia notes that the growth of independent regulatory commissions has led to a reduction in the discretionary power which characterised the "control" model of the former state monopolies and replaced it with a greater concern with fairness, competition, free access to markets and transparency. Many of the features to which she draws attention have similarities to aspects of the regimes governing the privatised regulated utilities in the United Kingdom. Professor Torchia argues that the creation of Community-wide systems which rely on national enforcement are creating the complementary institutions and principles and the familiarity with alternative ways of proceeding that are necessary for the deployment of comparative analysis, either in practice or by commentators.

Chapters 11 and 12, by Professor Bell and Dr Allison, are concerned with the distinction between transplantation and cross-fertilisation and the mechanisms for cross-fertilisation. Whereas transplantation is the direct and mechanical transposition of a doctrine from one system to another, cross-fertilisation is the indirect promotion through an external impetus of careful internal legal evolution fitted to a domestic tradition. Both agree that, because administrative law is more national-specific than private law, linked as it is to political processes, cross-fertilisation is safer and more likely than transplantation. Dr Allison sees the distinction between the two as a useful way of accommodating the views of Professor Kahn-Freund and Professor Watson in their famous exchange on legal transplantation.[26]

Professor Bell gives us an overview of the different European administrative law traditions and the extent to which there are common views as to the scope of administrative law, pointing, for example, to differences in the importance of administrative organisation, the courts, and alternative dispute resolution mechanisms such as the Ombudsman in the four legal families he identifies. The principal features of convergence are said to be a convergence of values and institutional arrangements and a similarity of political agendas. Professor Bell accepts that the notion of distinct legal cultures and institutional differences as well as the different political conditions determining the relationship of citizens and the state are significant features in making legal systems distinctive but does not accept that, as some argue, these preclude convergence. He notes that there is a difference between a system's self-presentation and what really goes on and that legal cultures are neither homogeneous nor unchanging. Dr Allison notes that those who emphasise the distinctness of legal systems do so by reference to culture or tradition, whereas

[26] *Infra* 171.

those who believe in the possibility of convergence point to the significant political convergence which has taken place in Europe. Both Professor Bell and Dr Allison do not adopt the pessimistic stance on convergence that Legrand has recently taken,[27] in part because they see the heart of a legal tradition as a set of practices among a caste of lawyers rather than a more intangible cognitive world view.

As far as the *mechanisms* for convergence are concerned, Professor Bell points to the pressure from the European Community and from the European Convention and Court of Human Rights, the latter of which has led to significant legislation in the United Kingdom[28] as well as changes in administrative practice. This legislation, which resulted from litigation in the Strasbourg Court, has been one of the factors producing a general climate of increased legalisation. There has also been a convergence of terminology and the development of a common legal culture fostered by the Community and Human Rights institutions, and increased numbers of exchanges of students, academics, lawyers and judges. But he accepts the different ways in which national systems integrate Community and European Convention of Human Rights developments in order to accommodate them into national institutional and conceptual structures.

Dr Allison argues that regard must be had to three considerations if cross-fertilisation is not to degenerate into hazardous transplantation; whether domestic legal doctrine can adapt to the external influence without imperilling its functions, whether the internal adaptation can be justified in the legal and political theories underpinning the receiving system, and whether domestic institutions and procedures can cope with the proposed doctrinal adaptation. He concludes his chapter by bringing the themes of the two conferences together and taking the case of state liability as a model for potential cross-fertilisation. In this section Dr Allison argues that Professor Craig's advocacy of cross-fertilisation in Chapter 6 does not have sufficient regard to the three considerations set out above. Thus, state liability depends on a concept of the state, a concept he sees as unfamiliar to the English legal tradition. Such liability also depends on a distinction between "public" and "private", again a matter on which English law has been sceptical, a scepticism reinforced by the experience of the procedural division created by Lord Diplock in *O'Reilly* v. *Mackman*.[29] Thirdly, he argues that state liability on the ECJ's model involves greater judicial activism than English judges are accustomed to, and may involve a wider view of what issues are justiciable. He notes that English courts have been preoccupied both with avoiding the non-justiciable and with not dictating financial priorities to government.

---

[27] "European Legal Systems are Not Converging" (1996) 45 *ICLQ* 52; "Against a European Civil Code" (1997) 60 *MLR* 44.

[28] E.g. Mental Health Act 1983, ss. 72–73; Criminal Justice Act 1991, s. 34; Contempt of Court Act 1981; Interception of Communications Act 1985; Education (No. 2) Act 1986, ss. 47–48.

[29] [1983] 2 AC 237.

2

Member State Liability in Damages for Breach of Community Law: An Assessment of the Case Law

TAKIS TRIDIMAS

The judgments in *Francovich*[1] and *Brasserie du Pêcheur*[2] eminently illustrate the extraordinary influence that the Court of Justice has had in the development of Community law. The establishment of state liability for breach of Community law and of the cognate right to reparation of injured parties represents a high point in the judicial quest for effective protection of Community rights and marks a new stage in the development of the law of remedies. State liability has attracted a vast bibliography.[3] This contribution focuses on the following issues. First, it examines the development of the law and the legal basis of liability. Then it discusses in some detail the conditions of liability. It continues by examining the national reaction to the judgment in *Brasserie* and, selectively, the relationship between state liability and other remedies. It concludes by making an assessment of the judgment in *Brasserie* and related case law.

---

[1] Joined Cases C–6 and 9/90 [1991] ECR I–5357.

[2] Joined Cases C–43 and 48/93 *Brasserie du Pêcheur* v. *Germany* and *The Queen* v. *Secretary of State for Transport, ex parte Factortame Ltd* [1996] ECR I–1029.

[3] See *inter alia*, the contributions in this volume and also: T. Heukels and A. McDonell (eds.), *The Action for Damages in Community Law* (Kluwer, 1997); P. Craig, "Once More unto the Breach: The Community, the State and Damages Liability" (1997) 113 *LQR* 67; M. Wathelet and S. Van Raepenbusch, "La responsabilité des États Membres en cas de violation du droit Communautaire. Vers un alignement de la responsabilité de l'État sur celle de la Communauté ou l'inverse?" (1997) 33 *CDE* 13; W. van Gerven, "Bridging the Unbridgeable: Community and National Tort Laws after *Francovich* and *Brasserie*" (1996) 45 *ICLQ* 507; N. Gravells [1996] *PL* 567; N. Emiliou (1996) 21 *ELRev.* 399; L. Neville Brown, "State Liability to Individuals in Damages: An Emerging Doctrine of EU Law" (1996) 31 *Ir.Jur.* 7; Tridimas (1996) 55 *CLJ* 412. For earlier contributions, see W. van Gerven, "Non-Contractual Liability of Member States, Community Institutions and Individuals for Breaches of Community Law with a View to Common Law for Europe" (1994) 1 *MJ* 6; P. Craig, "*Francovich*, Remedies and the Scope of Damages Liability" (1993) 109 *LQR* 595; C. Lewis and S. Moore, "Duties, Directives and Damages in European Community Law" [1993] *PL* 151.

THE LEGAL BASIS OF LIABILITY

The EC Treaty is silent on the issue whether Member States may be liable in damages to injured parties for breach of Community law. Traditionally, it was accepted that the matter was governed by national law. In its case law under Article 169, the Court repeatedly pointed out that a judgment finding an infringement of Community law may serve as the basis of liability that a Member State may incur under national law as a result of its infringement against private parties.[4] In *Russo* v. *AIMA*,[5] decided in 1976, an Italian producer claimed that he had suffered loss as a result of action by the Italian intervention agency which made available in the market products at prices lower than those guaranteed to producers by Community agricultural regulations. The Court held that under Community law a producer may claim that he should not be prevented from obtaining a price approximating to the target price and in any event not lower than the intervention price. It then stated that it was for the national court to decide, on the basis of the facts of each case, whether an individual producer has suffered damage. If damage had been caused through an infringement of Community law, the State was liable to the injured party in accordance with the provisions of national law on the liability of public authorities.[6] The traditional approach of the Court towards remedies was encapsulated in a dictum, made in *Rewe* v. *Hauptzollamt Kiel* in 1981, that the EC Treaty "was not intended to create new remedies".[7]

The issue of liability for breach of Community law was not addressed again by the Court until 1991.[8] In its seminal judgment in *Francovich*,[9] the Court established that a Member State may be liable in damages to an injured party for breach of Community law. The case concerned loss arising as a result of failure by a Member State to implement a directive. The Court based liability on two grounds: the principle of effectiveness and Article 5 EC. Its reasoning is instructive of the way it interprets the Treaty and of the way it understands its function in developing Community law. It first recalled that Community law gives rise to rights for individuals which become part of their legal heritage and that such rights arise not only where they are expressly provided in the Treaty but also by virtue of obligations which the Treaty imposes

---

[4] See e.g. Case 39/72 *Commission* v. *Italy* [1973] ECR 101, para. 11; Case 154/85 *Commission* v. *Italy* [1987] ECR 2717, para. 6.

[5] Case 60/75 *Russo* v. *AIMA* [1976] ECR 45.

[6] *Ibid.*, paras. 8–9. See also Case 181/82 *Roussel* [1983] ECR 3849 and the earlier dicta in Case 101/78 *Granaria* v. *Hoofdproductschap voor Akkerbouwprodukten* [1979] ECR 623, para. 14.

[7] Case 158/80 [1981] ECR 1805, para. 44.

[8] The question whether liability in damages may arise for breach of Community law by national administrative measures was referred in Case 380/87 *Enichem Base and Others* v. *Comune di Cinisello Balsamo* [1989] ECR 2491. The Court did not examine that question as it was not necessary to do so in the light of its reply to the other questions referred. The issue of damages as a remedy for breach of the Equal Treatment Directive was discussed briefly by van Gerven AG in Case C–188/89 *Foster and Others* v. *British Gas* [1990] ECR I–3301, at 3341.

[9] *Supra* n. 1.

on a clearly defined manner on Member States. It also stated that national courts must provide full protection to rights which Community law confers on individuals. It then continued:[10]

> "The full effectiveness of Community rules would be impaired and the protection of the rights which they grant would be weakened if individuals were unable to obtain redress when their rights are infringed by a breach of Community law for which a Member State can be held responsible.
>
> The possibility of obtaining redress from a Member State is particularly indispensable where, as in this case, the full effectiveness of Community rules is subject to prior action on the part of the State and where, consequently, in the absence of such action, individuals cannot enforce before the national courts the rights conferred upon them by Community law.
>
> It follows that the principle whereby a State must be liable for loss and damage caused to individuals as a result of breaches of Community law for which the State can be held responsible is inherent in the system of the Treaty."

The Court found a further basis of liability in Article 5, stating that among the measures which Member States must take to ensure fulfilment of their obligations, as required by Article 5, is the obligation to nullify the unlawful consequences of a breach of Community law.

The question may well be asked what changed between 1981, when the Court declared that the Treaty is not intended to create new remedies, and 1991 when the Court proclaimed that state liability in damages "is inherent in the system of the Treaty". Why did the Court take such a fundamentally different approach in *Francovich* than it had taken in previous years? The answer may be found only if one looks at the development of the case law on judicial remedies as a whole. In the early 1990s the case law moved from an approach based on rights to an approach based on remedies. Establishment of state liability in damages is the high point in the evolution of the principle of primacy from a general principle of constitutional law to a specific obligation on national courts to provide full and effective remedies for the protection of Community rights.[11] It has been noted that the principles of direct and indirect effect of directives were developed in the light of persistent failures by Member States to fulfil their obligations as expedients with a view to securing the enforcement of Community law.[12] *Francovich* could be seen as another

---

[10] *Ibid.*, paras. 33–35.

[11] Traces of the Court's approach in *Francovich* can already be found in the Opinion of the AG in *Russo* v. *AIMA*. Reischl AG stated that the issue of Member State liability was one for the national courts in accordance with the national legal system. He added however that, in order to avoid the risk of unequal treatment of individuals under the national legal system which applied to them, it was necessary to work out principles, as the Court had done in other cases, upon which a uniform and effective enforcement of Community rights could be established. *Russo* v. *AIMA, supra* n. 5, 62.

[12] J. Steiner, "From Direct effects to *Francovich*: Shifting Means of Enforcement of Community Law" (1993) 18 *ELRev.* 3, at 10. That view received judicial recognition by Léger AG in Case C–5/94 *The Queen* v. *Ministry of Agriculture, Fisheries and Food, ex parte Hedley Lomas (Ireland) Ltd* [1996] ECR I–2553, at 2575.

such "expedient". This analysis is correct but does not give the whole picture. It is an implicit premise in every legal system that the courts which are entrusted with upholding its laws must avoid consequences which would undermine its fundamental presuppositions. Viewed in that perspective, direct effect and state liability in damages can be seen merely as the means to achieve results or, to put it in a different way, as the directed use of judicial power. Such an analysis, however, is one-sided and liable to give the impression that judicial developments occur in a theoretical vacuum. That is not the case. The Court's approach can be encapsulated in the principle *ubi jus, ibi remedium*. According to this approach, the value of a right is determined by the legal consequences which ensue from its violation, namely the remedies available from its enforcement. The common thread underlying the Court's case law on remedies is the concern to ensure the availability of effective judicial protection. Such reasoning is by no means unique to the Community judicature. In his dissenting judgment in *Bourgoin*,[13] Oliver LJ (as he then was) followed a similar approach. At the risk of becoming "too metaphysical", he distinguished between a general right to have the provisions of the law observed, shared by everyone, and an individual right requiring protection. He then continued:

> "It is only when the breach of the public duty inflicts loss or damage on the individual that he has, as an individual, a cause of complaint. *If the law gives him no remedy for that damage then he would not ordinarily be said to have any 'individual right'*."[14]

In *Francovich* the Court viewed state liability as the natural consequence of the breach of individual rights granted by Community law.

The next step came in *Brasserie du Pêcheur and Factortame*.[15] In *Brasserie du Pêcheur*, a French company was forced to discontinue exports of beer to Germany because the German authorities considered that the beer it produced did not satisfy the requirements of German law. Earlier, in the *Beer case*[16] the Court had found in enforcement proceedings brought by the Commission that German law infringed Article 30 in two respects: (a) by prohibiting the marketing under the designation "beer" of beers lawfully produced in other Member States by different methods (the designation prohibition), and (b) by prohibiting the importation of beers containing additives (the additives prohibition). The French company brought an action for reparation of the loss that it suffered as a result of the import restrictions. In *Factortame*, the applicants sought to recover the loss that they incurred as a result of the registration conditions imposed by the Merchant Shipping Act 1988, which in

---

[13] *Bourgoin SA* v. *Ministry of Agriculture* [1986] 3 All ER 585.
[14] *Ibid.*, at 616, emphasis added.
[15] *Supra* n. 2.
[16] Case 178/84 *Commission* v. *Germany* [1987] ECR 1227.

previous proceedings had been found by the Court to be incompatible with Article 52 of the Treaty.[17]

The difference between *Francovich* and *Brasserie du Pêcheur* is that, whereas the former concerned liability arising from inaction, the latter concerned liability arising from an act of the national legislature. The Court did not find that to be a material difference. It held that, since the principle of state liability is inherent in the system of the Treaty, it "holds good for any case in which a Member State breaches Community law, whatever be the organ of the State whose act or omission was responsible for the breach".[18] It follows that a Member State is liable irrespective of whether the breach which gave rise to the damage is attributable to the legislature, the judiciary or the executive. The Court rejected the argument submitted by some Member States that, where a provision is directly effective, it is unnecessary to provide individuals who are affected by its breach with a right to reparation. It pointed out that direct effect cannot secure for individuals in every case the benefit of the rights conferred upon them by Community law nor can it avoid their sustaining damage as a result of a breach of Community law attributable to a Member State. The right of reparation is "the necessary corollary" rather than a substitute for direct effect.[19]

In *Brasserie*, the German government argued that a general right of reparation for individuals could be created only by legislation and that for such a right to be recognised by judicial decision would be incompatible with the allocation of powers between the Community institutions and Member States. Dismissing that argument, the Court held that the existence and extent of state liability for breach of Community law are questions of interpretation of the Treaty which fall within the jurisdiction of the Court. Referring to Article 164, it stated that since the Treaty contains no provision governing the consequences of breaches of Community law by Member States, it is for the Court to rule on such questions, in accordance with general principles of interpretation, by reference in particular to the fundamental principles of the Community legal system and, where necessary, legal principles common to the legal systems of the Member States.[20] That reasoning is indicative of the way the Court approaches Article 164 and understands its function in the development of Community law.

The extension of state liability to cases where a breach of Community law is the result of action by the national legislature was to be expected. Once the principle of state liability in damages was established in *Francovich*, there was no longer any valid reason why such liability should be restricted only to cases where a Member State had failed to take implementing measures to transpose

---

[17] See Case C–221/89 *Factortame II* [1991] ECR I–3905, Case C–246/89 *Commission* v. *United Kingdom* [1991] ECR I–4585.

[18] *Brasserie du Pêcheur*, *supra* n. 2, para. 32.

[19] *Ibid.*, para. 22.

[20] *Ibid.*, para. 27.

a directive into national law. However, the basis of state liability arising as a result of acts of the legislature is not identified with sufficient clarity in *Brasserie*. That basis is to be found in the distinct nature of Community law and in the principle of primacy. It is not based in principles common to the laws of the Member States as the Court implied. As Leger AG stated in *Hedley Lomas*, with regard to state liability arising from acts of the legislature "there are no general principles which are *truly common* to the Member States".[21]

THE CONDITIONS OF LIABILITY: AN OVERVIEW

The Court has repeatedly emphasised that the conditions which must be fulfilled in order for state liability to arise differ depending on the nature of the breach of Community law giving rise to the damage.[22] An attempt was made in *Dillenkofer*, however, to unify the conditions of liability and, as a general rule, the following conditions must be fulfilled:[23]

— the rule of law infringed must be intended to confer rights to individuals;
— the breach must be sufficiently serious;
— there must be a direct causal link between the breach of the obligation resting on the State and the damage sustained by the injured party.

So far, the Court has examined the following types of breach: failure to transpose a directive into national law; breach of a Treaty provision by the national legislature; breach of a Treaty provision by the national administration; and incorrect transposition of a directive into national law. These types of breach will be examined in turn in the sections that follow. It should be noted at this stage that the existence of a direct causal link[24] is a condition of liability common to all types of breach, on which the Court has not given specific guidelines. The Court has held that it is for the national court to determine whether there is a direct causal link between the breach of Community law and the damage sustained by the injured parties.[25] That reference is somewhat ambiguous. It must be accepted that it is for the national court to establish whether on the facts there is a causal link but the rules governing causation should not be left entirely to national law. That would amount to

---

[21] *Hedley Lomas, supra* n. 12, at 2579 (emphasis in the original) and see infra, pp. 23–24.
[22] See e.g. *Francovich, supra* n. 1, para. 35; *Brasserie, supra* n. 2, para. 31.
[23] Joined Cases C–178, 179, 188–190/94 *Dillenkofer and others* v. *Federal Republic of Germany* [1996] ECR I–4845, paras. 21–24. See also Joined Cases C–283, 291 and 292/94 *Denkavit Internationaal BV and others* v. *Bundesamt für Finanzen* [1996] ECR I–5063, para. 48.
[24] The term "direct" did not appear in *Francovich* where the Court referred to the "existence of a causal link": *supra* n. 1, para. 40. It was added in *Brasserie* and has appeared since in subsequent cases.
[25] *Brasserie, supra* n. 2, para. 65; *Hedley Lomas, supra* n. 12, para. 30.

a "re-nationalisation" of the conditions of liability. One would expect that subsequent case law will provide guidelines regarding the requirement of causation. In fact, as Professor Van Gerven has noted, it is surprising that the Court did not refer in the context of state liability to the principles governing causation laid down in its case law under Article 215(2).[26]

FAILURE TO TRANSPOSE A DIRECTIVE INTO NATIONAL LAW

Where a Member State fails to take implementing measures in order to transpose a directive into national law, the conditions of liability are the following:

(1) the result prescribed by the directive must entail the grant of rights to individuals;

(2) it must be possible to identify the content of those rights on the basis of the provisions of the directive, and

(3) there must exist a causal link between the breach of the State's obligation and the harm suffered by the injured parties.

Those conditions were laid down in *Francovich*[27] and, subsequently, reiterated in *Dillenkofer*,[28] a case which arose from Germany's failure to implement Directive 90/314 on Package Travel.[29] Directive 90/314 seeks to protect the purchaser of package travel in the event of the insolvency of the travel operator and, to that effect, Article 7 provides that the organiser or retailer of package travel must provide the consumer with "sufficient evidence of security for the refund of money paid over and for the repatriation of the consumer in the event of insolvency". The Directive required implementation by 31 December 1992 but it was not implemented in Germany until 1994. The applicants were purchasers of package tours who, following the insolvency of their tour operators in 1993, either never left for their destination or incurred expenses to return home. Having failed to obtain reimbursement of the sums paid to the operators or the repatriation expenses, they sought compensation

[26] See W. van Gerven, *infra* p. 38.

[27] In *Francovich* the Court drew a distinction between provisions which are sufficiently precise and unconditional so as to be able to produce direct effect and provisions which, although they lack sufficient precision for the purposes of direct effect, are nonetheless capable of giving rise to a right to reparation. The right to reparation is therefore a co-relative right, separate in law from direct effect. The provisions of Directive 80/987 in issue in *Francovich* were sufficiently precise with regard to the identity of the right holder and the content of the right but not with regard to the persons on whom the corresponding obligation was imposed. The right granted by the directive was therefore incomplete. The right to reparation however was complete since there can be no doubt about the identity of the person on whom the obligation to implement a directive is imposed. That obligation burdens *ex hypothesi* the State.

[28] *Supra* n. 23.

[29] Council Directive 90/314/EEC on package travel, package holidays and package tours [1990] OJ L158/59.

from the German State on the ground that, if Germany had implemented the Directive within the prescribed time-limit, they would have been protected against the insolvency of the tour operators.

In *Dillenkofer* it was argued by several governments that a State may incur liability for late transposition of a directive only where there has been a serious breach of Community law. The Court declined to accept that argument. It stated that failure of a Member State to implement a directive within the prescribed period is *per se* a serious breach and, consequently, it gives rise to a right of reparation for individuals subject to the conditions of liability provided for in *Francovich*. No other condition need be taken into consideration.[30] In particular, liability does not depend on the circumstances which caused the period of transposition to be exceeded. Also, liability does not depend on the prior finding by the Court of an infringement of Community law attributable to the State nor on the existence of intentional fault or negligence on the part of the State.[31] The Court proceeded to examine whether the first two conditions of liability provided for in *Francovich* were fulfilled in relation to the Package Travel Directive and found that Article 7 of the Directive entailed the grant to package travellers of rights the content of which was sufficiently identifiable.

Despite the generality of the judgment in *Dillenkofer*, which appears to recognize no exceptions, the question may be asked whether there may be circumstances in which failure to transpose a directive within the prescribed period does not in itself constitute a serious breach. The following cases may be examined.

Transposition through existing legislation. Where a Member State does not transpose a directive on the assumption that existing national legislation already complies with its provisions,[32] and subsequently it transpires that the existing legislation does not satisfy the requirements of the directive because the State misinterpreted the directive, it is submitted that liability should not be automatic.[33] That case should be equated with the situation where a Member State implements a directive incorrectly and should be subject, *mutatis mutandis*, to the same conditions of liability. It will be necessary therefore to establish that the error of interpretation committed by the Member State constitutes a serious breach.[34] The position is different where a Member State fails to comply with a directive not because it misunderstood the meaning of the directive but because it misunderstood the meaning of the existing national legislation. In such a case, the breach should be taken to be

---

[30] *Dillenkofer, supra* n. 23, para. 27.

[31] *Ibid.,* para. 28.

[32] The case law accepts that, subject to certain safeguards, where national law already complies with the requirements of a directive, a Member State need not take implementing measures. See e.g. Case 29/84 *Commission v. Germany* [1985] ECR 1661.

[33] For an example of unsuccessful transposition by existing legislation, see Case C–334/92 *Wagner Miret* [1993] ECR I–6911.

[34] See *infra* p. 25, the *BT case* and the guidelines given by the Court there.

serious since it is the responsibility of the Member State to ensure that its legislation complies with the requirements of directives.[35]

Failure to implement attributable to a Community institution. Where the implementation of a Community measure (e.g. an agricultural regulation) by the national authorities is subject to prior action by the Commission and the latter has failed to take the requisite action, it may be argued that the failure to implement is not attributable to the State but to the Commission. Any loss suffered therefore by an individual may not be causally linked to the State's but to the Commission's inaction. Whether such a defence may succeed will depend on the circumstances and on the obligations incumbent on the State in such a case.

Illegality of directive as defence. May a State plead as a defence in an action for damages against it that the unimplemented directive is vitiated by illegality? Examination of this question falls beyond the scope of this paper. Suffice it to say that one of the considerations to be taken into account is that a Community measure is voidable and not void, in that it can be annulled by the Court of Justice or the Court of First Instance only if it is challenged via certain procedural routes by an applicant having *locus standi* within the specified time-limit. A Member State which considers that a directive has been adopted in violation of an essential procedural requirement but does not bring an action for its annulment within the time-limit provided for in Article 173 and chooses instead not to implement it, may not necessarily succeed in pleading procedural impropriety as a defence in an action for damages brought against it by an individual. Since the directive was not annulled, it continues to produce legal effects. In any event, even if it had been annulled in proceedings under Article 173, the Court might have declared its effects definitive pursuant to Article 174. In such a case there would be an obligation on Member States to implement it. The individual's right to reparation should not depend on whether the State was diligent enough to seek clarification of the status of the directive by bringing an action for annulment.

BREACH OF COMMUNITY LAW AS A RESULT OF ACTION BY THE NATIONAL LEGISLATURE

In *Brasserie* the Court modelled the liability of Member States for breach of Community law on the liability of the Community institutions. Such an approach had been advocated by Mischo AG in *Francovich* but the judgment did not follow his view. This is probably because the breach in issue, namely failure to implement a directive, was of such a nature that it was not necessary for the Court to draw an analogy with Article 215(2). In *Brasserie* the Court stated that the conditions under which a State may incur liability to

---

[35] In such circumstances the question may arise which organ of the State is responsible for the breach, namely the legislature or the judiciary.

individuals for breach of Community law may not, in the absence of particular justification, differ from those governing the liability of the Community in like circumstances.[36] It then referred to its case law under Article 215(2) and stated that the strict approach which it has taken in relation to the liability of the Community institutions for legislative measures is justified by two considerations. First, the exercise of the legislative function must not be hindered by the prospect of actions for damages. The second reason follows from the first. It is in the public interest that, in taking policy decisions, the legislature must enjoy ample discretion. It follows that in a legislative context characterised by the exercise of a wide discretion, which is essential for implementing a Community policy, the Community may not incur liability unless the institution concerned has manifestly and gravely disregarded the limits on the exercise of its powers (*Schöppenstedt* test).[37] Turning to state liability, the Court held that where the breach emanates from the national legislature in circumstances where the legislature has wide discretion comparable to that of the Community institutions in implementing Community policies, Community law confers a right of reparation where three conditions are fulfilled:[38]

(1) the rule of law infringed must be intended to confer rights on individuals;
(2) the breach must be sufficiently serious;
(3) there must be a direct causal link between the breach of the obligation resting on the State and the damage sustained by the injured parties.

The Court stated that those conditions satisfy the need to ensure that Community provisions are fully effective and also that they correspond in substance to the conditions which must be satisfied in order for liability to arise on the part of the Community institutions as a result of legislative action.[39] In *Brasserie* the Court stated that the three conditions referred to above are necessary and sufficient to found state liability. It left open the possibility that liability may be incurred under less strict conditions on the basis of national law.[40] Presumably that possibility exists not only in relation to liability arising as a result of a breach by the national legislature but also in relation to liability arising from other types of breach.

For the first condition of liability specified above to be satisfied, it suffices that a provision is intended to confer rights on individuals. The fact that it may be designed to protect general, as opposed to individual, interests does

---

[36] *Brasserie, supra* n. 2, para. 42.
[37] See the test laid down in Case 5/71 *Zuckerfabrik Schöppenstedt* v. *Council* [1971] ECR 975, para. 11 as refined in Joined Cases 83/76, 94/76, 4/77 and 40/77 *HNL and Others* v. *Council and Commission* [1978] ECR 1209, paras. 5 and 6.
[38] *Brasserie, supra* n. 2, para. 51.
[39] *Ibid.*, paras. 52–53.
[40] *Ibid.*, para. 66.

not prevent the provision from being for the protection of individuals for the purposes of the right to reparation.[41] The first condition laid down in *Brasserie* is similar to the first two conditions of liability laid down in *Francovich* despite the fact that the Court used different language. There seems to be no reason why failure to implement a directive should be distinguished in this respect from breach of a Treaty provision by an act of the national legislature. The material requirement is the same, namely, that the rule of Community law in issue must be intended to confer rights on individuals. The reason the Court used different language in its judgments seems to be that it sought to emphasise different points. In *Francovich* it was material to distinguish between the right to reparation and direct effect.[42] By contrast, it was not necessary to draw such a distinction in *Brasserie*. In practice, the distinction between provisions which are directly effective and those which fall short of direct effect but intend to give rights to individuals seems to be more important in the case of failure to implement directives than in the case of Treaty provisions.

The most important condition of liability is the second one laid down in *Brasserie*. The extent of state liability will depend mostly on the interpretation to be given to the term "sufficiently serious". Drawing a parallel with the liability of the Community institutions under Article 215(2), the Court stated that the decisive test for finding that a breach of Community law is sufficiently serious is whether the Member State concerned manifestly and gravely disregarded the limits of its discretion.[43] The Court listed the following factors as being material in determining whether the infringement passes the threshold of seriousness:[44]

— the clarity and precision of the rule breached;
— the measure of discretion left by that rule to the national authorities;
— whether the infringement and the damage caused was intentional or involuntary;
— whether any error of law was excusable or inexcusable;
— the fact that the position taken by a Community institution may have contributed towards the omission;
— the adoption or retention of national measures or practices contrary to Community law.

In any event, a breach of Community law will be sufficiently serious if it has persisted despite a judgment which establishes the infringement in question or a preliminary ruling or settled case law of the Court on the matter from which it is clear that the conduct in question constitutes an infringement.[45]

---

[41] *Ibid.*, 1107, *per* Tesauro AG. This applies not only to Treaty provisions but also to provisions of directives. See *Dillenkofer, supra* n. 23, paras. 36–39.
[42] *Supra* n. 27.
[43] *Brasserie, supra* n. 2, para. 55.
[44] *Ibid.*, para 56.
[45] *Ibid.*, para. 57.

The notion of serious breach incorporates the notion of "fault". The Court stated that the obligation to make reparation cannot be made dependent on any notion of fault going beyond that of a sufficiently serious breach. Given that the notion of "fault" does not have the same meaning in the laws of the Member States,[46] the Court was keen to avoid reliance on concepts of national law which might lead to the right of reparation being subject to different conditions in the national legal systems.

In its judgment, the Court proceeded to give more specific guidelines with regard to the cases in issue. In relation to *Brasserie*, the Court drew a distinction between the provisions of German law prohibiting the marketing as beer of beverages which did not conform to the purity laws and those prohibiting the import of beers containing additives. With regard to the first, the Court held that it would be difficult to regard the breach of Article 30 as an excusable error, since the incompatibility of the purity requirements with Article 30 was manifest in the light of earlier case law. By contrast, in the light of the existing case law, the criteria available to the national legislature to determine whether the prohibition of the use of additives was contrary to Community law was significantly less conclusive until the judgment in the *Beer case*.

The Court also gave guidelines with regard to the situation in *Factortame*. It stated that different considerations apply to the provisions of the Merchant Shipping Act 1988 making registration of fishing vessels subject to the requirement of nationality and those imposing residence and domicile requirements for vessel owners and operators. The requirement of nationality constitutes direct discrimination manifestly contrary to Community law. The breach committed therefore by imposing that requirement is sufficiently serious. In assessing whether the requirements imposing residence and domicile are sufficiently serious the national court may take into account, *inter alia*, the particular features of the common fisheries policy, the attitude of the Commission, which made its position known to the United Kingdom in good time, and the assessments of the state of certainty of Community law made by the national courts in the interim proceedings brought by individuals affected by the Merchant Shipping Act. A further consideration to be taken into account is whether the United Kingdom failed to adopt immediately the measures needed to comply with the Order of the President of the Court made in proceedings for interim measures requested by the Commission.[47]

A CRITIQUE OF THE COURT'S REASONING

The notion of "serious breach" provides a flexible tool for the development of state liability in damages. However, the comparison drawn between the

---

[46] *Brasserie, supra* n. 2, para. 76. See further Craig, *infra* Chap. 6.
[47] Case 246/89 R *Commission* v. *United Kingdom* [1989] ECR 3125.

liability of Member States and the liability of Community institutions for legislative acts is not necessarily accurate. The *Schöppenstedt* formula has been developed by the Court in its case law under Article 215(2) in relation to Community legislative measures in the field of economic policy and has been applied primarily to measures of agricultural policy. The discretion of Member States when they act within the sphere of Community law remains both in terms of its nature and in terms of its extent different from the discretion exercised by the Community institutions in the field of agricultural law. It is doubtful therefore whether the discretion of Member States can be referred to as "comparable" to that of the Community institutions.

Also, it is not clear that the conditions of state liability for legislative acts do correspond in substance to those defined by the Court in relation to the liability of the Community institutions for legislative acts as the Court stated in *Brasserie*. In its case law under Article 215(2), the Court refers to two elements in determining whether there is a manifest and grave disregard of discretionary powers: (a) the effect of the measure on individuals, in other words, the degree of harm suffered by them as a result of the measure; and (b) the extent to which the law has been violated. The first element, which is a necessary condition for the establishment of unlawfulness, refers to the nature of the damage suffered rather than to the infringement *per se*. In particular, a requirement which consistently appears in the case law is that, in order for liability to ensue, the damage alleged by the applicants must go beyond the bounds of the economic risks inherent in the activities in the sector concerned.[48] That requirement, however, does not seem to be a prerequisite for the establishment of state liability in damages.

The case where Member State liability for breach of Community law may be most akin to the liability of the Community institutions is where a Member State exercises discretion conferred upon it by Community regulations in the field of the common agricultural policy in breach of one of the fundamental principles, e.g. equality or proportionality.[49] Even in such a case however considerable differences exist as the discretion of the national authorities is confined by the relevant Community measures.

The fundamental premise of the Court's rationale in *Brasserie* was that, unless specific reasons dictate otherwise, the liability of Member States and the liability of the Community institutions must be governed by the same principles. As a starting point, that is undoubtedly correct. As the Court pointed out, the protection of the rights which individuals derive from Community law cannot vary depending on whether a national authority or a Community authority is responsible for the breach.[50] There is however a fundamental

---

[48] See e.g. Joined Cases C–104/89 and 37/90 *Mulder v Council and Commission* [1992] ECR I–3061, para. 13.

[49] Cf. Case 5/88 *Wachauf v Bundesamt für Ernährung und Forstwirtschaft* [1989] ECR 2609.

[50] *Brasserie, supra* n. 2, para. 42.

difference between the liability of Community institutions arising from legislation and the liability of Member States for breach of Community law. That
difference was identified by Léger AG in *Hedley Lomas*. The Community
institutions act as a primary legislature. In the case of primary legislative
action, liability must be imposed, if at all,[51] only in exceptional circumstances
since, as the Court pointed out in *Brasserie*, the freedom of the legislature
must not be obstructed by the prospect of action for damages. As Capotorti
AG put it in an earlier case, the "power to express the sovereignty of the
people"[52] may justify immunity of the legislature from the general rules of liability. By contrast, within the scope of Community law, Member States do
not act as primary legislatures. They are confined by the norms of Community
law which, according to the principle of supremacy, are higher ranking. As
Léger AG stated it is no longer possible to seek refuge behind the sovereign
nature of legislation.[53] Reparation for damage is the corollary of the principle of primacy which requires not only that legislation contrary to
Community law should be disapplied but also that reparation must be made
for damages resulting from its past application.[54]

It is a pity that the Court did not expressly state the different legal foundation of state liability in damages for breach of Community law. As it stands,
the reasoning of *Brasserie* is inconsistent. On the one hand, the Court declares
that the liability of Member States for breach of Community law by acts of
the legislature must be governed by the same rules which govern the liability
of the Community institutions but, on the other hand, it specifies conditions
of liability which are not fully comparable. The Court acknowledges the differences between the liability of Member States and the liability of
Community institutions only indirectly by stating that the conditions must be
the same "in the absence of particular justification"[55] and that "the national
legislature . . . does not systematically have a wide discretion when it acts in
a field governed by Community law".[56] The judgment however does not
emphasise sufficiently the differences between Community liability and state
liability for breach of Community law.

BREACH OF THE TREATY BY THE NATIONAL ADMINISTRATION

Liability will be easier to establish where a Member State commits a breach
of Community law in circumstances where it has limited discretion or no

---

[51] The legal systems of many Member States do not recognise state liability for legislative
action: this is the case for example in Italy, Germany, Belgium, Ireland, Luxembourg and the UK.
See Léger AG in *Hedley Lomas*, *supra* n. 12, at 2579.
[52] See *HNL v. Council and Commission*, *supra* n. 37, at 1229.
[53] Léger AG, *supra* n. 12, 2580.
[54] *Ibid.*
[55] *Brasserie*, *supra* n. 2, para. 42.
[56] *Ibid.*, para. 46.

discretion at all. In *Hedley Lomas*[57] the United Kingdom imposed a general ban on the export of animals to Spain for slaughter on the ground that their treatment in Spanish slaughterhouses was contrary to Directive 74/577 which requires the stunning of animals before slaughter.[58] In accordance with the general ban, Hedley Lomas was refused an export licence for a quantity of sheep intended for slaughter in a Spanish slaughterhouse. The licence was refused even though the authorities had no evidence to suggest that the slaughterhouse involved was not complying with the Directive. Hedley Lomas applied for a declaration that the refusal to issue an export licence ran counter to Article 34 and for damages. The United Kingdom authorities conceded that the refusal to issue an export licence was contrary to Article 34 but claimed that it was justified under Article 36. The Court held that recourse to Article 36 is not possible where Community directives provide for harmonisation of the measures necessary to achieve the specific objective which would be furthered by reliance upon that provision. The fact that Directive 74/755 did not lay down any Community procedure for monitoring compliance with its provisions made no difference. The Court added that a Member State may not unilaterally adopt, on its own authority, corrective or protective measures to obviate any breach by another Member State of Community rules.

On the issue of damages, the Court found that the conditions of liability laid down in *Brasserie* were fulfilled. With regard to the first condition, the Court recalled that Article 34 creates rights for individual which national courts must protect. With regard to the seriousness of the breach, it held that where, at the time when it committed the infringement, the Member State was not called upon to make any legislative choices and had only considerably reduced discretion, or even no discretion, the mere infringement of Community law may be sufficient to establish the existence of a sufficiently serious breach. The Court noted that in the circumstances of the case, the United Kingdom authorities were not even in a position to produce any proof of non-compliance with the Directive by the slaughterhouse concerned.

INCORRECT TRANSPOSITION OF A DIRECTIVE

In *The Queen* v. *HM Treasury, ex parte British Telecommunications*[59] the Court held that the conditions provided for in *Brasserie* must also be fulfilled in order for liability to arise where a Member State incorrectly transposes a directive into national law. In such a case therefore liability does not ensue automatically and it must be established that the breach is sufficiently serious. The Court held that a strict approach to state liability in the case of

---

[57] Case C–5/94 *The Queen* v. *Ministry of Agriculture, Fisheries and Food, ex parte Hedley Lomas (Ireland) Ltd* [1996] ECR I–2553.
[58] Council Directive 74/577 on stunning of animals before slaughter [1974] OJ L316/10.
[59] Case C–392/93 [1996] ECR I–1631.

incorrect transposition of directives is justified for the same reasons as those given in *Brasserie*, namely the concern to ensure that the exercise of legislative functions is not hindered by the prospect of actions for damages.

In issue in *British Telecommunications* was Article 8(1) of Directive 90/531 on the procurement procedures of entities operating in the water, energy, transport and telecommunications sectors.[60] The Court found that the United Kingdom had interpreted the Directive erroneously and, as a result, it had implemented it incorrectly, but held that the incorrect implementation did not amount to a serious breach. The Court stated that Article 8(1) was imprecisely worded and was reasonably capable of bearing the interpretation given to it by the United Kingdom in good faith. That interpretation was shared by other Member States and was not manifestly contrary to the wording of the Directive and the objectives pursued by it. Also, no guidance was available to the United Kingdom from the case law of the Court with regard to the interpretation of Article 8. Finally, the Commission did not raise the matter when the implementing legislation was adopted. It is submitted that the last consideration is of lesser importance. The fact that the Commission considers that the interpretation which a Member State has given to a directive is incorrect is not conclusive as the Commission has no power to give authentic interpretation to Community law. The most important factors seem to be the existence of case law which can offer guidance on the issue and whether the interpretation given by the Member State is reasonable.

In *British Telecommunications* the Court equated with regard to the conditions of liability the incorrect transposition of a directive with a breach of Community law by the national legislature in circumstances where it enjoys wide legislative discretion. The two cases, however, are different. In the case of the incorrect implementation of a directive, liability arises as a result of an error of interpretation. The question turns on whether that error was justifiable. Where a Member State acts in a field where it has wide legislative discretion, liability arises because the Member State exercises its discretion in a way which is incompatible with Community law.

In *Denkavit*[61] the Court found that the incorrect transposition by Germany of a taxation directive[62] did not amount to a serious breach. The Court relied on the following considerations. First, it noted that the interpretation given to the directive by Germany, which proved to be incorrect, had been adopted by almost all other Member States which had exercised the option to derogate given by Article 3(2) of the Directive. Secondly, those Member States had

---

[60] [1990] OJ L297/1. That directive has now been superseded by Directive 93/38 coordinating the procurement procedures of entities operating in the water, energy, transport and telecommunications sectors [1993] OJ L199/84.

[61] Joined Cases C–283, 291 and 292/94 *Denkavit Internationaal BV and others* v. *Bundesamt für Finanzen* [1996] ECR I–5063.

[62] Council Directive 90/435 on the common system of taxation applicable in the case of parent companies and subsidiaries of different Member States [1990] OJ L225/6.

taken the view that they were entitled to adopt such an interpretation, following discussions within the Council. Thirdly, the incorrect interpretation furthered the objective of preventing tax fraud which was compatible with the Directive. Fourthly, the case law did not provide any indication as to how the contested provision was to be interpreted.

The second point mentioned above is of interest. In *Denkavit*, to support the interpretation of the Directive given by Germany, a number of Member States referred to discussions in the Council while the Directive was being adopted. Following its previous case law, the Court held that expressions of intent on the part of the Member States in the Council have no legal status unless they are actually expressed in the legislation. It seems then that discussions in proceedings of the Council bear no consequences on the interpretation of Community measures but may be of relevance in establishing excusable error on the part of a Member State in an action for damages.

THE RIGHT TO REPARATION: THE IMPORTANCE OF NATIONAL LAW

Although the conditions of liability are provided for by Community law, the remedy of reparation is subject to national law. In *Brasserie* the Court held that the State must make reparation for the consequences of the loss caused in accordance with the domestic rules on liability, provided that the dual requirement of non-discrimination and minimum protection laid down in the *Rewe* and *Comet* case law[63] are satisfied: the conditions for reparation laid down by national law must not be less favourable than those relating to similar domestic claims and they must not be such as in practice to make it impossible or excessively difficult to obtain reparation. The Court identified two such conditions which make the exercise of the right to reparation excessively difficult and are thus incompatible with Community law.[64] The first is a condition imposed by German law, and the second a condition imposed by English law. Under German law, where a legislative act is in breach of a higher-ranking national law, for example the Constitution, a right of reparation ensues only where the applicant can be regarded as the beneficiary of the obligation breached. The Court held that such a restriction would make it in practice impossible or extremely difficult to obtain effective reparation for loss or damage resulting from a breach of Community law, since the tasks falling to the national legislature relate in principle to the public at large and not to identifiable persons or classes of person. Referring to English law, the Court held that state liability for breach of Community law cannot be made subject to proof of misfeasance in public office as such a condition would make it in

---

[63] Case 33/76 *Rewe* v. *Landwirtschaftskammer für das Saarland* [1976] ECR 1989; Case 45/76 *Comet* v. *Productschap voor Siergewassen* [1976] ECR 2043.
[64] *Brasserie, supra* n. 2, paras. 71–73.

practice impossible to obtain reparation for loss arising from breach by the national legislature.[65]

With regard to the extent of reparation, the Court held that reparation for loss or damage caused to individuals as a result of breaches of Community law must be commensurate with the loss or damage sustained so as to ensure the effective protection of their rights.[66] The language in *Brasserie* may be contrasted with that in *Marshall II* where the Court held that the compensation awarded must be such as to enable the damage sustained as a result of discriminatory treatment to be made good in full.[67] In the absence of Community provisions, it is for the domestic legal system of each Member State to set the criteria for determining the extent of reparation. The Court laid down the following guidelines:

— the national court may inquire whether the injured person showed reasonable diligence in order to avoid the loss or damage or limit its extent and whether, in particular, he availed himself in time of all the legal remedies available to him.[68]

— total exclusion of loss of profit as a head of damage for which reparation may be awarded in the case of a breach of Community law is not acceptable. The Court pointed out that in the context of economic or commercial litigation, such a total exclusion of loss of profit would make reparation of damage practically impossible.[69]

— an award of exemplary damages pursuant to a claim or an action founded on Community law cannot be ruled out if such damages could be awarded pursuant to a similar claim or action founded on domestic law.[70]

Subject to those guidelines and the general conditions laid down in the *Rewe* and *Comet* case law, the remedy of reparation is governed by national law. One may take the view that reliance on national law is a source of divergence in an area where uniformity would be beneficial. Lack of uniformity however is inevitable given that the right to reparation is an entirely judge-made right. One would expect that, as the case law develops, Community law will gradually occupy some of the area currently left to national laws.

---

[65] *Brasserie* therefore put it beyond doubt that the judgment of the Court of Appeal in *Bourgoin* is no longer good law. After *Francovich*, doubt had already been expressed about the correctness of that decision by the House of Lords in *Kirklees MBC v. Wickes Building Supplies Ltd* [1992] 3 WLR 170.

[66] *Brasserie, supra* n. 2, para. 82.

[67] Case C–271/91 *Marshall v. Southampton and South West Hampshire Area Health Authority* [1993] ECR I–4367.

[68] *Supra* n. 2, para. 84.

[69] *Ibid.*, para. 87.

[70] *Ibid.*, para. 89.

THE NATIONAL REACTION

Following the judgment in *Brasserie and Factortame*, it fell upon the national courts which made the references to the Court of Justice to determine whether the applicants' claim for damages could succeed on the facts. In its judgment of 24 October 1996, the Bundesgerichtshof rejected the claim of Brasserie du Pêcheur for damages against the State as unfounded.[71] By contrast, in its judgment of 31 July 1997 in R. v. *Secretary of State, ex parte Factortame*, the Divisional Court held that the United Kingdom had committed a serious breach.[72]

The judgment of the Bundesgerichtshof merits close consideration. The Bundesgerichtshof referred to the judgment of the Court of Justice in *Brasserie* and held that the damage suffered by the applicant was the result of the additives prohibition imposed by German law, which was not a serious breach, and not the result of the designation prohibition which constituted a serious breach.[73] It could be argued that, since German law imposed the designation prohibition, the existence of a serious breach could not be negated by the fact that it also imposed another prohibition which was not sufficiently serious. The Bundesgerichtshof rejected that reasoning. It referred to the Opinion of Tesauro AG in *Brasserie* who stated that, if the damage suffered by the applicant was causally connected with the prohibition on additives rather than the designation prohibition, the failure of the claim "could not be ruled out".[74]

It should be accepted that, where there are separate breaches of Community law, only the damage which is actually causally connected with the serious breach must be compensated. In the case of overlapping breaches one of which is serious and the other of which is not, identifying the damage which is connected with the serious breach may give rise to difficulties. It appears odd however that the Bundesgerichtshof was unable to establish causal connection between any of the damage suffered by the applicant and the designation prohibition, given that the latter was in itself sufficient to restrict the importation of its products.

The Bundesgerichtshof also rejected the claim of the applicant for the damage which it allegedly incurred after 12 March 1987, the date when the judgment in the *Beer case* was delivered. Brasserie argued that it had suffered loss of profits during the transitional period that it needed after the judgment in the *Beer case* in order to build a distribution network. The Court accepted however that the German authorities took immediate steps to comply with the judgment and held that the loss suffered during the transitional period was

---

[71] See [1997] 1 CMLR 971.
[72] See below, Chapter 13.
[73] *Supra* p. 22.
[74] *Brasserie, supra* n. 2, 1126.

the result of the previous additives prohibition which was not a serious breach.

RELATIONSHIP WITH OTHER REMEDIES

State liability remains a new remedy the full ramifications of which are still to be determined. An important area which remains largely uninvestigated is the relationship between state liability and other remedies for breach of Community law.[75] The recent judgment in *R.* v. *Secretary of State for Social Security, ex parte Sutton*[76] appears to suggest that, at least for some purposes, the right to reparation is an independent remedy which may be sought in addition to other remedies available in national courts.[77] The case concerned Directive 79/7,[78] Article 7(1)(a) of which states that the directive is without prejudice to the right of Member States to exclude from its scope the determination of pensionable age for the purposes of granting retirement pensions and "the possible consequences thereof for other benefits". In *Secretary of State for Social Security* v. *Thomas and Others*[79] the Court gave a restrictive interpretation to that derogation, holding that it was limited to the forms of discrimination existing under the other benefit schemes which are necessarily and objectively linked to the difference in retirement ages. *Sutton* came as the aftermath of *Thomas*. Mrs Sutton was refused invalid care allowance on the ground that she had reached retirement age. Following the judgment in *Thomas*, the Social Security Commissioner held that Article 7(1)(a) of Directive 79/7 could not be relied on to refuse to award an invalid care allowance to women over sixty. He awarded to Mrs Sutton the allowance with effect from 19 February 1986, i.e. one year before her application. Mrs Sutton claimed interest on the arrears of benefit on the basis of Article 6 of Directive 79/7 or, alternatively, on the basis of the principle that a Member State is liable in damages for breach of Community law. Article 6 of the Directive requires Member States to introduce the necessary measures to enable persons who consider themselves wronged by failure to apply the principle of equal treatment to pursue their claims by judicial process. Despite the similarity between that provision and Article 6 of Directive 76/207 on Equal Treatment,[80] the Court refused to transpose the principle laid down in

[75] See further the contributions of Oliver, *infra* Chap. 4, and Eeckhout, *infra* Chap. 5.
[76] Case C–66/95, judgment of 22 Apr. 1997.
[77] See also the Opinion of Jacobs AG in Case C–188/95 *Fantask A/S and Others* v. *Ministry of Trade and Industry* delivered on 26 June 1997, discussed by Eeckhout, *infra* Chap. 5.
[78] Directive 79/7 on the progressive implementation of the principle of equal treatment for men and women in matters of social security, [1979] OJ L6/24.
[79] Case C–328/91 [1993] ECR I–1247.
[80] Council Directive 76/207 on the implementation of the principle of equal treatment for men and women as regards access to employment, vocational training and promotion, and working conditions [1976] (OJ L39/40.

Marshall II[81] to the effect that full financial compensation must include the award of interest. It held that *Marshall II* concerned the award of interest on amounts payable by way of reparation for damage sustained as a result of discriminatory dismissal. By contrast, the case in issue concerned the right to receive interest on social security benefits. According to the judgment, payment in arrears of such benefits is not compensatory in nature and therefore interest on them cannot be regarded as an essential component of the right to equal treatment. The Court, prompted by the Advocate General, seems to have followed an unduly restrictive interpretation of *Marshall II* and Oliver correctly criticises that part of the judgment[82] on the ground that it runs counter to the principle of effectiveness. The Court focused on the wrong criterion, since what matters is not the compensatory or otherwise nature of the claim but the need to ensure that the effluxion of time does not deprive a pecuniary right of its substance.

Having established that Mrs Sutton was not entitled to interest on the basis of Article 6 of Directive 79/7, the Court turned to examine whether the right to payment of interest on arrears of social security benefit could be based on the principle of state liability for breach of Community law. It did not give an answer to that issue but merely repeated the conditions of liability laid down in the case law and held that it was for the national court to determine whether Mrs Sutton was entitled to reparation for the loss which she claimed to have suffered. It is significant that the Court did not exclude the possibility that interest could be obtained on the basis of state liability in damages although it was invited to do so by the United Kingdom Government. It follows that the possibility of obtaining interest on arrears of social security benefit by way of a claim in damages where the delay in payment of the benefit is the result of discrimination prohibited by Community law remains open.

CONCLUSION

What conclusions can be drawn from the case law? Overall, it can be said that the recent judgments of the Court of Justice are balanced and do not result in an unwarranted extension of state liability. Liability is easy to establish where a Member State fails to take implementing measures in order to transpose a directive into national law but much more difficult to establish in any other case. Reasonable care on the part of the national authorities in enforcing Community obligations should ensure that the State does not incur liability.

A common theme which underlies national rules on the liability of public authorities is that such liability should have an exceptional character. The rationale is not difficult to understand: in making policy decisions, legislative

---

[81] *Supra* n. 67.
[82] See *infra* Chap. 4, pp. 60–61.

and administrative authorities should be able to enjoy wide discretion and their decision-making must not be inhibited by the threat of actions for damages in case where a measure is subsequently found to be illegal. In short, liability must not be a sword of Damocles over the administration and, *a fortiori*, the legislature. There is a second reason which justifies the exceptional character of liability. Where an action in damages is successful, it is ultimately the taxpayer who is called upon to cover the costs. Viewed from that perspective, a public authority should incur liability as a result of legislative action only where the interest of compensating a group of persons who suffer loss is judged as more worthy of protection than the interest of the taxpayer. In the context of Article 215(2), the *Schöppenstedt* formula is designed to meet those concerns. With regard to Member State liability in damages, however, the balancing exercise is heavily influenced by the requirement to provide effective protection of Community rights which acquires overriding importance. The legal basis of state liability for legislative acts is to be found in the principle of primacy and not in principles common to the laws of Member States. As the law stands at present, state liability for breach of Community law arising from legislative action is subject to less strict conditions than liability of Community institutions for legislative acts. It is perhaps an irony that the Community legislature, which is less democratically accountable than the national legislatures, enjoys a greater degree of immunity.

The test of serious breach is a flexible formula which enables liability to be assessed in the light of the nature of the breach and the discretion enjoyed by the national authorities in the circumstances of the case. Although in *Brasserie* the Court of Justice gave guidelines to be taken into account in order to determine whether a breach is sufficiently serious, the task of the national courts is not an easy one. The future of the remedy will depend to a large extent on the way it is applied by national courts. A point of particular importance is that the interaction between Community law and national law is surrounded by uncertainty. Although the conditions of liability are governed by Community law, the remedy of reparation is a matter for national law subject to the limitations imposed by the Court's jurisprudence. The case law in this area seeks to strike a balance between the need to ensure the effective protection of Community rights and respect for the autonomy of the national legal systems. The Court is increasingly willing to question the compatibility with Community law of national rules pertaining to procedure and remedies in order to secure the effective protection of Community rights. That in turn puts at risk the status under Community law of an even greater number of national rules. The resulting uncertainty is an inevitable consequence of the fragmentary development of the law inherent in the process of judicial harmonisation.

The recognition of a right to reparation for injured parties goes some way towards alleviating the adverse consequences which flow from the failure to recognise horizontal effect of directives. But it does not provide a full substitute for horizontal effect for the following reasons.[83] First, horizontal effect enables an individual to use a provision of Community law not only as a sword but also as a shield, that is to say, as a defence in proceedings initiated against him.[84] Secondly, where a directive imposes an obligation on an individual, the proper defendant is, by definition, that individual and not the State. The absence of horizontal effect may lead to the plaintiff being required to bring two separate sets of proceedings, one against the private defendant and the other against the State, which "would hardly be compatible with the requirement of an effective legal remedy".[85] Thirdly, the remedy of reparation may differ from State to State because of its dependence on national law. By contrast, the content of a right which a directly effective provision confers upon an individual is uniform throughout the Community. State liability therefore should not be seen as a panacea.

---

[83] For a fuller discussion, see T. Tridimas, "Horizontal Effect of Directives: a Missed Opportunity?" (1994) 19 *ELRev*. 621 at 634–5.

[84] See, e.g., the facts in Case C–91/92 *Faccini Dori* v. *Recreb Srl* [1994] ECR I– 3325.

[85] Case C–316/93 *Vaneetveld* v. *SA Le Foyer* [1994] ECR I–763, at 775, *per* Jacobs AG.

3

Taking Article 215(2) EC Seriously

W. VAN GERVEN

In its *Brasserie du Pêcheur and Factortame*[1] judgment (hereafter the *Brasserie* judgment) the European Court of Justice (hereafter ECJ or the Court) considerably extended the principle of state liability as laid down in *Francovich*[2] by declaring the principle applicable also in a situation of breach of directly applicable Treaty provisions, and by holding explicitly that the breach may also emanate from the national legislature. In the course of its reasoning the ECJ referred to Article 215(2) EC Treaty (hereafter Article 215) which it had not wished to do in *Francovich*. Article 215 refers to the principles common to the legal systems of the Member States in order to make out if liability of the Community arises for breaches of Community law by its institutions, and their civil servants.

The reference in *Brasserie* to Article 215, and the ECJ's case law relating thereto, was made in connection with a wrong committed by the national legislature (in *Brasserie* by omission, in *Factortame* by act). In that connection the reference was meant to make use of the so-called *Schöppenstedt* formula developed in the ECJ's case law[3] to gauge the legality of measures involving economic policy choices and thus characterised by the exercise of a wide discretion. For the Court to apply the *Schöppenstedt* formula also in the context of breaches committed by national authorities when implementing or applying—or failing to implement or to apply—Community law, it had to accept that the national authorities concerned were acting in the cases at issue, that is in *Brasserie* and in *Factortame*, in a situation of wide discretion. And indeed, the Court accepted that to be the case for both the German and the UK legislature (paragraphs 48 and 49 of *Brasserie*).

In this paper I intend to demonstrate that the reference to Article 215, as a model for defining the liability of Member States under *Francovich*, is not taken sufficiently seriously by the Court, as it is too limited in scope, in breadth and in depth.

---

[1] Joined Cases C–46/93 and 48/93 [1996] ECR I–1029.
[2] Joined Cases C–6/90 and 9/90 [1991] ECR I–5357. In that case the breach of Community law consisted in the complete non-implementation of a directive within the period prescribed.
[3] For the first time in Case 5/71, *Schöppenstedt* [1971] ECR 975, para. 11.

THE REFERENCE TO ARTICLE 215 IS TOO LIMITED IN SCOPE

Let us first explore the scope of the ECJ's reference to "Article 215 case law" in *Brasserie*, as it was made in connection with breaches of Community law by a national legislature. In its judgment, the Court distinguishes three points: (1) the existence of the principle of state liability (paragraphs 16 ff.); (2) the conditions for such liability to arise (paragraphs 37 ff.); and (3) the conditions under, and the extent to, which the remedy of reparation is to be put into effect (paragraphs 67 ff. and paragraphs 81 ff.). The role assigned to Article 215 is different for each of these three points.

As for the *principle* itself, the reference is, and can only be, of an exemplary nature since Article 215 deals with breaches by Community institutions, and not with breaches emanating from national authorities. To find liability in a situation of legislative wrong by a Member State the ECJ explains that it must:

> "rule on such a question in accordance with generally accepted methods of inter-
> pretation, in particular by reference to the fundamental principles of the Community
> legal system and, where necessary, general principles common to the legal systems
> of the Member States" (paragraph 27).

The Court elicits that ruling as follows. First it states that Article 215 "is simply an expression of [a] general principle familiar to the legal systems of the member States" (paragraph 29), whereby it refers undoubtedly to the liability of national public authorities *in general* to make good damage caused by an unlawful act or omission. Then it goes on to say, turning its attention to the *specific* situation of *legislative* wrong, that the principle of state liability holds good for any breach "whatever be the organ of the State whose act or omission was responsible for the breach" (paragraph 32). The problem with the latter statement is that the Court could indeed draw inspiration from Article 215 to acknowledge the principle of state liability on behalf of all organs, including the legislature—since Article 215 applies to all Community institutions, that is including the Council and the Parliament—*but* that it could not draw inspiration from Article 215 in so far as it refers to general common principles—because it is generally not in accordance with the general princi-ples common to the laws of the Member States to recognise liability for wrongs committed by the legislature proper.[4] Therefore, to justify the exten-sion of the principle of state liability to legislative wrongs proper, the Court had, on the one hand, to play down the role of general common principles of which the Court states, as recalled above, that they will only be used "where

---

[4] As the referring courts in *Brasserie* and in *Factortame* indicated it to be the case under German and English law respectively: see Tesauro AG's Opinion in *Brasserie* [1996] ECR I–1066, at paras. 4 and 7. See further Fernand Schockweiler, G. Wivenes and J. M. Godart, "Le régime de la responsabilité extra-contractuelle du fait d'actes juridiques dans la Communauté européenne"[1990] *Rev. trim. dr. eur.* 27 ff.

necessary", and, on the other hand, to find other grounds of justification, namely "the fundamental requirement of the Community legal order that Community law be uniformly applied" (paragraph 33), *and* the rules of international law which view a State "as a single entity, irrespective of whether the breach . . . is attributable to the legislature, the judiciary or the executive" (paragraph 34).[5]

As for the *conditions for state liability to arise*, particularly in a situation of legislative wrong, the ECJ felt more at ease in referring to Article 215 stating boldly that all breaches of Community law should be treated equally regardless, "in the absence of particular justification", of whether a national authority or a Community authority is responsible for the breach (paragraph 42). To bolster that position the Court emphasises that it draws inspiration from general common principles not only in the area of Article 215 liability but also in other areas of Community law, by which it means in this connection the area of state liability (paragraph 41). For indeed, once it is accepted that the liability of Community institutions under Article 215 and the liability of Member States under *Francovich/Brasserie* are to be founded on the same general common principles, the conditions for such liability to arise must be the same under both regimes, at least in principle, that is "in the absence of particular justification".

Having said that, the ECJ enunciates three conditions to be met for Community law to confer a right to reparation:

"the rule of law infringed must be intended to confer rights on individuals; the breach must be sufficiently serious; and there must be a *direct* causal link between the breach . . . and the damage sustained by the injured parties" (paragraph 51, emphasis added).[6]

Those conditions, the Court adds,

"correspond in substance to those defined by the Court in relation to Article 215 in its case law on liability of the Community for damage caused to individuals by unlawful legislative measures adopted by its institutions" (paragraph 53).

It is not the place here to go further into the substance of these conditions. A few remarks may suffice. Seen from the perspective of national laws, and from the Court's Article 215 case law itself, it is remarkable that the Court

---

[5] To document that statement, the Court refers to the AG's Opinion (see n. 4) at para. 38 where some references are found. *Adde* Draft Articles on State Liability, art. 6, prepared by the UN International Law Commission (see the Report of that Commission on the work of its 48th session, UN A/51/10 at paras. 57–64 (1996)). The Court could also have referred to Art. 50 of the European Convention on Human Rights (ECHR).

[6] In *Francovich*, cited *supra* n. 2, the ECJ did not mention the word "direct" (see para. 40). In Joined Cases C–178, 179/, 188/, 189/ and 190/94 *Dillenkofer* [1996] ECR I–4845, the Court mentioned the word "direct" where it quoted *Brasserie* (para. 21) but not where it quoted *Francovich* (para. 22) adding nevertheless that the conditions were substantially the same (para. 23). In the dictum of *Dillenkofer*, under 1, the word "direct" was omitted again. In the Court's Article 215 case law, it is specified that the damage must be a direct consequence of the unlawful conduct: see e.g. the judgment in *Dumortier Frères* [1979] ECR 3091, para. 21.

does not, at least not explicitly, name damage or injury as a condition for liability to arise, in addition to breach and causation—even though the condition of damage is a condition under the Court's Article 215 case law in
accordance with the laws of the Member States.[7] It is also interesting to note
that the Court, in spite of its intention to interpret the liability conditions in
the light of Article 215, does not follow that up when it deals with causation,
without giving any "particular justification" for it. On the contrary, in paragraph 65 of the *Brasserie* judgment, it states that "it is for the national courts
to determine whether there is a direct causal link between the breach of the
obligation borne by the State and the damage . . . ", by which the Court probably means that it is also for national law to determine whether there is such
a causal link.[8] It is also noteworthy that the Court, in order to define the first
two conditions (i.e. that of a rule intending to confer rights on individuals *and*
that the breach must be sufficiently serious), takes account only of the
Schöppenstedt part of its case law and makes no effort whatever to take
account of its Article 215 case law as a whole. We will deal with that point
further on.

As for the conditions and the extent of the *remedy of compensation*, which
the ECJ acknowledges exists as soon as the three aforementioned conditions
are fulfilled, the Court no longer refers, again without "particular justification", to Article 215, although its case law under that Article allows much
inspiration to be drawn from it.[9] It simply says that it is for the domestic rules
on liability to determine the conditions for reparation (paragraph 67) as well
as to set the criteria for determining the extent of reparation (paragraph 83)
subject, however, in both cases to the principle of equality of treatment
between Community based and similar domestic claims and to the principle
of minimal effectiveness, i.e. that reparation must not in practice be made
impossible or excessively difficult.[10]

To conclude this point, it appears from the foregoing that the reference in
Brasserie to Article 215 as a source of inspiration to elaborate the principle of

---

[7] The conditions under Art. 215 for liability to arise are: actual damage, a causal link between
the damage claimed and the conduct alleged against the institution, and the illegality of that conduct (see for an early example: Case 4/69 *Lütticke* v. *Commission* [1971] ECR 325, at para. 10.
See further my Opinion in Case 128/92 *Banks* v. *British Coal Corporation* [1994] ECR I–1209,
where all of these conditions, including the existence of actual damage, are dealt with at paras.
50–3 with many references to the Court's case law. See also A. G. Toth's article mentioned in n.
9 below.

[8] It is, indeed, hard to believe that it would be for the national courts to construe the condition of direct causation in conformity with Community law, that is in accordance with the general principles of the national laws, and not only their own law.

[9] See again my Opinion in *Banks*, cited *supra* n. 7, at para. 54. For a thorough investigation,
see A.G. Toth, "The Concepts of Damage and Causality as Elements of Non-contractual
Liability" and A. van Casteren, "Article 215(2) EC and the Question of Interest" in T. Heukels
and A. McDonnell (eds.), *The Action for Damages in Community Law* (Kluwer Law International,
1997), 179 and 199 respectively.

[10] On the origin of these principles, see M. Hoskins, "Tilting the Balance: Supremacy and
National Procedural Rules" (1996) 21 *EL Rev.*, at 365 ff.

state liability and the conditions for such liability to arise and for the remedy of compensation to apply is, to use a British understatement, rather limited in scope. The reference is made only to help the ECJ to define two out of the three conditions mentioned (breach of a rule intending to protect individuals and sufficiently serious fault). It is not used by the Court to define the third condition (causation), nor is it used to define the notion of damage or to establish the conditions and the extent of the remedy of compensation. The result is that much room is left to the national courts to define the conditions further, which does not help to ensure the uniform application of Community law throughout the Member States, a principle which the Court has repeatedly said is a fundamental requirement of Community law.[11] It is our conviction that the ECJ should go further in making the conditions for state liability more uniform, at least if it wishes to protect individuals and enterprises in the different Member States alike or, in other words, if it wishes to maintain the uniformity of Community law also in its enforcement, provided however, as emphasised later on, that such uniformity must be the result of a genuine search for common general principles underlying the national legal systems. If the Court does not wish to use Article 215 any further than it has done so far, it must give a "particular justification" for it, as it has itself emphasised in paragraph 42 of *Brasserie* (see above).

THE REFERENCE TO THE COURT'S ARTICLE 215 CASE LAW IS TOO LIMITED IN BREADTH

As mentioned already, the Court's reference in *Brasserie* to defining the conditions of liability is limited in breadth as it relates only to the so-called *Schöppenstedt* part of the Court's Article 215 case law.[12]

Obviously, that part of the Court's case law is most important as it involves (as in *Mulder*[13]) injury caused to potentially large groups of persons, which is the case, more often than not, when, as in *Brasserie*, the exercise of a legislative function is at issue. Nevertheless, one should not lose sight of the fact that the Court has also rendered many judgments outside the *Schöppenstedt* area of application of Article 215 in connection with the liability of Community

[11] Judgment of 21 Feb. 1991, Joined Cases C–143/88 and 92/89 *Zuckerfabrik Süderdithmarschen* [1991] ECR I–415, para. 26; see also *Brasserie*, cited *supra* n. 1, para. 33 quoted above.

[12] We are not dealing herein with the Court's case law relating to Art. 188(2) EAEC, or Arts. 34 and 40 ECSC, nor are we dealing with staff cases decided under Art. 179 EC *junto* 215(4). For the non-contractual liability of the EAEC and of the ECSC see respectively L. Hancher, "Issues of Non-contractual Liability under the EAEC Treaty", and G. Behr, "The Non-contractual Liability of the European Coal and Steel Community", at 41 ff. and 71 ff. of *The Action for Damages in Community Law*, *supra* n. 9.

[13] Joined Cases C–104/89 and 37/90 [1992] ECR I–3061.

institutions for individual acts of its organs (or servants[14]), of a legal or a purely factual nature. It may be correct to say that — because of the special nature of the Community which generally considers the application of rules in individual cases to be a matter for the Member States—most of the Court's case law under Article 215 concerns acts of a general nature;[15] however, that situation has gradually been changing, since the Commission is now more involved in the daily application of general rules.[16]

An example of a judgment relating to an individual act of a factual nature is the ECJ's decision of 8 October 1986 in *Leussink-Brummelhuis* v. *Commission*.[17] In that judgment the Court had to decide claims for compensation of a civil servant of the Commission who had suffered serious physical and non-physical injuries, and of his spouse and children who had suffered equally serious non-physical injuries, as a consequence of a traffic accident caused by another civil servant of the Community who drove a car owned by the Commission. The Court, following the Opinion of Advocate General Slynn (as he then was), decided that the Commission, because it had been negligent in maintaining the car, was liable in damages to the plaintiff civil servant (but not to his spouse and children) for both categories of injury. Another even more tragic example relating to an individual (semi-factual, semi-legal) act is the case decided by the Court on 7 November 1985 in *Adams* v. *Commission*.[18] In that case the Court ordered the Commission to compensate the plaintiff who, as a consequence of giving information to the Commission on an alleged violation by his employer of Article 86 EC, suffered considerable physical and non-physical injury (resulting finally in his wife committing suicide). The plaintiff's injury was held to be caused by the Commission having infringed its duty of confidentiality and more generally its duty of care towards the plaintiff. In either of these judgments, the Court founded its decision on negligence on the part of the defendant institution (*Leussink*, paragraph 15: "failure to exercise the diligence required . . . "; *Adams*, paragraph 44: "failing to make all reasonable efforts . . . ").[19]

---

[14] See H. G. Schermers and C. R. A. Swaak, "Official Acts of Community Servants and Article 215(4) EC", at 167 ff. of *The Action for Damages in Community Law, supra* n. 9.

[15] M. H. Van der Woude, "Liability for Administrative Acts under Article 21 (2) EC", at 109 ff., at 110–11, in *The Action for Damages in Community Law, supra* n. 9. This explains why problems relating to the application of Community legislation in individual cases also come mainly before national courts (*ibid.*, at 111).

[16] *Ibid.*, at 111–12. Further in his most instructive article, the author groups liability issues concerning individual acts, insofar as they come before the Community courts, in four categories: failure to exercise supervisory powers; factual conduct; public procurement problems; and funding operations: at 117 ff.

[17] Joined Cases 169/83 and 136/84 [1986] ECR 2801.

[18] Case 145/83 [1985] ECR 3539.

[19] For another case where factual conduct of the Commission (failure to take safety measures, and therefore to exercise the diligence required) was at issue, see the judgment in Case C–308/87, *Grifoni* v. *Commission* [1990] ECR I–1203 (rendered on the basis, though, of Art. 188 EAEC).

In an earlier judgment of 28 May 1970 in *Richez-Paris*,[20] relating this time to a (semi-)legal act of the Commission, the ECJ had to deal with a case in which the Commission had given wrongful information to the plaintiff due to an inaccurate interpretation of Community regulations. The Court held that interpreting a provision of law inaccurately does not in itself constitute a wrongful act (*"faute de service"*) giving rise to liability on the basis of Article 215 (paragraph 36),[21] but that a long delay in correcting the wrong information did constitute such a wrongful act (paragraph 42). And in a later judgment of 4 February 1975 in *Compagnie Continentale*[22] the Court said that the Council could be held liable under Article 215 EC for not having correctly fulfilled its mission of information by omitting to make a specific reservation as to the applicability of legislation, in a resolution intended to inform the enterprises concerned (paragraphs 20–21).[23] Also in these cases, a general criterion of wrongfulness was applied to assess the correctness of the institution's behaviour, which was applied in the framework of the classic legal test containing three conditions: illegality, causation and damage.[24]

There is a particular reason for mentioning the latter two cases: they relate both to the issue of liability of a public authority for injury caused by misleading information given on the basis of an incorrect or incomplete reading, i.e. interpretation, of Community law. That issue was raised in *Brasserie* itself but also, and more specifically, in two post-*Brasserie* judgments, namely *British Telecommunications*[25] and *Denkavit International*.[26] In *Brasserie* the ECJ held that (for one but not for another aspect of the litigation) the national legislatures could have acted on the basis of an excusable error (paragraph 59; compare paragraph 63). The reason therefore was that, for the matters concerned, the Member State acted in a field where it had "a wide discretion comparable to that of the Community institutions in implementing Community policies" (paragraph 47), and that Community law was yet in a state of uncertainty (paragraphs 59 and 63) and therefore difficult to assess. In *British Telecom* and *Denkavit* the situation was significantly different. In these cases relating to the incorrect transposition of a directive into national law, the margin of discretion was much more limited, circumscribed as it was by the

---

[20] Joined Cases 19, 20, 25 and 30/69 [1970] ECR 325.

[21] See also the judgment of 13 July 197 in Case 79/71, *Heinemann* [1972] ECR 579 where it was specified that this is so even when the authority had invited the persons concerned to ask for information.

[22] Case 169/73, [1975] ECR 117. No compensation was granted however, for lack of causal link.

[23] See also the Court's judgment of 9 November 1989 in Case 353/88, *Briantex* [1989] ECR 3623 where the Court held that the divulging of information of a general nature did not, under the circumstances of the case, amount to a wrongful act.

[24] As laid down in *Lütticke*, *supra* n. 7 and repeated e.g. in *Briantex*, cited in the preceding note, at para. 8. See further M. H. Van der Woude, *supra* n. 15, at 110 ff.

[25] Case C–392/93 R. v. *HM Treasury, ex parte British Telecommunications* [1996] ECR I–1631.

[26] Joined Cases C–283/94, 291 and 292/94, *Denkavit International and others* v. *Bundesamt für Finanzen* [1996] ECR I–5063.

alternative ways of implementation which the directive left to the Member States. Moreover, the error of the Member State occurred in the interpretation of a specific provision of the directive, which did not seem to raise more complicated problems of interpretation than those arising under other legal provisions of the same kind.[27] The Court nonetheless accepted in *British Telecom*—largely for policy reasons, that is in order not to hinder the exercise of legislative functions by the prospect of damage actions (paragraph 40)—that the Member State concerned had not committed a sufficiently serious breach of Community law, because the interpretation given by it to the "imprecisely worded" provision of the directive had been given "in good faith and on the basis of arguments which are not entirely devoid of substance" (paragraph 43 of *British Telecom*). In *Denkavit* the Court came to the same conclusion but on the basis of less explicit reasoning.[28]

Some may find it regrettable, as we do, that the Court made no attempt in its post-*Brasserie* case law, to look to the whole of its Article 215 case law (instead of looking only to the *Schöppenstedt* part). That would have enabled the Court to define *and* differentiate the liability conditions for breaches by Member States according to the type of situation involved, as the Court in *Francovich* had announced that it would do. Actually, the Court could have taken the opportunity, as suggested by Advocate General Tesauro in his Opinion,[29] to put more logic into its Article 215 case law by clarifying the scope of application of the *Schöppenstedt* test, that is by reserving it for measures, in particular legislative measures, involving a wide margin of discretion because of policy choices to be made.[30] As we have submitted elsewhere,[31] the Court could, indeed, have taken account of essential differences in the exercise of public authority, whether executive or legislative, by distinguishing between breaches of duty *simpliciter* (as in *Francovich*), breaches resulting from the misinterpretation of Community rules (as in *British Telecom*) and

---

[27] See, however, Paul Craig, "Once more unto the Breach: the Community, the State and Damages Liability" (1997) 113 *LQR* 67 ff.

[28] But see the ECJ's judgment of 22 Apr. 1997 in Case C–66/95, *Eunice Sutton*, not yet reported in ECR, where the Court leaves it entirely to the national court to find out whether the conditions for liability to arise are fulfilled (paras. 31–4).

[29] *Supra* n. 4, at paras. 64–9.

[30] In the same sense Darmon AG in his Opinion in Case C–282/90, *Vreugdenhil II* v. *Commission* [1992] ECR I–1947, at 1958, para. 45 and more recently M. H. Van der Woude in a well documented article, *supra* n. 15, in which he argues for the application of the *Schöppenstedt* test only to legislative acts involving choices of economic policy and to apply the classic test (using the general test of "illegality" as opposed to the more specific, and more rigorous *Schöppenstedt* "serious breach" test) also to legislative acts not involving policy choices (at 112–13). As pointed out by him, the Court of First Instance has adhered to this approach in its *Live Pigs* judgment of 13 Dec. 1995 (Joined Cases T–481 and 484/93, *Vereniging van Exporteurs in Levende Varkens and another* v. *Commission* [1995] ECR II–2941) wherein it established first (para. 83 ff.) that the decisions in question were general measures (on this notion, see further A. Arnull, cited in his contribution to *The Action for Damages in Community Law, supra* n. 9, at 131–6) and second (para. 89 ff.) that the Commission enjoyed broad discretionary powers.

[31] W. van Gerven, "Bridging the Unbridgeable: Community and National Tort Laws after *Francovich* and *Brasserie*" (1996) 45 *ICLQ* 507 ff.

breaches committed in the exercise of powers involving a wide discretion as to policy choices[32] (as in *Brasserie*) or, in more general terms,[33] by distinguishing between (i) breaches of a clear *"obligation de résultat"*, where no discretion at all exists, in which case, as the Court said in *Hedley Lomas* concerning a series of administrative decisions,[34] "the mere infringement of Community law may be sufficient to establish the existence of a sufficiently serious breach" (paragraph 28);[35] (ii) breaches of an "obligation de moyens", i.e. a duty of care, in which a failure to exercise the diligence required or to deploy all reasonable efforts (as in *Leussink* and *Adams*, mentioned above), or to pursue the correct interpretation of a rule of law with due care, amounts to illegal conduct;[36] and (iii) breaches in the exercise of wide discretion, in which case the more precise standard of "grave and manifest disregard of the limits on discretion"[37] is held to apply. To make these distinctions properly, it might help to use a less obscure standard than the "sufficiently serious breach" test which was devised by the Court in its Article 215 case law for the last category of breaches. That test is not an example of clarity or precision especially when one takes into account the terminology used in other language versions (*"violation suffisamment caractérisée"*, *"voldoende gekwalificeerde schending"*, *"violación caracterizada"*[38]), from which it appears that the test does not necessarily go hand in hand with the qualification of "grave and manifest disregard" but may also cover other (i.e. otherwise "characterised" or otherwise "qualified") types of infringements.[39]

The comparison of situations at stake in *Richez-Parise* or *Compagnie Continentale* with those at stake in *British Telecom* or *Denkavit*—in all of these cases operational (i.e. implementing or interpretative[40]) discretion rather than legislative discretion was exercised by the Community or national authority concerned—indicates in our view that the use of a more common

---

[32] We suggest that also non-legislative acts involving, exceptionally, a wide discretion should come in that category: *contra*, M. H. Van der Woude, *supra* n. 15, at 114.

[33] See, for a more "concretisied" categorisation in five sub-categories, my article, *supra* n. 31, at 521–2.

[34] Judgment of 23 May 1996 in Case C–5/94 [1996] ECR I–2553.

[35] It is not clear why the Court says "may be sufficient" instead of "is sufficient". Maybe to account for exceptional circumstances of *force majeure*, or for the pursuit of policy considerations of general interest acceptable under Community law: see my article, *supra* n. 31, at 522.

[36] See *infra* n. 41.

[37] See my Opinion in *Mulder*, *supra* n. 12, at I–3103 ff. paras. 15–18.

[38] The German text refers, like the English, to *"hinreichend schwere Verletzung"*: see further D. Edward and W. Robinson, "Is There a Place for Private Law Principles in Community Law?" in *The Action for Damages in Community Law*, *supra* n. 9, 339 ff., where other versions are quoted at 344.

[39] The words *"caractérisée"* or *"qualifiziert"* seem to refer to a breach being able to give rise to liability *under the specific circumstances of the situation type*. (According to Edward and Robinson, *supra* n. 38, at 345, it shows an analogy with the common law distinction between situations giving rise to strict liability and situations where the circumstances determine liability). That should not necessarily be a "serious" breach, a word which rather corresponds, in the languages quoted, to *"sérieux"*, *"ernstig"* or *"seria"*.

[40] The term is used by P. Craig in his article, *supra* n. 27.

standard would have been more appropriate, namely that of how "a normally (or reasonably) diligent authority would have acted under the circumstances".[41] That standard with which national courts are more familiar (than with the standard of "serious breach") would have enabled those courts to take a more flexible attitude and to adapt the standard more easily and comprehensibly to "each type of situation". Since that standard seems to coincide with the criterion of diligence (understood in an "objective" way), used in the "meta"-*Schöppenstedt* cases mentioned above, it would also have enabled the bringing closer together the whole of the two Community law regimes of extra-contractual liability, thereby promoting coherence and consistency at the level of Community law.

Such consistency between both Community law regimes of tort liability should be pursued not only in respect of the condition of breach, but also in respect of the other conditions for liability to arise (protective character of the rule breached, causation and damage) and in respect of the remedy of compensation. For indeed, since the Court has admitted in *Brasserie* that, "in the absence of particular justification", "the protection of the rights which individuals derive from Community law cannot vary depending on whether a national authority a Community authority is responsible for the damage" (paragraph 42), it should look systematically for inspiration to its Article 215 case law as a whole—with a view to achieving a maximum of consistency between both tort liability regimes in Community law—and only derogate from it for a particular reason to be indicated in the judgment.

Consistency of the law is an aim in itself as it promotes transparency and ensures a better comprehension of the law for all concerned. Such consistency must exist not only between the two Community law regimes of tort liability. It should also exist between Community law and the national legal systems, and *can* exist if the reference—in Article 215—to general principles is taken seriously. We will now turn to that point.

THE REFERENCE TO ARTICLE 215 IS TOO LIMITED IN DEPTH

One of the most surprising features of the Court's Article 215 case law, and as a consequence of the *Francovich/Brasserie* case law, is the little attention given in it to what Article 215 calls "the general principles common to the laws of the Member States". Obviously, that reference does not mean that the Court is under an obligation to look for "some sort of arithmetic mean",[42]

---

[41] A normally reasonably diligent authority should be deemed to be liable in damages in a situation involving the interpretation of a rule of law, when the interpretation given by it would, as the Court said in *British Telecom* (para. 43), be "manifestly contrary to the wording of the [directive] or to the objective pursued by it" or, as the Court held in *Richez-Parise*, when a wrongful interpretation was not corrected in time (para. 42).

[42] A. Arnull, *supra* n. 30, at 129–30.

or for the lowest common denominator, of the solutions adopted by all of the Member States.[43] Nor does it mean, on the contrary, that the Court may choose freely the national solution which it considers the most appropriate in its own discretion.[44] The Court's task is rather to look in the national legal systems for general principles (not specific rules) which are common to, and thus present in, several national legal systems, and which are capable of founding the interpretation of Community law rules which accords best with the structure and the fundamental principles of Community law.[45]

One may wonder, though, whether the Court searches enough for such common general principles. A case in point is the aforementioned *Leussink-Brummelhuis* judgment wherein the Court accepted the claim of the primary victim for physical and non-physical injury but dismissed the claim of the secondary victims for non-physical injury stating, almost in an *obiter dictum*, that the legal order of most of the Member States would not accept such claims (paragraph 22). Should the Court not have documented its position more explicitly by referring to common principles? As for the claim of the primary victim there is indeed *a general tendency* in many legal systems, already at the moment when the facts occurred and even more thereafter, to protect the victims of car accidents, including passengers, against interferences with physical integrity by allowing them damages for personal injury and economic losses consequential thereon, even to the point (in many legal systems) of placing the burden of proof, *de iure* or *de facto*, on the driver of the car and his/her insurer. And also for the dismissal of claims for pecuniary and non-pecuniary damage brought by the dependants of the primary victims, the Court could have attempted, and would most likely have succeeded, to find support for its ruling in several of the national legal orders.[46]

Also regarding the conditions for State and Community liability—including causation and damage, and more particularly, as indicated above, "sufficiently serious breach" when understood in the sense indicated above, that is as a subcategory of the general criterion of "acting as a normally diligent authority would have done under the circumstances"—the ECJ could have drawn much inspiration from the concepts and principles common to the legal systems of the Member States. As shown in an article by the much missed Judge

---

[43] See Gand AG in his Opinion, in Joined Cases 5, 7 and 13–24/66, *Kampffmeyer* [1967] ECR at 352; Roemer AG in his Opinion in Case 5/71, *Schöppenstedt*, *supra* n. 3, at 991.

[44] Fernand Schockweiler, G. Wivenes and J. M. Godart, *supra* n. 4, at 27 ff.

[45] Gand AG: "[*faire*] *œuvre de comparaison et de création*", in his Opinion, *supra* n. 43, at 352; see also J. Mertens de Wilmars, "Le droit comparé dans la jurisprudence de la Cour de Justice des Communautés Européennes" [1991] *J.T.* 37 ff.

[46] I can understand that the Court itself does not wish to incorporate explicit references to national laws in its judgment but would leave that to the AG to whose Opinion it could then refer. It is well known that the Court in some cases requests its Research and Documentation Department to prepare a comparative law note to describe the state of the national legal systems. Would it not be desirable to let the legal community benefit (under the usual reservations) from these notes which are now hidden in the archives of the Court?

Fernand Schockweiler published in 1990[47] (a publication most certainly known to the Court when it decided *Francovich*), common ground can be found in the legal systems of the (then twelve) Member States to define the condition of breach consisting in the violation of a Community rule aiming at the protection of the rights of individuals—which does not prevent that the rule may also aim at the protection of an objective of general interest.[48] Further comparative research would have allowed, we believe,[49] to find common general principles also to support the Court's position regarding the wrongful exercise of wide discretion—an issue which creates similar difficulties in all legal systems—as well as to define a common position regarding the notions of causation and damage (and the extent of compensation)—somewhere between the extremes (too generous or too restrictive) found in one or the other legal system.[50]

There are several reasons for the Court to follow such a comparative approach, as requested in Article 215 but also prevailing according to the Court "in other areas of Community law" (paragraph 41 of the *Brasserie* judgment). The first, and perhaps most important, reason is of a political nature. If the Court wishes to pursue its creative function in developing Community law, it must look systematically for common ground in the legal systems of the Member States on which it can build its edifice.[51] The second reason is of a purely legal nature. As explained elsewhere, there is a need to strengthen, within each legal system and between the legal systems of the European Union, those elements which preserve homogeneity in the face of growing divergencies, resulting partly from the fact that Community legislation regulates only limited areas of national laws, and leaves other similar ones untouched.[52] Indeed homogeneity or consistency is needed if we wish to avoid, as Advocate General Jacobs has labeled it, a new form of discrimination consisting of differences in legal protection when similar situations are governed by different rules.[53] The third reason is economic and goes hand in hand with the second. For economic operators to be able to function

---

[47] *Supra* n. 4.

[48] At 72.

[49] But see F. Schockweiler *et al.*, at 73.

[50] It is not correct in my view to leave the definition of these essential conditions entirely to the national legal orders (I hope that the recent Court judgment in *Eunice Sutton, supra* n. 28, is not to be regarded as a precedent therefor) because this would amount to a *de facto* "re-nationalisation" of the Community law principle of state liability, as illustrated by the judgment of the *Bundesgerichtshof* of 24 Oct. 1996, following *Brasserie* [1996] *EuZW* 761; [1997] *NJW* 123, and the English Court of Appeal's judgment of 10 June 1996 in R. v. *Secretary of State for the Home Department, ex parte John Gallaghan* [1996] 2 *CMLR* 951.

[51] That is another form of "subsidiarity in action", as the expression is used by David Vaughan in the editorial to [1997] *EuLR*.

[52] W. van Gerven, "Community and National Legislators, Regulators, Judges, Academics and Practitioners: Living Together Apart?" in B. Markesinis (ed.), *Law Making, Law Finding, and Law Shaping* (Clifford Chance Lectures, vol. II), 13 ff.

[53] F. Jacobs, "Remedies in National Courts for the Enforcement of Community Rights", in *Liber Amicorum for Don Manuel Diez de Velasco* (1993), at 969 and 982.

adequately within a single market, legal disparities must be kept to a minimum and must be kept within a general framework of common general principles. The fourth reason is of a cultural nature. According to Article 128 EC the Community

> "shall contribute to the flowering of the cultures of the Member States, while respecting their national and regional diversity and at the same time bringing the common cultural heritage to the fore".

Both the diversity of the legal systems of the EU and the general principles which they have in common notwithstanding the diversity, are an integral part of the cultural diversity and of the common cultural heritage to which Article 128 refers. As an institution of the Community, it is for the ECJ to help bring such common legal heritage to the fore while respecting national and regional diversity.

CONCLUSION

The reference in *Brasserie* to Article 215 is too limited in scope. The requirement of uniform application of Community law in the Member States implies that the reference, in the absence of particular justification to the contrary, should be extended to all conditions, and to the remedy of compensation, subject to what is said below.

The Court's reference to its Article 215 case law is too limited in breadth, as it focuses only on the *Schöppenstedt* part of that case law, thereby missing an opportunity to bring the two Community law regimes on tort liability closer to each other in all of their aspects—and, again, in the absence of particular justification to the contrary—and to achieve a much needed consistency at the level of Community law.

The Court's reference is also too limited in depth, as it should go hand in hand with a genuine search for general principles common to the legal systems of the Member States as is required by Article 215. For, indeed, if the Court wishes to promote the requirement of uniform application of Community law in the Member States by harmonising the conditions for liability and for compensation, it must look for sufficient support in the core principles of the national legal systems, and base its rulings on such principles as much as possible.

4

State Liability in Damages following Factortame III: A Remedy Seen in Context

PETER OLIVER*

Other papers in this volume examine the conditions of the State's liability in damages under the *Brasserie du Pêcheur* and *Factortame III* judgment,[1] and I would certainly not wish to encroach on their territory.[2]

Instead, I shall attempt to set this judgment within the context of the various remedies available before the national courts and before the European Court. To my mind, it is only by seeing state liability in damages in this context that its true role and importance can be properly appreciated.

---

* Member of the Legal Service, European Commission. The views expressed in this paper are personal to the author.

[1] Cases C–46/93 and 48/93 *Brasserie du Pêcheur* v. *Germany* and *The Queen* v. *Secretary of State for Transport, ex parte Factortame* [1996] ECR I–1029. See generally Barav, "State Liability in Damages for Breach of Community Law in the National Courts" in T. Heukels and A. McDonnell (eds.), *The Action for Damages in a Community Law Perspective* (Kluwer Law International, 1997); Craig, "Once More unto the Breach: The Community, the State and Damages Liability" [1997] *LQR* 67; Oliver casenote (1997) *CMLRev.* 635; Pardon and Dalcq, "La responsabilité des Etats membres envers les particuliers en cas de manquements au droit communautaire" [1996] *JTDE* 193; Reich, "Der Schutz subjektiver Gemeinschaftsrechte durch Staatshaftung" [1996] *EuZW* 709; Schockweiler, "La responsabilité de l'autorité nationale en cas de violation du droit communautaire" [1992] *RTDE* 27; Szyszczak, "Making Europe More Relevant to Its Citizens: Effective Judicial Process" [1996] *ELRev.* 351; Vandersanden, "Le droit communautaire" in Vandersanden and Dony (eds.), *La responsabilité des Etats membres en cas de violation du droit communautaire* (1997); van Gerven, "Bridging the Unbridgeable: Community and National Tort Laws after *Francovich* and *Brasserie*" [1996] *ICLQ* 507; Denis Waelbroeck, "Treaty Violations and Liability of Member States: the Effects of the Francovich Case Law" in *The Action for Damages in a Community Law Perspective* (*supra*); and Wathelet and Van Raepenbusch, "La responsabilité des Etats membres en cas de violation du droit communautaire. Vers un alignement de la responsabilité de l'Etat sur celle de la Communauté ou l'inverse?" [1997] *CDE* 13.

[2] See above Tridimas Chapter 2, below, Craig Chapter 6.

THE PRINCIPLES

At the outset, I feel it incumbent on me to recall—albeit very briefly—the principles relating to national remedies on which the Court built in *Factortame III.*[3]

Casting your minds back to the rulings in *Comet v. Produktschap voor Siergewassen*[4] and *Rewe v. Landwirtschaftskammer,*[5] you will recall that the remedies available in actions brought before national courts are governed by national law, as are the procedures to be applied in those courts. However, according to the same case law, this rule is subject to two extremely important provisos: first, an effective remedy must be available for the enforcement of a directly applicable Community provision ("the principle of effectiveness") and secondly, national law governing the enforcement of Community rights against the authorities of the State concerned must be no less favourable than those governing the same right of action on internal matters ("the principle of non-discrimination").

You will also recall the Court's statement in *Rewe v. Hauptzollamt Kiel* (butterboats)[6] that Community law "was not intended to create new remedies in the national courts to ensure the observance of Community law other than those laid down by national law". Subsequent rulings of the Court have cast the principles of effectiveness and non-discrimination so broadly that this statement has more or less been distinguished out of existence.[7] As Advocate General Tesauro was to put it in *Factortame III*, the autonomy of the legal systems of the Member States in this regard must yield to the requirements of Community law "in particular, whenever it is essential to derogate in order to ensure the proper implementation of Community law and correct, effective protection of the rights claimed by individuals under Community law".[8] In short, while the Member States may often be seen clinging for dear life on to the pronouncement in *Rewe*, in all probability that part of the judgment is no longer good law.

The Court has cited three distinct sources of law underlying these principles: Article 5 of the Treaty of Rome; the concept of direct applicability; and

---

[3] Recent literature includes: Brealey and Hoskins, *Remedies in EC Law* (1994); Caranta, "Judicial Protection against Member States: a New *Jus Commune* Takes Shape" (1995) *CMLRev.* 703; Fernandez Martin, "El principio de tutela judicial efectiva de los derechos subjectivos derivados del derecho comunitario" [1994] *Revista de Instituciones Europeas* 845; Hoskins, "Tilting the Balance: Supremacy and National Procedural Rules" [1996] *ELRev.* 365; Clive Lewis, *Remedies and the Enforcement of European Community Law* (1996); Oliver, "Le droit communautaire et les voies de recours nationales" [1992] *CDE* 348; and the proceedings of the 1992 FIDE Conference on "Enforcement of Community Law by Sanctions and Remedies".

[4] Case 45/76 [1976] ECR 2043.

[5] Case 33/76 [1976] ECR 1989.

[6] Case 158/80 [1981] ECR 1805 at 1838.

[7] Mischo AG in Cases C–6 and 9/90 *Francovich v. Italy* [1991] ECR I–5357 at 5385–6. See also Tesauro AG in *Factortame III* at 1093.

[8] *Factortame III, supra* n. 1.

human rights as recognised by its own case law and now enshrined in Article F(2) of the Treaty on European Union. As to direct applicability, it would be meaningless to say that certain provisions of Community law could be relied on before national courts, if the rules of procedure were so stringent as to defeat any action brought in reliance on them. In effect, the Court has merely applied the well-known maxim *"ubi ius, ibi remedium"*.

The Court of Justice will not stretch the scope of direct actions against the Community to compensate for any failure by national courts to provide effective remedies against the authorities of Member States. This is clear from the ruling in *Oleoficio Borelli* v. *Commission.*[9] The Commission had declined to grant the applicants an aid under EAGGF Guidance for the construction of a plant for producing olive oil. According to the Community legislation concerned, the Commission was not entitled to do otherwise following the negative opinion from the local Ligurian administration. Nevertheless, on the basis of Article 173 of the Treaty the applicants sought the annulment of the Commission's refusal, since in Italian law the negative opinion of the regional authorities was regarded as a preliminary act and thus did not give rise to a cause of action. The Court dismissed the action, on the ground that "any irregularity that might affect the opinion [of the regional authorities] cannot affect the validity of the decision by which the Commission refused the aid applied for"; and it was incumbent on the national courts to ensure that an action to quash such an opinion was available. By the same token, the claim for damages brought pursuant to the second paragraph of Article 215 of the Treaty was also dismissed on the grounds that the allegedly unlawful act was not attributable to the Commission.

I should also like to stress the recurrent theme in the case law that time may be of the essence. This was a crucial element in *Simmenthal*,[10] where the Court of Justice held that every national court must be empowered to set aside a national statute if it was incompatible with an earlier provision of Community law. Thus it would be contrary to Community law:

> "if the solution of the conflict were to be reserved for an authority with a discretion of its own [in this case the Italian Constitutional Court], other than the court called upon to apply Community law, *even if such an impediment to the full effectiveness of Community law were only temporary*" (emphasis added).

The Court later relied on that passage in *Factortame I*,[11] where it held that a party relying on directly applicable Community law rights must have the possibility of applying for interim relief with a view to enforcing those rights. By definition, the time factor was the cornerstone of that judgment.

---

[9] Case C–97/91 [1992] ECR I–6313.
[10] Case 106/77 *Amministrazione delle Finanze dello Stato* v. *Simmenthal* [1978] ECR 629.
[11] Case C–213/89 *The Queen* v. *Secretary of State for Transport, ex parte Factortame* [1990] ECR I–2433

Among the most significant aspects of the ruling in *Factortame III* was the Court's acceptance of the idea that its own case law on the non-contractual liability of the Community under Article 215 of the Treaty of Rome should, "in the absence of particular justification", be taken as a yardstick for determining the rules on state liability. This approach, which can be traced back to the majority judgment of the English Court of Appeal in *Bourgoin* v. *Ministry of Agriculture, Fisheries and Food*,[12] was first taken up by Advocate General Mischo in *Francovich*,[13] although it did not receive any endorsement from the Court in that case.

In contrast, in *Hedley Lomas*[14] Advocate General Léger baulked at this idea, for two reasons: in his view, state liability does not have the same foundation as the liability of the Community ("Member States are subject to a hierarchy of legal norms which does not exist in the Community"); and it would be "somewhat paradoxical to align state liability for breach of Community law with Article 215 rules which are judged to be unsatisfactory, unduly stringent and affording insufficient protection for the right to effective judicial relief, at least with regard to the condition concerning breach of Community law".

This negative view was not shared by Advocate General Tesauro, when he came to give his Opinion in *Factortame III*. While expressing disquiet at the unduly restrictive nature of the Court's case law on the second paragraph of Article 215,[15] he nevertheless regarded that case law as a suitable point of reference for the liability of Member States for the breach of Community law.

The Court was to endorse the basic approach in the following terms:

"First, the second paragraph of Article 215 of the Treaty refers, as regards the non-contractual liability of the Community, to the general principles common to the laws of the Member States

. . .

Second, the conditions under which the State may incur liability for damage caused to individuals by a breach of Community law cannot, in the absence of particular justification, differ from those governing the liability of the Community in like circumstances. The protection of the rights which individuals derive from

---

[12] [1986] 1 QB 716, [1986] 1 CMLR 267 ; see Oliver, "Enforcing Community Rights in the English Courts" [1987] MLR 881.

[13] From 5395 onwards; see also van Gerven AG in Case C–128/92 *Banks* v. *British Coal Corporation* [1994] ECR I–1212 at 1255.

[14] Case C–5/94 *The Queen* v. *Ministry of Agriculture, Fisheries and Food, ex parte Hedley Lomas (Ireland)* [1996] ECR I–2553. This Opinion was delivered before that of Tesauro AG in *Factortame III*.

[15] Needless to say, there is nothing novel in such criticism. More unusual is the recent suggestion that the Court's case law on Article 215(2) is actually growing more restrictive: see Fines, "A General Analytical Perspective on Community Liability" in *The Action for Damages in a Community Law Perspective, supra* n. 1.

Community law cannot vary depending on whether a national authority or a Community authority is responsible for the damage."[16]

Personally, I welcome that development, since in general it cannot be right to require national judges to be more stringent than the Court of Justice is itself. As is illustrated by the majority judgment of the Court of Appeal in *Bourgoin*, the opposite approach is likely to be perceived by national judges as involving double standards, and resented accordingly.

Having said that, a number of commentators have pointed to various discrepancies between the ruling in *Factortame III* and the conditions of non-contractual liability of the Community under Article 215.

For instance, Waelbroeck has remarked[17] that the Court has abandoned the requirement in its case law on Article 215 that the rule infringed must be "for the protection of the individual", which derives from the German *Schutznormtheorie*. In its place, it has substituted the less onerous requirement that the rule in question should "confer rights on individuals". This condition is automatically met, the Court has held, whenever the rule is enshrined in a directly applicable provision of Community law.

What is more, van Gerven[18] has pointed to a discrepancy between the Court's statement that the quantum of damages must be commensurate with the loss or damage sustained and its case law on Article 215: the Court has consistently ruled that, to recover damages against the Community, a plaintiff must show that the damage alleged goes beyond "the bounds of the normal economic risks inherent in the activities in the sector concerned";[19] but the Court did not apply this concept to state liability.[20]

In any case, the Court was surely right to leave itself room for manœuvre by saying that the same principles should be applied "in the absence of particular justification". It did not give any indication of the circumstances in which it might consider it appropriate for the conditions of liability to diverge. However, one member of the Court writing extra-judicially appears to consider that "particular justification" for treating Community institutions more leniently than Member States should not be found lightly.[21]

Finally, Waelbroeck has suggested[22] that the Court might begin to apply the second paragraph of Article 215 more strictly against the Community institutions, now that it has acknowledged a parallel between the non-contractual

[16] [1996] ECR I–1146–7.
[17] *Supra* n. 1, 328.
[18] *Supra* n. 1, 524.
[19] See e.g. Case 238/78 *Ireks-Arkady* v. *Council and Commission* [1979] ECR 2955. para. 11; Cases 241–2/78 *DGV* v. *Council and Commission* [1979] ECR 3017. para. 11; and case C–104/89 *Mulder* v. *Council and Commission* [1992] ECR I–3061, para. 13. The Court has also been known to take account of the fact that a "limited and clearly defined group of commercial operators" was affected by a measure (Cases 64 and 113/76 *Dumortier* v. *Council* [1979] ECR 3091 at 3114); but in *Mulder* damages were awarded, even though a large class of producers was affected.
[20] See also para. 92 of Tesauro AG's Opinion
[21] Judge Wathelet, writing with van Raepenbusch, *supra* n. 1, 41–3.
[22] *Supra* n. 1, 335.

liability of the Community and state liability for breach of the Treaty. Judge Wathelet and Van Raepenbusch have expressed the same idea, adding that the Community institutions might be regarded as being in a better position than national authorities to respect Community law.[23]

LOCUS STANDI IN ACTIONS TO QUASH NATIONAL MEASURES

One question which has scarcely been touched on by the Court is how generous the national rules on *locus standi* must be when a party seeks judicial review of the act of a public authority. Indeed, this is probably the most important aspect of national remedies which remains to be fully considered by the Court.[24]

A rather surprising pronouncement of the Advocate General in *Rewe* (butterboats)[25] undoubtedly deserves a mention here. It will be recalled that that case concerned cruises on the high seas carried out with the sole purpose of enabling passengers to purchase duty-free goods. The plaintiffs in the main action, who were competitors of the companies running these cruises, objected that this practice fell foul of a number of Community regulations. One of the questions posed by the court at Hamburg pursuant to Article 177 was whether breach of such regulations gave a right of action to a "person whose rights have been adversely affected" by an incompatible national measure. The referring court stated that in similar cases in German law plaintiffs in this situation would enjoy *locus standi*.

The Advocate General argued strongly that, although the Regulations were directly applicable, such litigants should be precluded from enforcing them, since they were not specifically concerned by the contested national measure. Happily, the Court declined to follow that path, stating:

> "the system of legal protection established by the Treaty, as set out in Article 177 in particular, implies that it must be possible for every type of action provided for by national law to be available for the purpose of ensuring the observance of Community provisions having direct effect, on the same conditions concerning the admissibility and procedure as would apply were it a question of ensuring observance of national law."

The Court's approach is surely sound: the purpose of Community law is not to restrict remedies which would otherwise be available under national law; rather, it lays down minimum remedies, leaving it open to the Member States to be more liberal if they wish. My point is precisely that there is a

---

[23] *Supra* n. 1, 41–2.

[24] Another unsolved question is the right of set-off: see Duncan and MacGowan "Is the Right of Set-Off Wholly a Matter of National Law?" [1994] *Irish Journal of European Law* 70; and see Case C–132/95 *Jensen* v. *Ministry of Agriculture* (pending), although that case turns primarily on issues peculiar to the Common Agricultural Policy.

[25] *Supra* n. 6.

dearth of authority on the minimum standards which national law must meet as regards *locus standi*. Rulings on this issue are scarce and are all limited to specific areas of the law.

Plainly, the addressee of an individual act or its "direct victim" must have the possibility of contesting it. Thus if an importer is required to pay an unlawful tax, he must of course have the possibility of recovering it. The Advocate General in *Rewe* conceded this.

Where an unnotified State aid is granted, must competitors have *locus standi* to contest that aid? In my view, the answer must unquestionably be "yes", even though the Court has not expressly decided this point.[26]

In *Heiderijk*[27] the Court had occasion to consider this matter in relation to a wholly different area of substantive law, namely Council Directive 79/7 on equal treatment between men and women in matters of social security.[28] The Dutch court hearing that case had asked whether an individual might rely on that Directive when he suffered the effects of a discriminatory national provision applying to his spouse, who was not a party to the proceedings. The Court replied that "the right to rely on the provisions of Directive 79/7 is not confined to individuals coming within the scope *ratione personae* of the directive, in so far as the possibility cannot be ruled out that other persons may have a direct interest in ensuring that the principle of non-discrimination is respected as regards persons who are protected". It followed, the Court held, that the plaintiff could bring an action based on the Directive, provided that his wife fell within the scope of its provisions. Unfortunately, the Court's reasoning was so general that it is not easy to extrapolate from it any principles which might apply in other contexts.

A similar question was posed by the High Court in *Coloroll Pension Trustees* v. *Russell*,[29] namely: can dependents of employees rely on Article 119 of the Treaty to contest an occupational pension scheme involving discrimination between the sexes? After referring to an earlier ruling to the effect that a survivor's pension provided by an occupational pension scheme falls within the scope of that provision, the Court held:

> "It follows that since the right to payment of a survivor's pension arises at the time of the death of the employee affiliated to the scheme, the survivor is the only person who can assert it. If the survivor were to be denied this possibility, this would deprive Article 119 of all its effectiveness as far as survivors' pensions are concerned."

---

[26] Yet this seems implicit in the judgment in Case C–254/90 *Fédération Nationale du Commerce Extérieur* v. *France* [1991] ECR I–5505 at 5528, where the Court said: "National courts must offer to individuals in a position to rely on such a breach the certain prospect that all the necessary inferences will be drawn, in accordance with their national law, as regards the validity of measures giving effect to the aid, the recovery of financial support granted in disregard of that provision and possible interim measures"; see also Case C–39/94 *Syndicat Français de l'Express International* v. *La Poste* [1996] ECR I–3547.

[27] Case C–89/90 *Heiderijk* v. *Sociale Verzekeringsbank* [1991] ECR I–3757.

[28] [1979] OJ L6/24.

[29] Case C–200/91 [1994] ECR I–4389.

In a sense, this question was more straightforward than that in *Heidorijh*, since here the survivor was alleged to be the "direct victim" of the discriminatory measure—just like the importer who is required to pay an unlawful tax.

Where the question becomes much more difficult is in relation to the environment. For instance, if a Member State infringes a Community environmental directive, must all the inhabitants of the area have *locus standi* to contest the measure concerned before the national courts? And what about environmental groups such as Greenpeace and Friends of the Earth?[30]

These issues cannot be pursued any further here, but one important general point should be noted: in this area of the law, any attempt to use the situation as regards direct actions before the European Court as a yardstick breaks down. In other words, it cannot in my view be argued that, because the rules on *locus standi* under Article 173 of the Treaty are restrictive, the same should apply before the national courts. To my mind, quite the reverse is the case: it is precisely because direct actions before the European Court are to be regarded as only *part* of the remedies available that effective remedies must be available in the national courts. Thus an individual who is affected by a regulation and who cannot contest it in proceedings based on Article 173 must be able to attack before the national courts the act applying that regulation.

Finally, recent developments in England in this field give some grounds for optimism, as the English courts have delivered some liberal rulings of late on *locus standi* in cases involving Community law.[31]

IS THE ACTION FOR DAMAGES SUBSIDIARY TO OTHER REMEDIES?

In *Denkavit Internationaal* v. *Kamer van Koophandel*,[32] Advocate General Jacobs spoke of the "exceptional character" of state liability in damages "as a remedy which goes beyond ordinary administrative remedies". Advocate General Tesauro expressed much the same idea when he suggested in *Factortame III*[33] that the action for damages might be regarded as ancillary to other remedies. It followed in his review that, "the Member States cannot reasonably be debarred" from making the right to damages dependent on the applicant having brought an action for annulment, where available, provided that the same rule applied to purely domestic claims. In other words, a litigant who has

---

[30] See generally the Order of the Court of First Instance in Case T–585/93 *Stichting Greenpeace and others* v. *Commission* [1995] ECR II–2205, from which an appeal is currently pending before the Court (Case C–321/95P).

[31] *R.* v. *Secretary of State for Employment, ex parte Equal Opportunities Commission* [1995] AC 1, [1994] 1 All ER 910 (HL) and *R.* v. *Secretary of State for Employment, ex parte Seymour-Smith* [1997] 1 WLR 473, [1997] IRLR 315 (HL) (see the case note on the judgment of the Court of Appeal in that case by Villiers and Woods [1997] *MLR* 110).

[32] Case C–2/94 [1996] ECR I–2827.

[33] Paras. 100–4 of his Opinion.

failed to mitigate his loss by seeking to have the contested measure quashed in due time may be denied damages. Although the Court held generally that the plaintiff owed a duty to take reasonable care to mitigate his loss, it did not touch on this specific issue.

Although the Court has yet to endorse this approach, it has much to commend it in that it precludes parties from sitting back and waiting for the damage to occur, rather than giving the authorities the opportunity to put an end to unlawful conduct more speedily. It might also be noted that this very same principle is enshrined in Article 839(3) of the German Civil Code which precludes the recovery of damages for the acts of public authorities where the plaintiff has "deliberately or negligently failed to avert loss by seeking another remedy".[34] Moreover, as Advocate General Tesauro pointed out, the Court has arguably followed the same approach with respect to non-contractual liability under Article 215.

If it exists, this principle constitutes an incentive to Member States not to make the rules on *locus standi* too restrictive as regards actions to quash national measures: an action for damages can surely not be dismissed on the grounds that the plaintiffs ought to have brought an action for the annulment of the act of the national authorities, when in fact such an action for annulment was not available.

NATIONAL MEASURES IMPLEMENTING COMMUNITY ACTS

Do the principles laid down in the judgment discussed here also hold good where the wrongful act of a Member State consists in nothing more than the faithful implementation or application of an act of the Council or the Commission, which subsequently turns out to be unlawful? Although the Community institution concerned will be primarily liable, the conditions laid down in *Factortame III* for state liability will often be met, especially as in such cases the Member State will not have enjoyed a wide margin of discretion.

No doubt the simplest solution would be to find, with Advocate General Capotorti, that "the Member State has not committed any wrongful act by implementing a regulation in force, even if it is defective because it is at variance with higher rules of Community law" (*Granaria v Hoofdproduktschap voor Akkerbouwprodukten*).[35] However, I would venture to suggest that, on closer examination, that view appears somewhat simplistic: under the EAGGF Guarantee at least, the Court has held in many cases that the injured party

---

[34] "*Die Ersatzpflicht tritt nicht ein, wenn der Verletzte vorsätzlich oder fahrlässig unterlassen hat, den Schaden durch Gebrauch eines Rechtsmittels abzuwenden.*" This rule is derived from the principle of good faith; see Ossenbühl, *Staatshaftungsrecht* (4th edn. 1991), 75; Wilms, "Le droit allemand" in Vandersanden and Dony, *supra* n. 1, 73.

[35] Case 101/78 [1979] ECR 623 at 644.

must bring his action against the national authorities before the national courts, not against the Community institution pursuant to Article 215.[36] Furthermore, if a Member State is held liable in damages in such circumstances, it may then recover an indemnity for the same amount from the Community budget pursuant to Council Regulation 729/70 on the financing of the Common Agricultural Policy.[37]

Whether adequate mechanisms exist for the Member State to be indemnified in this way in sectors other than the CAP is a moot point.[38] Moreover, a detailed analysis of these issues would be out of place here.[39] Suffice it, then, to refer to two judgments in which such issues have already been considered. In *Granaria* it was decided that "a question relating to the *application* of the second paragraph of Article 215 cannot be determined in proceedings under Article 177 of the Treaty" (emphasis added). Consequently, a national court cannot ascertain with certainty whether the Community will be, or would be, held liable pursuant to Article 215. In *Asteris* v. *Greece and EEC*[40] the Court held that, where a party had failed in an action under Article 215 on the ground that the Community had not manifestly and seriously disregarded the limits on its powers, that party could not bring an action before the national courts against the Member State on the same grounds.

IS THERE A RIGHT TO INTERIM DAMAGES IN NATIONAL PROCEEDINGS?

In his recent Order in *Antonissen* v. *Council and Commission*,[41] the President of the Court has now held that the Court of First Instance has jurisdiction to grant provisional damages by way of interim measure in proceedings brought pursuant to Article 215.[42] He did so in the following terms:

"an absolute prohibition on obtaining a measure of that kind, irrespective of the circumstances of the case, would not be compatible with the right of individuals to complete and effective judicial protection under Community law, which implies in

---

[36] Indeed, it has been said that there is a presumption to the effect that, wherever possible, the plaintiff must bring his action against the authorities of the Member States before the national courts, rather than bringing proceedings pursuant to Art. 215: see Warner AG in Case 126/76 *Dietz* v. *Commission* [1977] ECR 2431 at 2447 and Slynn AG in Case 59/83, *Biovilac* v. *Commission* [1984] ECR 4057 at 4085.

[37] [1970] JO L94/13 ([1970] OJ English Special Edition, 218), subsequently amended.

[38] Mechanisms for a Member State to obtain an indemnity also exist under Council Decision 94/728 on the Community's own resources ([1994] OJ L293/9), implemented by Council Regulation 1552/89 ([1989] OJ L155/1) as amended. In other fields, a Member State would appear to have no choice but to bring proceedings against the Commission under Art. 175 of the Treaty.

[39] See Oliver, "Joint Liability of the Community and the Member States" in *The Action for Damages in a Community Law Perspective, supra* n. 1, 285.

[40] Cases 106–120/87 [1988] ECR 5515.

[41] Order of 29 Jan. 1997 in Case C–393/96 P(R) [1997] ECR I–441.

[42] This development had been anticipated by Hoskins, "The Relationship between the Action for Damages and the Award of Interim Measures" in The *Action for Damages in a Community Law Perspective, supra* n. 1.

particular that interim protection be available (see, *inter alia*, the judgments in Case 213/89 *Factortame and Others* [1990] ECR I–2433, paragraph 21, and in Joined Cases C–143/88 and C–92/89 *Zuckerfabrik Süderdithmarschen and Zuckerfabrik Soest* [1991] ECR I–415, paragraphs 16 to 18, and the order in Case C–399/95R *Germany* v. *Commission* [1996] ECR I–2441, paragraph 46).

It is therefore not possible to rule out in advance, in a general and abstract manner, that payment, by way of an advance, even of an amount corresponding to that sought in the main application, may be necessary in order to ensure the practical effect of the judgment in the main action and may, in certain cases, appear justified with regard to the interests involved . . .

It is true that recourse to such a type of measure, which is more likely than others to give rise to irreversible effects, in particular in the event of the applicant's subsequent insolvency, must be restricted, and should be confined to cases where the *prima facie* case appears particularly strong and the urgency of the measures sought undeniable."[43]

Does this mean that such relief must also be available before the national courts? I would suggest that the arguments in favour of such a view are extremely strong. This is all the more so as the President of the Court referred in his Order to *Factortame I*, which related to interim relief before national courts.[44]

INTEREST ON DAMAGES

Finally, I should like to draw your attention to the vexed question of when interest is to be awarded, an important area which has scarcely been explored to date.[45]

Plainly, interest does not constitute a free-standing remedy in itself, but is dependent on the right to damages. To some extent, interest might be compared to mistletoe on the tree of damages. Yet in one significant respect the analogy is inadequate: unlike mistletoe, the award of interest cannot be regarded merely as an adornment, but should be seen as an indispensable measure to take account of the passage of time. This was recognised in *Marshall II*,[46] where the Court said:

"suffice it to say that full compensation for the loss and damage sustained as a result of discriminatory dismissal cannot leave out of account factors such as the effluxion of time, which may in fact reduce its value. The award of interest in accordance with the applicable national rules must therefore be regarded as an *essential component of compensation* for the purposes of restoring real equality of treatment." (emphasis added)

---

[43] The case was referred back to the Court of First Instance, whose President declined to grant interim relief (Order of 21 Mar. 1997 in Case T–179/96R)

[44] Interim damages are available in England by virtue of RSC Order 29, rule 11.

[45] For an all too rare examination of this subject, see van Casteren, "Article 215(2) and the Question of Interest" in *The Action for Damages in a Community Law Perspective, supra* n. 1.

[46] Case C–271/91 *Marshall* v. *Southampton Health Authority* [1993] ECR I–4367.

Marshall II was a case which related to damages. The plaintiff's contract of employment had been terminated because she had reached the retirement age for women, which was lower at the material time than the retirement age for men. The Court had ruled[47] that the employer's action fell foul of Council Directive 76/207 on equal treatment of men and women.[48] There could be no doubt that some compensation was due to Mrs. Marshall in view of Article 6 of that Directive, which required that an effective remedy be available in the national courts for any breach of its substantive provisions.

However, there was a dispute *inter alia* as to whether interest must be paid on such compensation. For the reasons given in the passage quoted here, the Court found that interest was indeed due.

Sutton[49] is a case referred from England which is still pending and which is marginally different. The plaintiff there had received an invalid care allowance (ICA) which had initially been withheld contrary to Council Directive 79/7 on equal treatment for men and women in matters of social security.[50] She is now claiming interest on that sum pursuant to Article 6 of that Directive, which is identical in all material respects to Article 6 of Directive 76/207. In the light of *Marshall II*, the Commission submitted to the Court that her claim should be upheld. In contrast, Advocate General Léger has taken the view that interest is not payable; he has sought to distinguish *Marshall II* on the basis that the sum in issue here is not damages. The crucial passage of his Opinion reads as follows:

> "In [*Marshall II*] the Court in no way laid down a general principle to the effect that any restoration of equality of treatment presupposes payment of interest on account of effluxion of time. The Court laid down such a requirement only when such restoration took the form of financial compensation imposed as a penalty, and it emphasized that 'the particular circumstances of each breach of the principle of equal treatment should be taken into account' . . .
>
> The arrears of ICA paid by the United Kingdom to Mrs. Sutton cannot be treated in the same way as damages granted as compensation for loss. Payment of those arrears merely restored to Mrs. Sutton her right to an award by an administrative authority of benefit to which she was entitled under a system of social protection."

I do not believe that I stand alone in being unconvinced by this reasoning. In the first place, there seems little force in the distinction between interest on damages and interest on a social security allowance to which the plaintiff is entitled as of right. Moreover—and this is of course the fundamental point—depriving a party of interest in this way scarcely seems compatible with the principle of effectiveness. It cannot be over-emphasised that, if the Advocate

---

[47] Case 152/84 *Marshall* v. *Southampton and South West Area Regional Health Authority* [1986] ECR 723 (*Marshall I*).

[48] [1976] OJ L39/40.

[49] Case C–66/95 *The Queen* v. *Secretary of State for Social Security, ex parte Sutton, infra* n. 50. For a discussion of the case see also above, Tridimas at p. 30 and below, Eeckhout at p. 68.

[50] *Supra* n. 28.

General's approach is followed, a Member State can refuse with impunity to pay sums due for many years, *even where the plaintiff has brought proceedings in good time.*[51] As the Court has pointed out on several occasions, a remedy cannot be effective if it takes no account of the effluxion of time.

I would remind you that, in the *Woolwich Building Society*[52] case, Lord Goff relied on the case law of the European Court in support of the proposition that interest must be due on sums reimbursed by the Inland Revenue after having been paid in taxes charged unlawfully. It is hard to see any material difference between *Sutton* and *Woolwich Building Society*. So it would be embarrassing now if the ECJ were to follow the approach suggested by the Advocate General.[53]

CONCLUSION

At the outset I said that state liability in damages for breach of Community law should not be seen in isolation, but must be viewed as part of the web of remedies available to aggrieved parties both in the national courts and before the two Community courts. I hope that that statement is now vindicated: once state liability in damages is understood in this light, it becomes easier to determine the proper scope of that remedy.

I hope also to have demonstrated that, to be effective, a remedy must take adequate account of the effluxion of time. This was the basis of the Court's rulings that *any* national court must be able to set aside a national measure contrary to Community law (*Simmenthal*); and that interim relief must be available in national courts (*Factortame I*). The time factor has rightly been a recurring theme in the case law of the Court, and it is likely to remain so.

---

[51] Thus the situation is wholly different from that which arose in Case C–208/90 *Emmott* v. *Ireland* [1991] ECR I–4269.

[52] *Woolwich Equitable Building Society* v. *Inland Revenue Commissioners* [1992] 3 WLR 366.

[53] Regrettably, in its judgment of 22 Apr. 1997 in *Sutton*, the Court has indeed followed the approach suggested by Léger AG. However, the Court proceeded to temper this ruling by saying that it was "for the national court to assess", in the light of *Factortame III* and its other judgments on state liability, whether the Member State was liable in damages for failure to implement and apply the Directive correctly throughout. Presumably, the quantum of damages, if awarded, would be equivalent to the interest lost—although the Court did not make this clear.

Would it not have been simpler, and more in keeping with the principle of effectiveness for the Court to have followed its earlier ruling in *Marshall II*?

5

Liability of Member States in Damages and the Community System of Remedies

PIET EECKHOUT*

INTRODUCTION

The context in which the Court of Justice first developed the principle of liability of Member States for damage caused to individuals by breaches of Community law (hereafter "liability") was clearly one of remedies: in *Francovich* the Court was forced to admit that the directive in issue did not have direct effect, and compensation for damages was the only remedy available for the individuals in question.[1] More broadly, there has been until now a strong link between the Court's case law on liability and the issue of non-implementation of directives. In *Faccini Dori*,[2] where the Court confirmed that directives do not have so-called horizontal direct effect (i.e. they cannot as such impose obligations on individuals), the Court referred to liability as a second type of safety net for the lack of horizontal direct effect (the first being consistent interpretation). The 1996 case law on liability confirms that one of the Court's main concerns is the proper implementation of Community law, and the corresponding protection of the rights of individuals.[3] It is thus one of the basic conditions for liability that "the rule of law infringed must have been intended to confer rights on individuals".[4] Further, the Court expressly links the liability of Member States with the liability of the Community itself:

"The protection of the rights which individuals derive from Community law cannot vary depending on whether a national authority or a Community authority is responsible for the damage".[5]

* All views are personal.

[1] Case C–6/90 [1991] ECR I–5357.

[2] Case C–91/92 [1994] ECR I–3325.

[3] See Joined Cases C–46 and 48/93 *Brasserie du Pêcheur and Factortame* [1996] ECR I–1029, para. 39, referring to "the full effectiveness of Community rules and the effective protection of the rights which they confer" as one of the bases for the principle of liability.

[4] Joined Cases C–178/, 179, 188, 189/ and C–190/94 *Dillenkofer and Others* v. *Federal Republic of Germany* [1996] ECR I–4845, para. 21.

[5] See *Brasserie du Pêcheur and Factortame, supra* n. 3, para. 42.

The liability of Member States is therefore but one side of the coin of the Community law principle of liability for damage caused by public authorities in general: the other side is the non-contractual liability of the Community, governed by Articles 178 and 215 of the Treaty. Those are indeed two sides of one coin, and they should both find currency in the system of remedies against breaches of Community law.

The aim of this contribution is to formulate some thoughts on the position of liability in the system of remedies for breaches of Community law and, more broadly, in the system of enforcement of Community law, and on how that position might develop. There is no doubt that, as a specific remedy, liability will lead its own life (it started walking and talking in 1996), but it should none the less be emphasised that it is part of a broader system. Against that background the following sections look at the potential use of liability as a pre-litigation tool and the relationship between liability and other national remedies.

LIABILITY AS A PRE-LITIGATION TOOL

In cases of alleged breaches of Community law the prospect for governments of possibly incurring liability should certainly concentrate their minds. In all cases where government authorities are accused by individuals of violating Community law it is possible for lawyers to refer to liability as a (more or less) plausible outcome of continued non-compliance. Given governments' interests in maintaining control over their finances, arguments to that effect are likely to have them re-examine their legal position. It is true of course that liability will be incurred only in case of a serious and manifest breach of Community law. However, in the early phases of a dispute, when the precise factual and legal issues may not yet be fully defined, it will often not be clear whether there is such a type of breach. If governments act on the basis of the principle of due care (as they normally should), liability claims are bound to have some impact.

That may be so in particular where administrative action by government authorities is in issue. Examples are cases such as *Hedley Lomas*[6] and *Brasserie du Pêcheur*[7] where government authorities apply legislation against companies or individuals in a manner contrary to Community law. A refusal to grant export licences or a prohibition on marketing imported products will often give rise to damage (loss of profit to start with) and may therefore set in motion exchanges on possible liability. Such cases will often be concerned with barriers to trade. From that perspective, the liability prospect might in the first place induce better compliance with the rules of the single market, and in particular with the basic freedoms.

[6] Case C–5/94 *The Queen* v. *MAFF, ex parte Hedley Lomas* [1996] ECR I–2553.
[7] *Supra* n. 3.

Administrative action also extends to cases where Community law itself is implemented by Member States. It should indeed be remembered that that is the standard way of implementing Community policies. Again one may think of licences not being granted,[8] or of subsidies which are refused, etc.

With respect to administrative action two areas perhaps deserve special mention. The first is the area of state aids.[9] Where for example aids are granted in breach of Article 93(3) of the Treaty (i.e. without notification to the European Commission) competitors of the aided undertaking may ask for the aid to be repaid. If the government does not comply, it may well incur liability towards those competitors. The second area is that of public procurement, which is to a large extent governed by Community rules. In that area there are specific rules on remedies, the so-called Remedies Directives, which provide for the award of damages to persons harmed by an infringement.[10] It would be logical to interpret those rules in the light of the Court's liability case law.

It will probably be less effective for individuals to brandish the liability weapon in cases of legislative action (i.e. where new legislation contrary to Community law is developed and enacted, or where legislation is not enacted where it should be). It is true that in the legislative process there is often effective lobbying by business or interest groups, but it is hard to conceive of lobbyists explaining the legal ramifications of legislative action in terms of liability. However, there is little doubt that the European Commission, in its role of Community law watchdog, will aim to refer to the prospect of liability, in particular in cases where directives are not implemented (i.e. legislative inaction). In some cases the risk of incurring liability may even concentrate the minds of governments more than the risk of being fined under Article 171 of the Treaty.

The issue of non-implementation of directives calls for a side-remark. Where individuals cannot invoke non-implemented directives against other individuals because they lack horizontal direct effect liability will often be the last resort remedy. In those cases Member States are likely to suffer from the lack of horizontal direct effect.[11] In the light of that, should those Member States not review their negative position on horizontal direct effect?[12]

---

[8] See e.g. Case C–124/95 *Centro-Com* [1997] ECR I–81 (although it is by no means suggested here that the UK's action amounted to a serious and manifest breach).

[9] Cf. Case C–39/94 *SFEI and Others* [1996] ECR I–3547.

[10] See e.g. Art. 2 of Council Directive 89/665/EEC of 21 Dec. 1989 on the co-ordination of the laws, regulations and administrative provisions relating to the application of review procedures to the award of public supply and public works contracts (OJ [1989] L359/33).

[11] See *Francovich*, *supra* n. 1, and *Dillenkofer*, *supra* n. 4.

[12] Cf. L. Van Den Hende, "Derdenwerking van richtlijnen? Diagonale werking van richtlijnen? Hoog tijd voor een verdragsherziening", [1997] *SEW* 196. See also Tridimas, above, pp. 32–33.

LIABILITY AND OTHER NATIONAL REMEDIES

Community law does not as a rule provide for procedures for the enforcement of Community rights by national courts. It is up to each domestic legal system to organise judicial process and claims based on Community law are subject to national procedural rules, provided those rules do not discriminate against such claims and do not render the exercise of Community rights unduly difficult.[13] Liability is essentially an exception to that principle of procedural autonomy in that it is, in part, subject to common rules defined by the Court of Justice. Thus liability is the only remedy for violations of Community rights by national authorities which is truly common in origin, even though many of its aspects are governed by national law.

As stated, the principle of procedural autonomy is not absolute. It is not that Community law simply turns a blind eye to national procedural rules. There is more and more case law by the Court of Justice which examines particular aspects of those rules in order to assess whether they are compatible with the above conditions of non-discrimination and effective protection.[14] Therefore, with the advent of the liability remedy there are two strands of case law on remedies: case law on the adequacy of national remedies and case law on the European liability remedy. The aim of the present section is to look at the relationship between those national remedies and liability.

Case law

In *Brasserie du Pêcheur and Factortame* Advocate General Tesauro discussed the subject of "Remedies in damages and administrative remedies: independent or ancillary?"[15] The starting-point of that discussion was the question whether, if the damage could be avoided by the injured party by means of other domestic judicial remedies, a failure to have recourse to such remedies did not break the necessary chain of causation between the breach of Community law and the damage. The Advocate General did not reach a conclusive view on that question, but was inclined to allow national rules which make actions for damages dependent on a previous action for annulment having been brought. He did not however suggest that that question is governed by Community law.

In its judgment the Court took a slightly different angle. It held that, in the context of an action for damages, the national court could inquire whether

---

[13] See Case 33/76 *Rewe* v. *Landwirtschaftskammer Saarland* [1976] ECR 1989 and Case 45/76 *Comet* v. *Produktschap voor Siergewassen* [1976] ECR 2043.

[14] See e.g. Case C–312/93 *Peterbroeck* v. *Belgian State* [1995] ECR I–4599 and Joined Cases C–430 and 431/93 *Van Schijndel and Van Veen* v. *SPF* [1995] ECR I–4705. For comments see M. Hoskins, "Tilting the Balance: Supremacy and National Procedural Rules" [1996] *ELR*, 365–77.

[15] Paras. 100–4 of the Opinion.

the injured person showed reasonable diligence in order to avoid the loss or damage or limit its extent and whether, in particular, he availed himself in time of all the legal remedies available to him. The Court added that it is a general principle common to the legal systems of the Member States that the injured party must show reasonable diligence in limiting the extent of the loss or damage, or risk having to bear the damage himself.[16] Those statements did not however make clear whether the requirement of reasonable diligence (or, in other words, the duty to mitigate one's loss) is a requirement actually imposed by Community law, nor what the exact implications of that requirement are.

A subsequent case in which there was some discussion of the relationship between liability and national remedies was *Denkavit Internationaal*.[17] In that case Advocate General Jacobs examined the issue of time-limits imposed by national law (and their compatibility with Community law) and the conditions for liability. The Netherlands and the United Kingdom had argued that the Court's judgment in *Emmott*[18] (where the Court stated that, as long as a directive is not properly transposed, a period laid down by national law within which proceedings must be initiated cannot begin to run) should be qualified along the lines of liability: the principle would apply only where there is a serious and manifest breach. The Advocate General did not agree. In his view, the remedy against the State in damages must be "of an exceptional and complementary nature and in particular should not be available as a means of circumventing time-limits for other remedies against administrative decisions".[19] The Court, however, did not need to express itself on that point in light of the interpretation given to the substantive rules in issue.

The above statement by the Advocate General could be read as meaning that the liability remedy should not be available in all cases of manifest and serious breach; it should be available only where no other remedies are available under national law, or where such remedies do not permit the full protection of rights derived from Community law. In other words, the liability remedy should not be concurrent with other remedies. An argument in favour of such an approach could be that the rights of the individual must be balanced against the general interest. Where national law imposes limitations on rights of action those will normally be in the public interest. In tax matters, for example, time-limits for taking legal proceedings will often be short in the interest of legal certainty, which, as Advocate General Jacobs emphasised in *Denkavit Internationaal*, protects both individuals and administrations.[20] In matters of social security, for example, there will often be limitations on

---

[16] Paras. 84 and 85 of the judgment. The Court also referred to Joined Cases C–104/89 and C–37/90 *Mulder and Others* v. *Council and Commission* [1992] ECR I–3061, para. 33.

[17] Case C–2/94 *Denkavit Internationaal and Others* v. *Kamer van Koophandel en Fabrieken voor Midden-Gelderland and Others* [1996] ECR I–2827.

[18] Case C–208/90 [1991] ECR I–4269.

[19] Para. 80 of the Opinion.

[20] Para. 64.

claims for arrears of benefits.[21] The approach of Community law is to accept such limitations, subject to the principles of non-discrimination and effectiveness. In other words, even before the liability remedy was developed Community law offered full guarantees of protection of Community rights where national remedies were available. If the liability remedy could be used concurrently with other national remedies, then in many cases the balance between the rights of the individual and the general interest (and the right of Member States to strike that balance through the adoption of procedural rules) could be lost.

However, more recent case law seems to go in a different direction. In *Société Comateb and Others* v. *Directeur Général des Douanes et Droits Indirects*[22] the Court considered the issue of repayment of charges on imports levied in breach of Community law. The judgment mainly deals with the conditions under which repayment can be refused where the charges were passed on to the purchaser (unjust enrichment). The Court substantially clarified those conditions, and imposed strict limitations on refusal to repay in national proceedings for recovery. At the end of the judgment, however, the Court added a paragraph on liability:[23]

> "Furthermore, traders may not be prevented from applying to the courts having jurisdiction, in accordance with the appropriate procedures of national law, and subject to the conditions laid down in . . . *Brasserie du Pêcheur and Factortame* . . . , for reparation of loss caused by the levying of charges not due, irrespective of whether those charges have been passed on."

Further signals were sent out by the Court in *The Queen* v. *The Secretary of State for Social Security, ex parte Eunice Sutton*.[24] That case concerned the right to receive interest on arrears of social security benefits. In the national proceedings Mrs Sutton had obtained an Invalid Care Allowance on the basis of Council Directive 79/7/EEC on equal treatment in the field of social security,[25] including arrears for the year prior to the date of her claim. Subsequently Mrs Sutton also claimed interest on those arrears, for which the relevant national rules did not provide. The High Court of Justice referred two questions to the European Court of Justice. The first question was whether the directive imposed the payment of interest on arrears of benefits. The Court found that that was not the case.[26] The second question was whether payment of interest flows from the principle that Member States are liable for breach of Community law.

[21] See Case C–338/91 *Steenhorst-Neerings* [1993] ECR I–5475; Case C–410/92 *Johnson* [1994] ECR I–5483.
[22] Joined Cases C–192 to 218/95, judgment of 14 Jan. 1997.
[23] Para. 34.
[24] Case C–66/95, judgment of 22 Apr. 1977.
[25] Council Directive 79/7/EEC of 19 Dec. 1978 on the progressive implementation of the principle of equal treatment for men and women in matters of social security [1979] OJ L6/24.
[26] For criticism see B. J. Drijber and S. Prechal, "Gelijke behandeling van mannen en vrouwen in horizontaal perspectief" [1997] *SEW* 156–7.

In relation to that second question Mrs Sutton claimed that the United Kingdom had not properly transposed the directive and that she suffered loss on account of the belated payment (some seven years after she had entered her claim) to which she was entitled. Inflation had eroded the real value of the amount in question, and the United Kingdom was required to compensate her, by paying a sum corresponding to the interest due, for the loss caused. However, the United Kingdom Government argued that liability could not apply in the present case, because the result prescribed by the directive, namely the payment of social security benefits, had been achieved (as stated, the directive does not require the payment of interest on arrears).[27]

The Court did not agree with the United Kingdom. It referred to the principle of Member State liability, and to the three basic conditions for liability: the rule of law infringed must be intended to confer rights on individuals; the breach must be sufficiently serious; and there must be a direct causal link between the breach and the damage. The Court also recalled that, notwithstanding those three conditions, the national law on liability provides the framework for making reparation, and then left it to the national court to decide whether Mrs Sutton was entitled to reparation and to determine, if appropriate, the amount of such reparation.[28]

Both judgments suggest that liability is a remedy which is wholly independent from other, national remedies, such as for recovery of charges or taxes, or for payment of arrears of social security benefits. That is also the view taken by Advocate General Jacobs in *Fantask A/S and Others* v. *Ministry of Trade and Industry*.[29] He states that repayment or entitlement claims and damages claims are claims of a different nature, and that what is recoverable under each may differ.[30] In matters of taxation and social security an individual should be able, where the liability conditions are met, to obtain full compensation for loss or damage incurred, including the amount of the tax overpaid or benefit withheld. The duty to mitigate loss or damage by using other remedies has no relevance to the restitutionary or entitlement element of the claim (the amount of the overpaid tax or benefit denied): whereas the duty to mitigate will be relevant in the case of loss of profits, the loss corresponding to overpaid tax or denial of benefits will not be aggravated by the delay in bringing proceedings.[31] The Advocate General adds that the existence of a wholly independent claim for damages, subject to longer time-limits than the comparatively short ones prescribed for restitutionary and entitlement claims in many Member States, is consistent with the different nature of the claim. The basis of that claim is not merely the unjust enrichment of the State resulting from simple error in the routine application of technical legislation

---

[27] Paras. 29 and 30 of the judgment.
[28] See paras. 30–34 of the judgment.
[29] Case C–188/95, Opinion of 26 June 1997, paras. 78–84.
[30] At para. 81.
[31] At para. 82.

but a serious violation of individual rights, calling for the re-appraisal of the balance between such rights and the collective interest in a measure of legal certainty for the States.[32]

It therefore appears that Advocate General Jacobs does not take the view, in contrast with the above reading of his remarks in *Denkavit Internationaal*, that the liability remedy is only available where no other remedies could be used which offer the same amount of protection. In cases of serious violation of individual rights it is no longer possible to defend procedural limitations in the context of ordinary remedies as expressing the correct balance between the rights of the individual and the general interest. That balance must then be re-appraised in favour of the individual.

An appraisal

What principles can be derived from the above case law? It seems clear now that liability is an autonomous, independent remedy, in so far as those terms express the principle that its use is not conditional on any prior or simultaneous use of other (national) remedies. Liability is subject to its own, specific conditions, and it is in the framework of those conditions alone that a person's claim must be dealt with. As such, the relationship between the liability remedy and other national remedies is the same as the relationship between the non-contractual liability of the Community (Articles 178 and 215(2) of the Treaty) and actions for annulment (Article 173 of the Treaty), where the Court has also stated that the action for damages is autonomous.[33] And from a purely legal perspective it seems inconceivable not to treat liability as an autonomous remedy. Liability is essentially a self-contained system, based on principles which, as the Court has held, are inherent in the system of the Treaty. Thus, liability claims have to be assessed on their own merits, and on those merits alone.

However, autonomy is, generally speaking, a concept which will often be difficult to define. That is also true of the autonomy of the liability remedy, as the following observations may serve to illustrate.

In *Brasserie du Pêcheur and Factortame* the Court does refer to the duty to mitigate, which may extend to the timely use of available remedies. That duty is not contrary to the autonomy of the liability remedy. It is, as the Court stated, inherent in a liability system, as witnessed by the fact that it is common to the legal systems of the Member States. But through the duty to mitigate there is none the less a link between liability actions and other national

---

[32] At para. 83.

[33] See Case 4/69 *Lütticke v. Commission* [1971] ECR 325, para. 6. See for a discussion of the case law P. Mead, "The Relationship Between an Action for Damages and an Action for Annulment: The Return of Plaumann", in T. Heukels and A. McDonnell (eds.), *The Action for Damages in Community Law* (The Hague, Kluwer Law International, 1997), 248–53.

remedies. In that respect many questions may arise. For example, in *Fantask* Advocate General Jacobs took the view that the duty to mitigate could not affect the restitutionary element of a claim: where a tax was paid in violation of Community law the damage (i.e. the overpaid tax) could not have been avoided by immediately instituting proceedings for repayment. If the taxpayer failed to do so within the applicable time-limits then he must still be able to recover the tax through an action in damages (provided there is a sufficiently serious breach). However, a different type of reasoning is not unthinkable. Some national courts might take the view that the taxpayer, by failing to institute proceedings for recovery, has not taken appropriate action to remove the damage (the overpaid tax). If he had, the damage would no longer have existed at the time of the action in damages, and therefore the taxpayer has failed to observe the duty to mitigate and his action must fail. It would seem that, in the current state of the law, such reasoning cannot be discarded as being clearly wrong. The example illustrates that at present the exact scope of the duty to mitigate is all but certain.

There are perhaps some analogies with the Court's case law on Community liability. In that respect the Court made some interesting statements in *Krohn* v. *Commission*.[34] The case concerned the refusal to grant import licences by national authorities in application of Community legislation. The Commission advanced several arguments against the admissibility of the action for compensation, one of which was that the applicant should first exhaust national remedies against the national authorities' decision. The Court pointed out that the action for damages under Articles 178 and 215, second paragraph, of the Treaty was an autonomous form of action. It none the less added:[35]

> "that such actions must be examined in the light of the whole system of legal protection for the individual established by the Treaty and that the admissibility of such an action may in certain cases be dependent on the exhaustion of national rights of action available to obtain the annulment of a national authority's decision. In order for that to be the case, however, it is necessary that those national rights of action should provide an effective means of protection for the individual concerned and be capable of resulting in compensation for the damage alleged."

Again, it is not clear what the exact scope of that statement is, but it does suggest that there may be further links between actions for damages and other national remedies.

It is also not clear which role national law will have to play in the relationship between liability and other national remedies. Would the Court for example accept a national rule which does not admit an action in damages where other remedies were available and have not been used? Or would it hold that, since the liability remedy is autonomous, such a national rule

---

[34] Case 175/84 [1986] ECR 754. See also Mead, *supra* n. 33, 250–3.
[35] At para. 27.

cannot be applied? And as regards the duty to mitigate, which the Court accepts as being common to the legal systems of the Member States, is it up to national law to determine its exact scope, or will it be determined by the Court as an essential element of the liability remedy? Again the answers to those questions may substantially affect the relationship between the liability remedy and other national remedies.

Another factor is the potential factual link between liability and other remedies in that liability could be used to complement other remedies. *Sutton*[36] illustrates that: Mrs Sutton could not obtain interest on arrears of benefits on the basis of the relevant directive, but the Court held that that did not preclude her from obtaining such interest by way of compensation for damage (provided of course that the various conditions for liability were met). Thus liability may operate as a complementary remedy, permitting the full compensation of damage incurred through sufficiently serious violations of Community law. In many cases, however, a plaintiff will have to initiate separate proceedings because the courts having juridisction to hear the "basic action" (e.g. for recovery of tax or for the granting of benefits) do not have jurisdiction to hear the action for damages. From the point of view of the effectiveness of remedies that does not seem fully satisfactory, and on that basis there may be scope in certain cases for setting aside procedural rules which preclude the court hearing the basic action to rule also on damages.[37]

LIABILITY AS THE CAP ON THE SYSTEM OF REMEDIES?

It can be seen from the preceding discussion that, although the Court of Justice confirmed the autonomous character of the liability remedy, the latter will not operate in a vacuum. Accordingly, there are bound to be many questions on the relationship between liability and other national remedies.

Because the liability remedy is autonomous it may serve as the "ultimate" remedy which is available, in cases of a sufficiently serious breach, (a) to complement other remedies by compensating for damage which cannot be recovered through those remedies and (b) to set aside procedural limitations (such as time-limits) governing other remedies. Thus understood liability is, as the only Community-law-based remedy against violations of Community law by national authorities, the crowning cap on the complex of varying national remedies. As such it counterbalances the lack of a Community-based system of remedies in national courts: where a serious violation by national authorities of an individual's rights derived from Community law has occurred there is always the guarantee of the liability remedy which permits the recovery of all damage caused by the violation.

[36] *Supra* n. 24.
[37] Compare with Case C–213/89 *Factortame and Others (Factortame I)* [1990] ECR I–2433.

If the above view is correct, then there are forceful arguments for creating more uniformity in the assessment of liability. Until now, the Court of Justice has stuck to the position that only the basic conditions for liability are governed by Community law, and that other conditions are subject to national law.[38] It is to be feared, however, that that approach will create many imbalances and therefore a rather uneven application of the liability remedy throughout the Community. One obvious example is time-limits. In a country like Belgium actions in damages are generally subject to a thirty-year time-limit, whereas in some other Member States time-limits may be much shorter (five years for example). From the perspective of the common character of the liability remedy such differences are difficult to defend.

There are two possible routes towards achieving more uniformity. The Court of Justice could itself gradually determine more of the rules governing liability. The obvious model for doing that would be its own case law on Community liability. Or there could be legislative action. In that respect there may be scope for some creativity. Where legislative action in the field of remedies is suggested the standard reply is that harmonisation of national systems of remedies is too complex, intrusive, that the efforts are not in proportion with the value added, and that there is no political willingness to achieve harmonisation. However, where the liability remedy is concerned it might be possible to lay down only some basic conditions, based on the Court's case law, and to provide for mechanisms permitting the incorporation of liability in national systems of judicial process.

---

[38] Subject, as always, to the principles of non-discrimination and effectiveness. For applications of those principles in the field of liability see Joined Cases C–94 and 95/95 *Bonifaci and Others* v. *INPS*, Case C–261/95 *Palmisani* v. *INPS* and Case C–373/95 *Maso and Others* v. *INPS*, judgments of 10 July 1997, not yet reported discussed below in Chapter 13.

6

The Domestic Liability of Public Authorities in Damages: Lessons from the European Community?

PAUL CRAIG

The impact of the recent decision of the European Court of Justice in *Brasserie du Pêcheur* and *Factortame*[1] raises a number of important issues concerning state liability in damages for breach of Community law. The object of this paper is not to examine in detail the nature of the test adopted by the ECJ itself. My views on this issue have been set out elsewhere.[2] It is rather to consider the possible implications of the decision for domestic law in the United Kingdom, both in those cases which have and in those cases which do not have a Community law component. A bare outline of the ECJ's reasoning is however necessary in order to assess its possible relevance and utility for United Kingdom domestic law.

1. AN OUTLINE OF THE ECJ'S DECISION IN *BRASSERIE DU PECHEUR* AND *FACTORTAME*

The decision of the ECJ may be summarised in the following manner. It should be emphasised that this is only a summary, and that more detailed examination of particular points will be considered later where necessary.

(a) The principle of state liability in damages was held to be general in nature and existed irrespective of whether the Community norm which had been broken was directly effective or not.

(b) The Court adopted what might be termed a *unitary conception of the state*: liability could be imposed irrespective of which organ of the state was responsible for the breach, the legislature, the executive or the judiciary.[3] The rationale for this was that all State authorities were bound, when performing

---

[1] Cases C–46 & 48/93, *Brasserie du Pêcheur SA v. Germany, R. v. Secretary of State for Transport, ex parte Factortame Ltd* [1996] 1 CMLR 889, [1996] All ER (EC) 301.

[2] This paper draws upon a more general article, "Once More unto the Breach: The Community, the State and Damages Liability" (1997) 113 *LQR* 67.

[3] *Supra* n. 1, para. 32.

their tasks, to comply with the rules laid down by Community law which governed the situation of individuals.[4]

(c) The ECJ set out the criteria to determine when the state could incur liability for acts and omissions of the national legislature which were contrary to Community law. The ECJ followed the general line of reasoning suggested by Tesauro AG who insisted that the tests for State and Community liability should be linked.[5] The ECJ held[6] that in determining the conditions for state liability it *was* pertinent to refer to its case law under Article 215(2) of the Treaty.[7] The rationale for this connection was that the protection which individuals derived from Community law could not, in the absence of some particular justification, vary depending upon whether a national authority or a Community institution was responsible for the breach.[8]

The system of rules developed under Article 215(2) took account, said the Court, of the wide discretion possessed by the Community institutions in implementing Community policies. This was particularly so in relation to liability for legislative measures.[9] The relatively strict approach to the Community's own liability under Article 215(2) in the exercise of its legislative activities was, the Court said, justified by the following consideration:[10] the exercise of legislative functions must not be hindered by the possibility of actions for damages whenever the general interest of the Community requires legislative measures which may adversely affect individual interests. The consequence of this was that, in a legislative context characterised by the exercise of wide discretion, the Community could not incur liability unless a Community institution had manifestly and gravely disregarded the limits on the exercise of its powers.

Member States do not always possess such a wide discretion when acting in areas covered by Community law, since the relevant Community norm may restrict this discretion to a significant degree, as was so on the facts of *Francovich* itself.[11] However, where a Member State acted in an area in which it did have a wide discretion, comparable to that of the Community institutions when implementing Community policies, the conditions for liability in damages must, said the ECJ, be the same as those applying to the Community itself.[12]

The right to damages was dependent upon three conditions.[13] First, the rule of law which was infringed must have been intended to confer rights on

---

[4] *Supra* n. 1, para. 34.

[5] Tesauro AG, *supra* n. 1, paras. 60, 80, 81, 84.

[6] ECJ, *supra* n. 1, para. 42.

[7] For general discussion of Art. 215(2) see, Heukels and McDonnell (eds): The Action for Damages in Community Law, (Kluwer Law International, 1997); Craig and de Burca, *EC Law, Text, Cases and Materials* (Oxford, Oxford University Press, 1995), chap. 12.

[8] ECJ, *supra* n. 1, para. 42.

[9] *Ibid.*, para. 43.

[10] *Ibid.*, para. 45.

[11] *Ibid.*, para. 46.

[12] *Ibid.*, para. 47.

[13] *Ibid.*, para. 51.

individuals. Secondly, the breach of this rule of law must have been sufficiently serious. Finally, there must have been a direct causal link between the breach of the obligation imposed on the State and the damage which was sustained by the injured parties.

The second of these conditions is of particular importance. As regards both Community liability under Article 215(2) and state liability in damages, the decisive test for deciding whether the breach was sufficiently serious was whether the Community or the Member State had manifestly and gravely disregarded the limits of its discretion.[14] The following factors could, said the ECJ, be taken into account when deciding upon this issue:[15] the clarity and precision of the rule which had been breached; the measure of discretion left by the rule to the national or Community authorities; whether the breach and consequential damage were intentional or voluntary; whether any error of law was excusable or inexcusable; whether the position adopted by a Community institution contributed to the act or omission causing loss committed by the national authorities; and whether on the facts the national measures had been adopted or retained contrary to Community law. A breach of Community law would, the ECJ said, be sufficiently serious if the State persisted in its behaviour notwithstanding the existence of a judgment by the ECJ which found the infringement of Community law to have been established. It would be equally so where there was settled case law of the Court making it clear that the action by the Member State constituted a breach of Community law.[16]

(d) It is important to highlight an ambiguity in the conditions for the application of the test set out above. Does this test apply only where the form of state action is legislative in nature *and* there is some significant measure of discretion, or can it be applicable even where the form of State action is administrative or executive provided that the significant measure of discretion exists?

The ECJ's judgment points to the latter formulation. The exercise of legislative power in areas where there is wide discretion is the form of State action most likely to render the preceding test applicable, but the fact that the State action is not legislative will not be conclusive provided that the requisite discretion exists.[17] That this is so is apparent from the ECJ's articulation of the Article 215(2) test itself. The ECJ, having stated that the test for liability cannot vary depending upon whether the Community or a Member State is responsible for the damage,[18] then states:[19]

"The system of rules which the Court has worked out with regard to Article 215 of the Treaty, *particularly in relation to liability for legislative measures*, takes into account, *inter alia*, the complexity of the situations to be regulated, difficulties in

[14] *Ibid.*, para. 55.
[15] *Ibid.*, para. 56.
[16] *Ibid.*, para. 57.
[17] I have argued that this is the correct approach in principle: Craig, *supra* n. 2, 81–3.
[18] ECJ, *supra* n. 1, para. 42.
[19] *Ibid.*, paras. 43–44. Emphasis added.

the application of the texts and, more particularly, the margin of discretion available to the author of the act in question.

Thus, in developing its case law on the non-contractual liability of the Community, *in particular as regards legislative measures involving choices of economic policy*, the Court has had regard to the wide discretion available to the institutions in implementing Community policies."

The ECJ's judgment in the *Lomas* case[20] is consistent with this view. In that case the Ministry of Agriculture refused licences for the export of live animals to Spain on the ground that the animals were suffering treatment contrary to a Community directive. The Ministry sought to justify the ban on the basis of Article 36. The ECJ found that this was not warranted. When considering the subsequent damages action the ECJ began by holding that the three limbs of the *Brasserie du Pêcheur* test applied to the instant case.[21] Given that the impugned act in *Lomas* was executive rather than legislative this would seem to confirm the view presented above, that the form of the state action was not in itself a condition precedent for the application of the test. When considering the second limb of the *Brasserie du Pêcheur* test, (the requirement of serious breach), the ECJ held that at the time of the infringement the United Kingdom "was not called upon to make any legislative choices and had only considerably reduced, or even no, discretion" and therefore that the mere infringement of Community law could suffice to establish the serious breach.[22] The most natural reading of this passage is that because the ECJ found that there was *neither* a legislative choice, *nor* any real discretion, therefore an infringement *per se* of Community law could be sufficient to establish the existence of a serious breach for the purposes of damages liability.

(e) Having established the general conditions for state liability in damages, the ECJ in *Brasserie du Pêcheur* and *Factortame* then made some observations on the relevance of fault. It held, in essence, that the finding of a serious breach might well involve "objective and subjective factors connected with the concept of fault",[23] but that liability could not depend on any concept of fault *going beyond* the finding of a serious breach of Community law.[24] The import of this part of the Court's judgment might easily be misunderstood.

Fault is a word which is given different meanings in different legal systems. It may be treated as equivalent to illegality, which is the approach adopted in some civil law systems.[25] Fault may be seen as distinct from illegality, which is the general approach taken in common law jurisdictions: proof of an *ultra vires* act will not be treated as the equivalent of objective fault, in the sense

---

[20] Case C–5/94, R. v. *Ministry of Agriculture, Fisheries and Food, ex parte Hedley Lomas (Ireland) Ltd* [1996] All ER (EC) 493.

[21] *Ibid.*, paras. 25–26.

[22] *Ibid.*, para. 28.

[23] ECJ, *supra* n. 1, para. 78.

[24] *Ibid.*, paras. 78–79.

[25] Thus in France the starting point is that "*toute illégalité constitue par elle-même une faute*".

of breach of an Atkinian duty of care.[26] Fault may also be defined in a more subjective sense, which connotes either some wrongful intent or some consciousness of the wrongdoing in question.

The term strict liability is also open to a range of meanings which are related to the interpretation of fault which a particular legal system adopts. Thus in the United Kingdom system, for example, the term would normally be employed (in non-criminal cases) to denote those areas where liability can be established without proof of fault, in the sense that no breach of a duty of care is required.[27]

When the *Francovich* case was decided one of the issues which prompted discussion was whether state liability in damages would be what is termed in United Kingdom law as strict, or whether some element of fault would be required. On the former view, the breach *per se* of a Community norm could render a State answerable in damages irrespective of whether, for example, the Community norm in question contained a broad discretion and/or was open to a spectrum of possible reasonable meanings. On the latter view, something more than illegality or invalidity *per se* would be required before a State could be liable in damages.

Now it is quite clear from the judgment in *Brasserie du Pêcheur* and *Factortame* that liability will *not* normally be strict in the sense articulated in the preceding paragraph. This is made clear both by the ECJ itself and the Advocate General. The Court's judgment and the Opinion of the Advocate General both state explicitly that, at least in cases where there is some significant measure of discretion and/or where the meaning of the Community norm is imprecise, illegality *per se* will not suffice for liability. The applicant will have to prove that the breach was sufficiently serious. This is further confirmed by the fact that the ECJ states, in its discussion of fault, that there is no requirement of fault *going beyond* proof of the serious breach of Community law.

However, once it is shown that the State did indeed commit a serious breach of the relevant Community norm, there is no room for any further inquiry. It is not open to the State to argue that there should be no monetary liability because there was no subjective fault relating to the conduct which led to the breach.[28]

(f) The general principle laid down by the ECJ was that the reparation for loss or damage caused to individuals flowing from a breach of Community law must be commensurate with the loss or damage which had been sustained.[29] In the absence of Community rules on this issue, it was for the

---

[26] See e.g. *X (Minors)* v. *Bedfordshire County Council* [1995] 2 AC 633.

[27] The plaintiff would, of course, have to establish that the criteria contained in the relevant statutory or common law rule had been broken.

[28] Tesauro AG chose to characterise this position as being one of strict liability. It is however clear that he is not using this phrase to mean damages liability for illegality *per se* by state authorities, but rather the absence of any requirement to prove subjective fault by the state: para. 88.

[29] ECJ, *supra* n. 1, para. 82.

domestic systems of each Member State to establish the criteria for determining the extent of the reparation. This was subject to the qualification that these criteria must not be less favourable than those which were applied in similar claims based on domestic law, and that they must not be such as to make it impossible or excessively difficult to obtain monetary compensation.[30]

The ECJ gave legal guidance on four more specific issues concerning damages: national courts could have regard to principles concerning mitigation;[31] reparation could not be limited to certain protected interests, such as property interests, if the consequence of this was to exclude totally the possibility of claiming loss of profit;[32] exemplary damages could in principle be recovered, if they could be awarded pursuant to a similar action in domestic law;[33] and the obligation to make reparation could not be limited to losses which were sustained after the delivery of the judgment finding the infringement of Community law.[34]

2. THE IMPACT ON DOMESTIC LAW: CASES WHICH HAVE A COMMUNITY LAW COMPONENT

The impact of the ECJ's jurisprudence on domestic law is clearly a matter of some importance. The nature of this impact may well differ as between those cases in which there is a Community law component and those in which there is not. These will be considered in turn.

The national courts are bound to apply the decisions of the ECJ in cases which have a Community law component. This is self-evident. The real issues are the cause of action in domestic law and the extent of the reparation. It is clear from the ECJ's ruling in *Brasserie du Pêcheur* and *Factortame* that both of these are matters for national legal systems, subject to the same provisos: that the conditions for recovery laid down by national law must not be less favourable than those which relate to similar domestic claims, and must not be such as to make recovery impossible or excessively difficult.[35]

There are two different ways in which the ECJ's decision can be applied in cases which have a Community law component.

The first, and most straightforward, would be to treat such cases as giving rise to an autonomous cause of action, without the necessity of fitting them into pre-existing heads of liability. On this view, a new tort will have been

---

[30] ECJ, *supra* n. 1, para. 83.

[31] *Ibid.*, para. 85.

[32] *Ibid.*, paras. 86–87.

[33] *Ibid.*, para. 89.

[34] *Ibid.*, para. 94. The general principle was that losses would be recoverable from the date of the infringement of Community law.

[35] ECJ, *supra* n. 1, paras. 67, 83. The national autonomy over the form of action and the extent of reparation is further bounded by guidance on matters of principle provided by the ECJ, concerning mitigation of damages, heads of recoverable loss and the like: paras. 68–73, 84–9.

created and liability in damages will sound in the United Kingdom if the three conditions set out by the ECJ are met. There is certainly some authority for treating liability in damages flowing from a breach of Community law in this manner.[36] The development of the law in this way would avoid the difficulties of adapting existing causes of action to this new situation, more particularly since there may be elements within such causes of action which do not sit easily with the requirements imposed by EC law in this area.

The second way in which the ECJ's jurisprudence could be fitted into domestic law would be via the action for breach of statutory duty.

This was suggested as the conceptual basis for a damages claim founded upon a breach of Article 86 in the *Garden Cottage Foods* case.[37]

As is well known, this case was distinguished in *Bourgoin*,[38] where the Court of Appeal held that the reasoning in the *Garden Cottage* case was limited to damages actions in private law, and did not apply to those cases where the defendant was a public body. In such instances the Court of Appeal held that a damages action would require proof of something more than a mere breach of a Treaty Article, and that a proven abuse of power, as required by the tort of misfeasance in a public office or some other recognised tort, would be needed.

It is clear that to limit applicants *only* to a misfeasance cause of action would not satisfy the ECJ since the restricted test for liability under this tort would make it "impossible or excessively difficult" for applicants to obtain compensation. There could be situations in which the State would be held to have committed a serious breach for the purposes of the *Brasserie du Pêcheur* test, and yet there would be no cause of action, since the breach may have been neither knowing nor malicious in the sense demanded by the tort of misfeasance.

It should, however, immediately be pointed out that the application of a breach of statutory duty test, properly structured in the manner to be described below, would meet the concerns expressed in *Bourgoin*. The essence of those concerns can be conveyed quite simply: if a State could be liable in damages for any breach of Community law *per se*, then this would not only be extremely burdensome, but it would also be subjecting the state to a more onerous liability than the Community itself under Article 215(2) of the Treaty. This objection was undermined by the approach adopted in *Brasserie du Pêcheur* and *Factortame*, since, as we have seen, the ECJ applied the same test for both State and Community liability, which test will often require more than proof of illegality *per se*.

---

[36] In *Application des Gaz* v. *Falks Veritas* [1974] Ch. 381, 395–6, Lord Denning MR spoke of Arts. 85 and 86 of the Treaty as creating new torts which would be actionable in domestic law, although he also stated that national courts would have to use the remedies which were available.

[37] *Garden Cottage Foods Ltd* v. *Milk Marketing Board* [1984] AC 130.

[38] *Bourgoin SA* v. *Ministry of Agriculture, Fisheries and Food* [1986] QB 716.

It is, nonetheless, extremely important to realise that the action for breach of statutory duty must be adapted to meet the needs of this area, since otherwise confusion and error will result. The normal criteria for the application of this action are well known, including the need to prove that Parliament intended to create private rights, that the damage was of the kind that the statute was intended to guard against, and that once the breach has been proven there is no further requirement for a showing of fault.[39]

These criteria would have to be adapted in the following manner. The national action for breach of statutory duty operates in this context as the vehicle through which the EC principle of state liability is applied at national level. This must, therefore, be reflected in the constituent elements of the breach of statutory duty action in this context. More specifically this means that the three key elements of the Community test of liability must be met before the national action can be sustained. The first of these, whether the Community law norm which was infringed was intended to confer private rights, is for the ECJ. The second condition, the requirement that the breach be serious, is for the national courts to assess, subject to guidance provided by the ECJ. The final limb of the test, causation, falls once again to the national court. The national action for breach of statutory duty will, therefore, operate differently here from in many other purely domestic contexts. It will *not* function as a strict liability tort. Where there is a significant measure of discretion, proof that a Community law norm has been broken will *not* suffice for liability. The plaintiff will have the onus of proving the seriousness of the breach.

There is no doubt that the breach of statutory duty action could be modified in this manner. The tort is intended to capture and reflect legislative intent as to whether an action should exist at all, *and*, if so, on what conditions. The normal presumption is that an affirmative answer to the first of these issues will lead to liability being conditioned on breach of the statute *per se*. The only difference here is that an affirmative answer on the first issue generates different conditions of liability which require in many cases proof of a serious breach.

While the tort of breach of statutory duty could be modified, there is little doubt that the development of an autonomous cause of action would be preferable. Such a development would thereby avoid some of the technical difficulties which might arise from basing liability on breach of statutory duty.[40] It would, moreover, avoid straining the idea which lies behind breach of statutory duty. The tort is based to some extent on the intent of the legislature. While there are well known difficulties in divining legislative intent as to whether a cause of action should exist or not, the idea nonetheless retains some importance. If we did employ breach of statutory duty in this context

---

[39] For a recent application of these criteria, see *X (Minors)* v. *Bedfordshire CC* [1995] 2 AC 633, 731–2.

[40] Hoskins, "Rebirth of the Innominate Tort", *infra* Chap. 7.

then we would be doing so in a manner which largely stripped away ideas of legislative intent, given that the operative decision whether a Community norm would be held to generate potential liability in damages would be for the ECJ, and this determination would clearly not be based upon any ideas of domestic legislative intent.

3. THE IMPACT ON DOMESTIC LAW: CASES IN WHICH THERE IS NO COMMUNITY LAW COMPONENT

(a) The basic foundations of domestic law

It is axiomatic that in formal legal terms the ECJ's decisions will have no impact in cases where there is no Community law component. It is equally clear that this formal legal result may not reflect reality. Even if the national courts are under no duty to apply EC law they may well consider it, particularly if they believe that it may be of assistance in developing domestic law. The possibility of a spillover impact from EC law cannot, therefore, be ignored.

The detailed domestic rules concerning the liability of public bodies are not of concern to us here. It is the underlying principles which are of relevance. These may be stated succinctly. The basic premise is that an *ultra vires* act *per se* will not give rise to damages liability. This has long been the basis of the common law, and the principle was recently explicitly reaffirmed by the House of Lords.[41] A corollary of this is that for a plaintiff to succeed the claim must be capable of being fitted into one of the recognised causes of action which exist, such as negligence.

It has long been recognised that the system has shortcomings. It can be difficult to prove these causes of action where the defendant is a public body. Perhaps more important is the fact that it may be difficult to fit certain fact patterns within the established causes of action at all.[42]

Three possible reforms have been proposed.[43] Arguments have been advanced for a new head of liability based upon *ultra vires per se*; for the adoption of a risk theory under which certain species of lawful governmental action would nonetheless require the payment of compensation; and for greater usage of *ex gratia* payments of compensation where this was felt to be warranted.

There is merit in these suggestions. They are not, however, unproblematic. This is especially so in relation to the reform which would have the greatest impact if generally adopted, state liability for losses caused by *ultra vires*

---

[41] X, *supra* n. 39, 730G.

[42] The *ultra vires* deprivation of benefits afforded by the State, such as welfare payments, licences, or aid may not be easily fitted into the traditional causes of action.

[43] Craig, *Administrative Law* (3rd edn., London, Sweet and Maxwell, 1994), 646–51.

action *per se*. The reasons such a test would be unduly onerous have been charted in detail elsewhere.[44] It is not a satisfactory *general* test of liability, which is not to say that it might not be appropriate within certain limited areas. It should not, moreover, be forgotten that the Community has resisted the wholesale adoption of this strict criterion.

Whether one feels that we in the United Kingdom have anything of value to learn from the ECJ's approach to the problems of state liability will obviously depend upon one's view as to the test which ought to operate in this area. It might, for example, be felt that a generalised regime of strict liability would be a preferable way forward. Yet it is clear that the United Kingdom courts have never taken this general approach to the liability of the state in damages. They have, as we have seen, resisted the equation between a finding of *ultra vires* and consequential liability in damages, and have insisted upon the plaintiff fitting the facts into an established cause of action. The pattern of thinking in terms of existing causes of action has also meant that on some occasions this has resulted in, for example, the imposition of strict liability through the finding of a breach of statutory duty; while on many other occasions the plaintiff has had to prove fault in the sense of negligence.

(b) Lessons from the ECJ's jurisprudence?: the action for breach of statutory duty

Given the basic doctrinal starting point of United Kingdom law, the jurisprudence of the ECJ may be of assistance, in that it increases the options at our disposal. It shows a way of adding to or modifying the existing heads of liability, without thereby imposing excessive burdens upon the public authorities. The dichotomy drawn by the ECJ between those cases where the public body has some significant measure of discretion and those where it does not may be helpful. It would allow us to develop, in the former type of case, an action based upon the serious breach of a domestic norm. In the latter type of case breach of the norm in and of itself should suffice for liability. In both types of case the plaintiff would also have to prove that the rule infringed was intended to confer rights and causation.

There is little doubt that the United Kingdom courts could develop the law in this way. There are in fact already some elements pointing in this direction. Specific authority for an approach akin to that developed by the ECJ can be found in the case law concerning the liability of judicial authorities. While United Kingdom law accords immunity to many judicial authorities, some are still open to damages liability when they act *ultra vires* and cause loss. The courts have, however, made it clear that the sense of invalidity which will be required for a damages action is narrower than that which applies in the

---

[44] Craig, *supra* n. 43, 648–50.

normal context of judicial review.[45] Only serious invalidity will suffice for a damages action.

The utility of developing a test analogous to that employed in the European Community can be exemplified by considering the important decision in *X (Minors)* v. *Bedfordshire CC*,[46] and comparing the reasoning used by the House of Lords with that of the ECJ. There were five actions, two of which concerned claims for damages arising out of mistakes in the application of legislation to prevent child abuse, the other three arising out of mistakes in the application of legislation concerning children with special educational needs. Space precludes a detailed analysis of this complex decision. It is, however, the structure of the Lords' reasoning which concerns us here.

Lord Browne-Wilkinson gave the unanimous judgment of the House of Lords. He reaffirmed the principle that proof of an *ultra vires* act would not, in and of itself, suffice for liability.[47] A plaintiff would still need to bring the claim within one of the recognised private law causes of action, such as breach of statutory duty, or negligence.[48]

The discussion of breach of statutory duty was orthodox. The plaintiff would have to show that the statute was intended to confer private rights of action, and that he or she came within the protected class. The normal rules of construction were applied to the instant cases. His Lordship found, however, that general legislation of the type in question here, although passed for the protection of those affected by it, was really enacted for the benefit of society as a whole, and therefore no action for breach of statutory duty would lie.[49]

Their Lordships may well have reached the same conclusion even if the test employed by the ECJ had been available to them. The ECJ's criterion does, nonetheless, give a court room for manœuvre which the standard breach of statutory duty doctrine does not readily provide. Part of the reason which may have convinced the House of Lords not to find for the plaintiffs was that this would impose strict liability on the defendants. Lord Browne-Wilkinson made it clear that this cause of action was not dependent on proof of carelessness.[50] The prospect of imposing such an onerous strict duty on the defendants in areas where they had to make complex discretionary determinations was not an attractive one for the House of Lords. A test akin to that used by the ECJ would have given their Lordships an extra option: they could have held that the statute was intended to give rights to individuals, but that proof of a serious breach was required for a damages action.

---

[45] *Re McC (A Minor)* [1985] AC 528; Craig, *supra* n. 43, 635–6.

[46] [1995] 2 AC 633.

[47] *Ibid.*, 730G.

[48] Lord Browne-Wilkinson made it clear in his judgment that there was no cause of action based upon careless performance of a statutory duty: the plaintiff always had to show that a common law cause of action in negligence existed, and this requirement could not be bypassed simply by averring that the statutory duty had been performed carelessly: *ibid.*, 732–5.

[49] *Ibid.*, 731–2.

[50] *Ibid.*, 731.

The interesting question is whether there is any conceptual obstacle to treating the action for breach of statutory duty in this manner? More specifically, is there any reason why this tort has to be one of strict liability? The answer must surely be no, for two related reasons.

In terms of decided cases, there are indeed cases of breach of statutory duty where the court has decided to impose a test other than strict liability. The approach has been to consider the relevant statute, its wording and its context, and from this to determine whether liability should be imposed at all, and if so on what terms.[51]

In terms of principle, it is difficult to see any objection to reasoning in this manner. The decision whether an action for breach of statutory duty lies at all is, as is well known, dependent upon construction of the relevant statute to determine legislative intent. Such intent is often difficult to divine, and therefore the court will often impute an intent to Parliament whether an action should lie or not, based upon certain principles of interpretation, such as the size of the class affected, whether there were existing penalties provided for in the legislation, and whether the damage which occurred was of the kind which the statute was intended to guard against. Given this approach, it is difficult to see why it would not be open to a court to find that an action could lie, but that it would do so only upon a finding of something more than illegality *per se*.

It should be emphasised that this might have made no difference to the actual result reached in the X case: their Lordships might still have decided against the imposition of any liability on the public authority under the head of breach of statutory duty. It is equally clear that the possibility of imposing such liability, but conditioning it on a finding of a serious breach of the statutory duty, would have given the court additional room for manœuvre.

(c) Lessons from the ECJ's jurisprudence?: the negligence action

It might also be argued that United Kingdom law could learn from European Community law concerning the way in which we approach the negligence action. This can be seen by focusing upon the discussion by Lord Browne-Wilkinson of *negligence* in the X case. The reasoning of his Lordship can be summarised as follows.

(i) Where a public authority had a statutory discretion it was for that body and not the courts to exercise the discretion. Therefore nothing which the body did within the ambit of its discretion could give rise to an action at common law. In determining whether the challenged action was outside its statutory discretion, the court could not assess factors which were felt to be non-

---

[51] Markesinis and Deakin, *Tort Law* (3rd edn., Oxford, Clarendon Press, 1994), 318–19; Horton Rogers (ed.), *Winfield and Jolowicz on Tort* (13th edn., London, Sweet and Maxwell, 1989), 179–80.

justiciable, or within the policy category of the policy/operational dichotomy. In that sense, "a common law duty of care in relation to the taking of decisions involving policy matters cannot exist".[52] Moreover, it seems clear from the judgment that even if a matter is justiciable, the plaintiff, in seeking to show that the authority has acted outside its discretion, will have to prove that it acted manifestly unreasonably so that its action falls entirely outside the ambit of the statutory discretion.[53]

(ii) If the challenged decision does fall outside the statutory discretion, it may give rise to a common law duty of care. Whether it will do so depends upon the application of the standard tests for the determination of such a duty,[54] taking into account, in particular, whether the existence of this common law duty would be inconsistent with or discourage the performance of the statutory duties.[55]

If one stands back from this formulation two elements for a successful action can be identified. First, the plaintiff will have to show what is, in effect, a serious breach of the statutory power. This follows necessarily from the requirement that the plaintiff prove that the defendant has acted outside the relevant statutory discretion in a manner which was manifestly unreasonable.[56] Other heads of *ultra vires* are insufficient for these purposes. Secondly, the plaintiff will then also have to show the requisites of a common law duty of care, in particular satisfying the requirement that it is fair, just and reasonable to impose this duty.

When viewed in this manner the gap between the ECJ's criterion and that which emerges from the House of Lords is not as great as might have been thought. It is moreover, clear that the three part test derived from the ECJ is capable of accommodating the concerns of our domestic courts.

The ECJ's requirement that the rule of law infringed should be intended to confer rights on individuals could, without difficulty, accommodate many of the issues which are presently considered under the heading of whether it is fair, just and reasonable to impose a duty of care.[57] Moreover, this element of the test should focus on whether there should be a right *to damages*.

The second limb of the ECJ's test, the requirement that the breach be serious is, as we have seen, echoed by the House of Lords. There are two aspects of this part of the test which are worthy of note.

---

[52] *Ibid.*, 738.

[53] *Ibid.*, 736H–7A, 749C–D, 761A–B.

[54] Was the injury foreseeable; were the parties sufficiently proximate; was it fair, just and reasonable to impose a duty of care?: *Caparo Industries plc* v. *Dickman* [1990] 2 AC 605.

[55] *X* v. *Bedfordshire CC, supra* n. 39, 739.

[56] *Ibid.*, 749, 761.

[57] In denying such a duty of care in the abuse cases the House of Lords was influenced by the following factors: there were a number of bodies responsible for this social service and therefore it would be wrong to impose damages liability on one particular body, the local authority; the delicacy and difficulty of the task performed in this area; and the fact that liability might render the local authority more wary of exercising its powers to protect children: [1995] 2 AC 633, 749–51.

On the one hand, it is true that when deciding whether the breach was serious the ECJ does not explicitly employ the language of justiciability in order to exclude from consideration factors which United Kingdom courts would deem unsuited to judicial resolution. This should not blind us to similarities which exist even on this issue. The ECJ will utilise analogous techniques, in determining whether there was a breach of Community law at all. This is exemplified by the fact that the ECJ will apply varying intensities of review to decide whether there has been a breach by the Commission of Community law, depending principally on the extent to which the ECJ feels suited to re-assessing the initial discretionary choice made by the Commission.[58] Low intensity judicial review in order to determine whether there has been a breach of Community law at all fulfils, therefore, much the same function in European Community law as does the explicit usage of justiciability in the United Kingdom.

On the other hand, it is difficult not to recognise that the ECJ's concept of serious breach is richer and better worked out than its domestic counterpart. The United Kingdom courts content themselves with linking the seriousness of the breach to proof of something akin to *Wednesbury* unreasonableness. To prove a serious breach, in the sense of *Wednesbury* unreasonableness, would, if this test is taken seriously, render it extremely difficult for a plaintiff ever to prove liability. The meaning of serious breach in Community law has been set out above. The inclusion of factors such as the clarity and precision of the rule broken and the extent to which the error of law was excusable or not, are of particular significance for much public law litigation. They provide a better and fairer touchstone of what should have to be proven, in addition to a finding of *ultra vires*, before liability in damages should be imposed, than does the bare invocation of *Wednesbury* unreasonableness. The point can be intuitively tested by asking oneself what types of factors does one think ought to be of relevance in a public law case, in addition to a finding of *ultra vires*, before liability should be imposed? It would be surprising if the types of factors mentioned by the ECJ did not feature in any such list.

The third limb of the ECJ's test, the causation requirement, is clearly a necessary component of any criterion for monetary liability. In the United Kingdom it is presently included as an aspect of the duty of care, but there is no reason in principle why it could not be regarded as a separate factor in its own right.

It might be objected that this recasting of domestic doctrine has failed to reconcile the fact that United Kingdom law requires proof of negligence in addition to the seriousness of the breach, whereas European Community law imposes no such condition on a damages action. There are two answers to this point. One is to acknowledge its correctness as a matter of formal legal doctrine. This precondition is a reflection of the fact that plaintiffs have to fit

---

[58] Craig and de Burca, *supra* n. 7, 501–5.

their claims into traditional causes of action in United Kingdom law. Negligence is the most plausible category in most instances.

The other possible response is more interesting. Leaving aside the formal legal reason for negligence, what would be lost if United Kingdom law dropped this stipulation? We have already seen that many of the issues presently considered under the heading of negligence can be integrated into the first and third limbs of the ECJ's approach. It has, moreover, been demonstrated that there are clear connections between the ECJ's second limb, the need for a serious breach, and the approach of the United Kingdom courts. If the United Kingdom were then to define the notion of serious invalidity in the richer manner adopted by the ECJ what exactly would be lost by dropping negligence as a distinct condition of liability?

4. CONCLUSION

Time will tell whether domestic law will develop along the lines charted above. Internal impetus for such a development will come from the fact that United Kingdom law will have to be modified to accommodate those cases which *do* have a Community law element. At the very least this will make our courts aware of the EC law approach, and mindful of its potential.

Opinions will doubtless differ as to whether it would be desirable for any such spillover effect to occur. Much will depend upon personal views concerning the correctness of the Community test itself. It has been argued elsewhere that the test does encapsulate an appropriate balance between the need to render government financially liable for its actions, and the equally important necessity of not imposing on the government a too onerous regime of liability, which could hinder it in the discharge of its responsibilities.[59] The approach of the ECJ does, moreover, allow for differentiation between those cases where there is some significant measure of discretion and those where there is not. In the former type of case the three part test developed by the ECJ will be applied. In the latter type of case, assuming that the rule of law was intended to confer rights on the individual, and that there was a causal link between the breach and the loss, it will be held that any breach was *ipso facto* a serious breach.

In reaching a conclusion as to the desirability of any spillover impact two points should perhaps be borne in mind.

When we look to other legal systems we should do so with an open mind. We should not approach any legal problem on the assumption that our current doctrine is necessarily defective, nor should we be so insular as to assume that we have nothing to learn from the way in which other legal systems deal with the same problem. Thus, even if it is decided that on balance we wish

---

[59] Craig, *supra* n. 2, 77–87.

to preserve the structure of the traditional common law mode of thought as captured in the negligence action, and that we wish to continue to apply it to public bodies in the manner set out in the X case, this does not mean that we should automatically shut our minds to, for example, the richer notion of serious breach developed by the ECJ.

The other point to bear in mind in this respect is that there may be other catalysts for re-thinking the criteria which we apply to determine the damages liability of public bodies. The incorporation of the European Convention on Human Rights (ECHR) into domestic law will inevitably raise the issue of remedies and the place of a damages action within any such scheme. Experience from other common law jurisdictions shows the difficulties which fashioning any such remedy can involve.[60] It also shows the importance of clarity on the government's part (in the enabling legislation) as to the test for liability which it would like to see imposed. The Labour Government has already given some indication that it does not wish to exclude such a remedy in all cases, but nor does it believe that a damages action for any and every breach of the incorporated ECHR is necessarily appropriate or desirable. The language used by the Labour consultation paper was that it would be "wrong to rule out compensation in very serious and exceptional cases".[61] This objective may well point to the adoption of a test similar to that adopted by the ECJ. Indeed, given the currently expressed governmental objectives, it is difficult to see how it could not be analogous. If this were to happen then there would, of course, be the possibility of a spillover impact from this to other parts of United Kingdom law.

[60] See e.g. in New Zealand, *Simpson* v. *Attorney-General (Baigent's Case)* [1994] 3 NZLR 667.
[61] See *Bringing Rights Home: Labour's Plans to Incorporate the European Convention on Human Rights into UK Law* (Dec. 1996), 8.

7

Rebirth of the Innominate Tort?

MARK HOSKINS*

1. INTRODUCTION

The principle of state liability for breach of Community law is not expressly provided for in the EC Treaty, but has been developed by the case law of the Court of Justice beginning with the judgment in Joined Cases C–6/90 and C–9/90 *Andrea Francovich* v. *Italy*.[1] Now that the fundamental conditions of liability have been established, the focus will switch to the practical application of those conditions by the national courts. One of the issues for the English courts to consider will be the identification of the appropriate cause of action for such a claim. Whilst preparing this paper for the conference, I was slightly concerned that everyone attending would consider this to be a non-issue on the basis that breach of statutory duty was the obvious candidate.[2] To my relief, the majority of the delegates seemed to share my view that serious consideration should be given to the idea of the innominate tort as the appropriate solution.

However, on 31 July 1997, a three judge Divisional Court delivered a judgment in *R* v. *Secretary of State for Transport, ex parte Factortame* in which it indicated that the appropriate cause of action should be breach of statutory duty. The main issue in the case was the assessment of whether the United Kingdom Government had committed a sufficiently serious breach of law to give rise to liability in damages by enacting the Merchant Shipping Act 1988. The Divisional Court found that it had. The Court also considered whether exemplary damages were available in the context of a claim against the State for breach of Community law and held that they were not.

In relation to the appropriate cause of action the Court held that:

> "In Community law, the liability of a State for a breach of Community law is described as non-contractual. In English law there has been some debate as to the correct nature of the liability for a breach of Community law. In our judgment it is best understood as a breach of statutory duty.

* Barrister, Brick Court Chambers, London.

[1] [1991] ECR I–5357.

[2] Arguments in support of breach of statutory duty as the appropriate cause of action can be found in the excellent article by Jane Convery, "State Liability in the United Kingdom after *Brasserie du Pêcheur*" (1997) 34 CML Rev. 603.

. . . whilst it can be said that the cause of action is *sui generis*, it is of the character of a breach of statutory duty. The United Kingdom and its organs and agencies have not performed a duty which they were statutorily required to perform [by the European Communities Act 1972]."

2. CASE LAW OF THE COURT OF JUSTICE

The Court of Justice has established that a Member State will incur liability for breach of Community law whenever the following three substantive conditions are satisfied:[3]

(a) the rule of law infringed must have been intended to confer rights on individuals;
(b) the breach must be sufficiently serious; and
(c) there must be a direct causal link between the breach of the obligation resting on the State and the damage sustained by the injured parties.

However, these conditions are not sufficiently detailed to cover all of the substantive and procedural issues which will arise from a state liability claim in the national courts of the Member States. Therefore, subject to the reservation that the three conditions laid down by the Court are "necessary and sufficient" to give rise to a right to damages founded directly on Community law,[4] the Court also held that, in the absence of Community legislation, it is for the internal legal order of each Member State to provide the detailed substantive and procedural conditions for reparation of loss. Any action for damages for state liability in the national courts will therefore be a hybrid of Community and national rules. In order to establish a right to damages, a plaintiff will have to show that the three conditions laid down by the Court have been satisfied. Thereafter the nature and content of the right will be defined by national substantive and procedural rules. However, the national rules applied must not be less favourable than those relating to similar domestic claims and must not make it virtually impossible or excessively difficult to obtain reparation.[5]

[3] Joined Cases C–46 and 48/93 *Brasserie du Pêcheur* v. *Germany and R.* v. *Secretary of State for Transport, ex parte Factortame Ltd* [1996] ECR I–1029, paras. 50–1; Case C–392/93 *R.* v. *HM Treasury, ex parte British Telecommunications plc* [1996] ECR I–1631, paras. 39–40; Case C–5/94 *R.* v. *Ministry of Agriculture, Fisheries and Food, ex parte Hedley Lomas (Ireland) Ltd* [1996] ECR I–2553, paras. 25–6; Joined Cases C–178/94 etc. *Erich Dillenkofer* v. *Germany* [1996] 3 CMLR 469, paras. 21–3.
[4] Joined Cases C–6 and 9/90 *Andrea Francovich* v. *Italy, supra* n. 1, para. 41; Joined Cases C–46 and 48/93 *Brasserie du Pêcheur and Factortame, supra* n. 3, para. 66.
[5] Joined Cases C–6 and 9/90 *Francovich, supra* n. 1, paras. 42–3; Joined Cases C–46 and 48/93 *Brasserie du Pêcheur and Factortame, supra* n. 3, paras. 67–8 and 83; Case C–5/94 *Hedley Lomas, supra* n. 3, para. 31.

This formulation is one which has consistently been employed in the past in relation to national *procedural* rules,[6] however, in the context of State liability, the Court of Justice has expressly indicated that the national legal systems are to lay down the detailed *substantive* and procedural conditions necessary to enable a plaintiff to bring an action for damages in the national courts.

3. POTENTIAL CAUSES OF ACTION

In the context of English law, it has been accepted without debate that a state liability claim should be categorised as a tort. However, the detailed substantive rules applicable to such a claim will be largely determined by the nature of the "cause of action" under which the claim is brought. There appear to be four possible causes of action in English law for giving effect to state liability. These are misfeasance in public office, breach of statutory duty, innominate tort and negligence.

(a) Negligence

Negligence can be discounted from the outset as, by definition, it will only be applicable where it is possible to establish negligence on the part of the relevant public body. It is clear from the case law of the Court of Justice that state liability under Community law does not depend on fault in the sense in which it forms part of the common law of negligence. In Joined Cases C–46 and 48/93 *Brasserie du Pêcheur and Factortame*,[7] the Court held that "reparation of loss or damage cannot be made conditional on fault (intentional or negligent) on the part of the organ of the State responsible for the breach, going beyond that of a sufficiently serious breach of Community law". Furthermore, it would be exceptionally difficult to apply the common law of negligence to legislative acts of Parliament, which are capable of giving rise to state liability as a matter of Community law. (*Factortame* concerned liability for adoption of the Merchant Shipping Act 1988.) Finally, in the context of claims based on negligence, as a general rule the English courts have been unwilling to recognise a right to damages for economic loss as opposed to damages to compensate for physical harm or damage. In short, the basic nature of the tort of negligence is too dissimilar to the principles underpinning state liability for breach of Community law for this cause of action to provide an appropriate vehicle for state liability claims in the English courts.

---

[6] See, in particular, Case 33/76 *Rewe* [1976] ECR 1989 and Case 45/76 *Comet* [1976] ECR 2043.

[7] *Supra* n. 3, para. 80 of the judgment.

(b) Misfeasance in public office

In *Bourgoin* v. *Ministry of Agriculture, Fisheries and Food*,[8] MAFF had introduced a system of licences for the import of turkeys into the United Kingdom ostensibly to deal with the problem of Newcastle disease. The Court of Justice held that the system was contrary to Article 30 of the EEC Treaty and was in reality a disguised restriction on trade designed to protect British poultry producers from French competition.[9] Certain French turkey producers commenced an action for damages in the English courts. They claimed damages for breach of statutory duty, innominate tort and misfeasance in public office. The majority of the Court of Appeal held that there was no cause of action for breach of statutory duty or an innominate tort. They found that the only possible cause of action for a breach of Community law by the Minister was misfeasance in public office.

In order to found a cause of action upon the tort of misfeasance in public office, it is necessary to prove that the defendant acted with the intention of injuring the plaintiff (ie. targeted malice) or that the defendant acted with actual knowledge of the *ultra vires* or unlawfulness of his act and knew that the act would probably cause damage to the plaintiff.[10] In Joined Cases C–46 and 48/93 *Brasserie du Pêcheur and Factortame*,[11] the Court of Justice held that to impose such a condition where the breach is attributable to the national legislature would make it impossible or extremely difficult in practice to obtain effective reparation for loss or damage. Thus, although there may be particular situations where it is possible to claim damages against the State for a breach of EC law on the basis of misfeasance in public office, it will not be appropriate as a cause of action in most cases where state liability has been incurred as a matter of Community law.

(c) Innominate or Euro tort

The concept of "innominate" or Euro "torts" was first raised, *obiter*, in 1974 by Lord Denning MR in *Application des Gaz SA* v. *Falks Veritas Ltd*,[12] where he stated that, as Articles 85 and 86 of the EEC Treaty had direct effect, they were part of English law and created new torts or wrongs called "undue

---

[8] [1986] QB 716.

[9] Case 40/82 *Commission* v. *United Kingdom* [1982] ECR 2793.

[10] *Bourgoin, supra* n. 8, at 740E–F, *per* Mann J and at 777H, *per* Oliver LJ; *Three Rivers District Council* v. *Bank of England (No. 3)* [1996] 3 All ER 558 at 594A–C, *per* Clarke J.

[11] *Supra* n. 3, at para. 73. Even before this judgment of the Court of Justice, Lord Goff had doubted whether *Bourgoin* could still be considered good law as a result of the judgment of the Court of Justice in Joined Cases C–6 and 9/90 *Factortame*: see *Kirklees Metropolitan Borough Council* v. *Wickes Building Supplies Ltd* [1993] AC 227 at 281C–2C. The appropriateness of misfeasance in public office as a cause of action for state liability under Community law was also doubted by Clarke J in *Three Rivers, supra* n. 10, at 624C–E.

[12] [1974] 1 Ch. 381 at 395H–6C.

restriction of competition within the common market" and "abuse of a dominant position within the common market". However, this approach was firmly rejected by Lord Diplock in *Garden Cottage Foods Ltd* v. *Milk Marketing Board*,[13] who stated that there was no reason to invent a wholly novel cause of action in order to deal with breaches of the EEC Treaty which have the same effect in the United Kingdom as statutes.

In the specific context of state liability, Mann J, at first instance in *Bourgoin*,[14] described the formulation of a claim based on an innominate tort as "obsolete". However, more recently in *Three Rivers*, Clarke J observed:[15]

> "It appears to me that in such a case the claim should not be regarded as a claim for damages for the tort of misfeasance in public office, but rather as a claim of a different type not known to the common law, namely a claim for damages for breach of a duty imposed by Community law or for the infringement of a right conferred by Community law."

(d) Breach of statutory duty

In *Garden Cottage Foods*,[16] Lord Diplock held that:

(a) Article 86 of the EEC Treaty has direct effect and therefore creates rights for individuals;

(b) Section 2(1) of the European Communities Act 1972 provides that such Community rights are without further enactment to be given legal effect in the United Kingdom and enforced accordingly;[17]

(c) Therefore, a breach of the duty imposed by Article 86 can be categorised in English law as a breach of statutory duty.

In principle, there is no reason why state liability claims should not be categorised in a similar way. Indeed, this was the view taken by Oliver LJ (dissenting) in *Bourgoin*.[18]

The judgment of the Court of Justice in *Francovich* establishes that state liability may also arise in respect of failure by a Member State to implement a directive which does not have direct effect. However, reliance on breach of

---

[13] [1984] 1 AC 130 at 144F–G.

[14] [1986] 1 QB 716 at 734B–F, following a concession by counsel. See also *per* Oliver LJ at 775C–G.

[15] *Supra* n. 10, at 624C–D.

[16] *Supra* n. 13, at 141C–F.

[17] S. 2(1) of the European Communities Act 1972: "All such rights, powers, obligations and restrictions from time to time created or arising by or under the Treaties, and all such remedies and procedures from time to time provided for by or under the Treaties, as in accordance with the Treaties are without further enactment to be given legal effect or used in the United Kingdom shall be recognised and available in law, and be enforced, allowed and followed accordingly; and the expression 'enforceable Community right' and similar expressions shall be read as referring to one to which this subsection applies."

[18] *Supra* n. 8.

statutory duty need not be restricted to directly effective rights The right to damages for breach of Community law is "a right founded directly on Community law"[19] and section 2(1) of the 1972 Act gives effect to all rights and remedies arising under the Treaties.

4. BREACH OF STATUTORY DUTY VERSUS INNOMINATE TORT

At first sight, it might appear that breach of statutory duty is the most appropriate and indeed the only possible cause of action for giving effect to state liability. However, this assumption requires further consideration.

Breach of statutory duty is not a tort which was specifically created to deal with unlawful acts by the State and/or public authorities. Indeed, it is most commonly associated with cases involving private parties. A typical case would be where an employer has failed to comply with statutory health and safety requirements with the result that an employee has been injured. *Clerk and Lindsell*[20] notes that "There would appear to be today a significant trend against finding that a remedy in breach of statutory duty lies against public authorities charged with the protection of the public welfare." Furthermore, in *X (Minors)* v. *Bedfordshire County Council*[21] Lord Browne-Wilkinson observed that:

> "The cases where a private right of action for breach of statutory duty have been held to arise are all cases in which the statutory duty has been very limited and specific as opposed to general administrative functions imposed on public bodies and involving the exercise of administrative discretions."

Section 2(1) of the European Communities Act 1972 does not impose a "very limited and specific" statutory duty. On the contrary its purpose and scope are general in nature. The artificiality of basing the right to damages on a breach of the "duty" imposed by section 2(1) of the 1972 Act is demonstrated by the approach of the Divisional Court in *Factortame* in relation to exemplary damages. The Court began by recognising that various domestic statutes provide for the recovery of exemplary damages. However, it found that state liability for breach of Community law is a breach of the statutory duty imposed by section 2(1) of the European Communities Act 1972 and the 1972 Act does not contain any express provision for the award of penal or exemplary damages. It therefore drew the conclusion that exemplary damages were not available for breach of Community law by the State. However, this argument is largely self-justifying because the 1972 Act is not the sort of Act which on its own could ever give rise to a cause of action for breach of statutory duty. It is too general in nature. It is therefore hardly surprising that it does not specifically provide for the availability of exemplary damages.

---

[19] Joined Cases C–6 and 9/90 *Francovich*, *supra* n. 1, para. 41.
[20] *Clerk and Lindsell on Torts* (17th edn., London, Sweet and Maxwell, 1995), 11–14.
[21] [1995] 2 AC 633 at 732B.

Whilst it is true that the basis of state liability is breach of a duty, the primary duty breached is one imposed by Community law, whether it be the EC Treaty itself or an act of secondary legislation. Liability arises as a result of a breach of *Community law*, not English law. Furthermore, the remedial right to damages arises solely from the case law of the Court of Justice, not from any English law concept of tortious liability. The common law simply does not have any notion of state liability in the sense in which it exists in Community law. This is exemplified by the fact that, under Community law, a Member State may incur liability in damages for the adoption of primary legislation. The idea that the State can be liable for legislative acts is something which is wholly alien to English domestic law, as it conflicts with the concept of the sovereignty of Parliament.

As a matter of logic, it is difficult to justify an analysis which is based on the notion that Parliament is liable in damages for breach of a particular domestic statute (the European Communities Act 1972) by virtue of the fact that it has adopted a subsequent statute which is contrary to Community law. It is a fundamental part of the United Kingdom's constitutional principles that Parliament is free to legislate how it wishes and may overturn or amend any previous statute. In truth, it is not the 1972 Act which has a special status in English law, it is Community law which is supreme.[22]

It follows that, as a matter of constitutional theory, the notion that a breach of Community law gives rise to a right to damages in the English courts because there has been a breach of the European Communities Act 1972 is a fiction, albeit a convenient one. Both the primary substantive law duty and the obligation to pay damages as a result of a breach of that duty arise from Community law, not English law. *Factortame* itself involved this sort of issue as the breach of Community law was occasioned by the adoption of the Merchant Shipping Act 1988. However, the constitutional problems of analysing the right to damages as a breach of statutory duty were not addressed by the Divisional Court in its judgment.

Rather than relying on the fiction of a breach of statutory duty arising from section 2(1) of the 1972 Act, it would be preferable to recognise that we are dealing with a wholly novel situation and to establish the existence of a new type of tortious cause of action which could be called the tort of "state liability for breach of Community law". If such an approach were to be adopted, the detailed substantive rules necessary to give effect to the notion of state liability could be drawn from the Court of Justice's case law on the liability in damages of the Community institutions (Articles 178 and 215 of the EC Treaty), rather than from the domestic tort of breach of statutory duty. In contrast to breach of statutory duty, the case law of the Court of Justice on Article 215 has been developed specifically to deal with the liability of public authorities (i.e. the Community institutions), including liability for legislative acts.

[22] For an argument to the contrary, see the article by Convery, *supra* n. 2, at 630–2.

The choice of cause of action is not purely theoretical; it has important practical effects. This is because the detailed substantive conditions for breach of statutory duty differ in certain respects from the substantive conditions relating to Article 215 of the EC Treaty. In particular,

(a) *Causation*—under Article 215, the damage suffered must be a sufficiently direct consequence of the unlawful conduct.[23] This is an apparently stricter test than that applied to breach of statutory duty where the plaintiff must show that, on a balance of probabilities, the breach of duty caused, or materially contributed to, his loss.[24] There is no need to show that any loss suffered was a reasonably foreseeable result of the breach.

(b) *Mitigation*—under Article 215, the plaintiff must show reasonable diligence in limiting the extent of his loss. However, any losses incurred in attempting to mitigate loss are not recoverable as there is no direct link between such loss and the unlawful Community act.[25] In relation to breach of statutory duty, the general principle is the same in that a plaintiff cannot recover damages for any loss which he could have avoided by taking reasonable steps. However, in contrast to the position under Article 215, where a plaintiff incurs additional loss or expense as a result of taking reasonable steps to mitigate the original loss, he may recover the additional loss or expense from the defendant.[26]

(c) *"Defences"*—in relation to breach of statutory duty, the defences available, such as *volenti non fit injuria* and contributory negligence, reflect the fact that this cause of action has been developed in the context of actions brought by private individuals against other private individuals. Such defences are not particularly appropriate to public bodies, depending as they do on notions of subjective intention or fault. In contrast, in relation to Article 215, the Court of Justice has developed particular principles which take account of the special considerations which attach to liability of public bodies. For example,

(i) *Assumption of normal risks*—in Joined Cases 83/76 and others *HNL* v. *Council*,[27] the Court stated that, " . . . individuals may be required, in the sectors coming within the economic policy of the Community, to accept within reasonable limits certain harmful effects on their economic interests as a result of a legislative measure without being able to obtain compensation

---

[23] Joined Cases 64/76 & 113/76 *Dumortier Frères* v. *Council* [1979] ECR 3091, para. 21.

[24] *Bonnington Castings Ltd* v. *Wardlaw* [1956] AC 613.

[25] Joined Cases C–104/89 and C–37/90 *Mulder* v. *Council and Commission* [1992] ECR I–3061, para. 33.

[26] See *Clerk & Lindsell, supra* n. 20, at 27–06; *Chitty on Contracts* (27th edn., London, Sweet and Maxwell, 1994) at 26–050).

[27] [1978] ECR 1209, paras. 6–7.

from public funds even if that measure has been declared null and void". As a result, although the relevant regulation was found to be unlawful as it discriminated against the applicants, no damages were payable *inter alia* as the financial effect of the regulation did not exceed the bounds of the economic risks inherent in the activities of the agricultural sector concerned.

(ii) *Overriding public interest*—the Court of Justice has held that the Community will not be liable to pay compensation where there is an overriding consideration of public interest.[28] For example, where there are serious disturbances in the market or where the market is operating artificially, the Community may have to act in the interests of the Community as a whole, rather than in the individual interests of a particular group of traders.

In Joined Cases C–46 and 48/93 *Brasserie du Pêcheur and Factortame*, the Court of Justice, as part of its justification for the adoption of the three "necessary and sufficient" conditions giving rise to state liability in damages, held[29] that:

"the conditions under which the State may incur liability for damage caused to individuals by a breach of Community law cannot, in the absence of particular justification, differ from those governing the liability of the Community in like circumstances. The protection of the rights which individuals derive from Community law cannot vary depending on whether a national authority or a Community authority is responsible for the damage."

Although the Court of Justice expressly recognised that the remaining substantive rules of liability could be provided by the Member States' own domestic legal systems, the goal of uniformity for Community and state liability is clearly a desirable one. However, for the reasons outlined above, adoption of breach of statutory duty as the appropriate cause of action in English law would mean that actions for damages in the English courts would not proceed on the same basis as actions for damages against the Community institutions in the Court of Justice and Court of First Instance.

The adoption of breach of statutory duty as the appropriate cause of action by the Divisional Court in *Factortame* could lead to further problems. The Court of Justice has established that, whilst it is for the national legal systems of the Member States to lay down the detailed substantive conditions to be applied to claims in the national courts based on the principle of state liability, the conditions imposed must not be less favourable than those relating to similar domestic claims. Application of this principle could lead to a situation where lawyers acting for a plaintiff conduct a comparison of Article 215 and

[28] Case 74/74 *CNTA* v. *Commission* [1975] ECR 533, para. 43; Case 97/76 *Merkur* v. *Commission* [1977] ECR 1063, para. 5.

[29] *Supra* n. 3, para 42.

breach of statutory duty and "cherry-pick" the most favourable elements from each cause of action. Such a patchwork cause of action would be highly undesirable as it would prevent a principled approach to state liability from being developed. This provides a further reason why it would have been preferable if the Divisional Court had held that the concept of state liability was something previously unknown to the common law and adopted a specific tort tailored to meet that concept.

5. CONCLUSION

It would be unfair to seek to criticise the Divisional Court in *Factortame* for adopting an approach based on breach of statutory duty. The question of the appropriate cause of action does not appear to have been one of the main areas of dispute in the case. It was only considered by the Court in the context of the availability of exemplary damages. Indeed, the judgment does not refer at all to the possibility of adopting the innominate tort approach. However, it would be regrettable if national courts felt bound to adopt the breach of statutory duty approach because of existing judicial pronouncements to that effect without there being a detailed analysis of the issue. It is important, not least from a constitutional perspective, that the principles relating to state liability should be developed in a coherent and justifiable manner. This is more likely to be achieved if the English courts adopt the innominate tort approach and recognise the existence of a specific tort of "state liability for breach of Community law" based on the Court of Justice's case law on Article 215 of the EC Treaty.

8

Give and Take: Cross-fertilisation of Concepts in Constitutional Law

EIVIND SMITH

Most of us still regard constitutions mainly as national phenomena.[1] As such, they are eminently dependant upon the historical, political, etc. context in the States that they are supposed to govern.

At the same time, however, few legal instruments—and few fields of legal and political studies—are more indebted to concepts and ideas from foreign countries, or—better—to the common heritage of mankind dating back to the Century of Enlightenment and beyond. Whereas the early Constitutional developments in the USA were largely inspired by French political thinking, the French Revolution got inspiration from the other side of the Ocean, whereas one of the most influential constitutional writers of the eighteenth Century (Montesquieu) frequently referred to the British "constitution"—as Montesquieu thought it was—the Westminster model of Parliamentary sovereignty has served as a powerful source for those who did *not* cherish the development of strong versions of the "separation of powers" doctrine, and so on.

The tension between "national" and "comparative" (or "international") elements in constitutional law will not always be strongly felt: *au jour le jour*, the local—i.e. national—context and local problems will normally dominate the minds of those interested in the operation of a given constitution. But exceptions are easy to find, above all in times of national crises, like the recent ones in Eastern Europe or in South Africa. And, more generally, elements of "New Europe" contributes strongly to making words like "constitution" and "judicial review" most well-chosen keys to studies of "cross-fertilisation". As a matter of fact, the influence exercised on national debates on constitutional

---

[1] Of course, this traditional approach is not the only one present in current debate—how about a "constitution" for the European Union, for instance, or for the World? One should equally be aware of the discussion on the applicability of measures inherited from national constitutions on figures like the "democratic deficit" in European integration (see for instance several contributions in E. Smith, *National Parliaments as Cornerstones of European Integration* (The Hague/London/Boston, Kluwer Law International, 1996). But in the present context, I will confine myself to a more or less clear-cut comparative approach to the study of national constitutions.

issues by, for instance, discussions about the "constitutional" character of the European Union, the growing jurisprudence of the European Court of Human Rights and personal contacts between politicians, civil servants and scholars from different countries is much more intense at present than it has been for a very long time.

Of course the abovementioned key words point at different levels of analysis, "cross-fertilisation" being a concept about processes whereas words like "constitution" and "judicial review" address legal and political institutions. Before contemplating a few key concepts about institutions, I would like to say a few words about the dynamic aspect of our subject-matter.

"FERTILISATION"

"Fertilisation" and "Cross-Fertilisation"

"Fertilisation" is commonly perceived as an entirely positive phenomenon (albeit fertilisation by accident is of course known). The concept of cross-fertilisation is probably less well-known—from my school days I believe I remember that, in nature, such a phenomenon may only take place among bisexual forms of life such as certain classes of plants and certain classes of animals commonly regarded as "lower" forms. For this reason, it is likely that "cross-fertilisation"—even if sharing the positive value of one-way "fertilisation"—is not benefiting from the same degree of positive connotation. But this is of little importance for the following discussion.

It may of course be argued that genuine "cross-fertilisation" supposes interaction between two or more constitutional systems of more or less equal health. It seems evident, for example, that the idea of mutual influence gives a profoundly different meaning when applied to the relationship between more or less embryonic constitutional systems in Eastern Europe just after the communist break-down and self-confident Western constitutional systems from when applied to the relationship between some of the members of the European Union. But the difference should not be over-estimated: even in this respect, it is important not to forget the tempering influence that acclimatisation to local conditions will always have (see below). Even when it comes to new constitutions of Eastern Europe, it is neither possible nor desirable to irradiate every local influence; legal or political institutions "transplanted" from another constitutional system are most unlikely to become exact replicas of those institutions as the donor used to know them. And, the other way round, regimes in crisis may at least give more settled constitutional systems very healthy lessons about the importance of principles.

For my purpose, I thus prefer to say that unilateral and mutual fertilisation is of equal interest to us. Consequently, I do not need to discuss how one would eventually draw the boundaries between mutual learning and influence—for instance through studies in comparative law or through jurisprudence at European level—and influences of a more straightforward unilateral character ("transplants"). In any event mechanisms of cross-fertilisation are discussed by Professor Bell in Chapter 11 below.

Fertilisation and change

What *may* actually be of some importance, on the other hand, is that the concept of fertilisation is inevitably dynamic in the sense of necessarily entailing changes: if A fertilises B, it means that B is submitted to change and that B—if all goes well—will give birth to new phenomena (e.g. babies). As already pointed out, I suppose that such changes will normally be perceived as positive.

In the cultural field to which constitutional institutions belong, however, such a perception should not at all be taken for granted. After all, successful "fertilisation" in this field means opening up for new attitudes, concepts or institutions (including legal and other social norms). By the same token, it means giving up pre-existing patterns or—at least—accepting that they co-exist with new ones.

Even if rather banal, the observation seems to be fundamental that human beings will not always regard cultural or social changes as entirely positive. It is equally fundamental to remember that such changes *should* not always be regarded as positive: for example, why should cultural homogeneity always be preferred to difference, Coca-Cola to local beverages or English to French? To the contrary, it is perfectly legitimate to believe that one or more of the institutions that exist in a given society should be preferred to phenomena that others would like to transplant into that society, and to argue that such "fertilisation" ought not to take place.

We thus see that qualifications as "positive" or "negative" are relative to the observer. They are relative also in the sense that the choice may vary according to the position of the observer, namely between the donor and the receiver.

Throughout history, colonial powers quite typically have appreciated their "gifts" differently from the colonised populations. More recently, those who met a certain type of United States constitutional "missionary" in Eastern Europe during the first years after the break-down of the communist order will easily grasp my point: active attempts to "fertilise" solely in one direction will often provoke negative reactions—in legal and other cultural relations as well as between human beings.

Fertilisation through negative reactions

The presence of negative reactions is certainly not enough, however, to block every influence of foreign origin. In many fields of life, growth through conflict is a well-known feature—others would speak of dialectic methods of learning. This may take different forms, including the role that foreign examples may play for making domestic changes less likely or frankly impossible, or—in other words—in strengthening the existing national solutions.

An excellent illustration is offered by the way United States Supreme Court practice regarding judicial review of legislation—especially some parts of the *New Deal* story of the 1930s—has been used in much European debate, On a number of points, the American experience in this field—or, better, the *impressions* which this experience made on Europeans—has been important for the development of judicial review of legislation in Europe. Such impressions are certainly one of the prominent factors in understanding how and why—or why not—judicial review emerged in continental Europe and the way it developed in a country like Norway, where such a system was already established.

For some, the United States experience has been an illustrious example to be copied as soon as possible. But for a very long time, what I believe to be the majority of scholars and politicians interested in such questions rather invoked the "political" role of the Supreme Court as a powerful argument in the opposite sense: look what might happen if similar institutions were to be introduced in our system or if the judge did not unconditionally submit to the opinions of succeeding majorities in Parliament (or even to the opinions of ministers and civil servants).

Well-known critical notions like *"gouvernement des juges"*[2] that have served throughout most of the century are inspired from such impressions. Since World War II, the *New Deal* experience has no doubt contributed massively to strengthening the scepticism[3] (and to some extent, it undoubtedly still does). And at a more recent stage, the "preferred position" principle and other creatures of US doctrines on judicial supremacy have inspired much debate on a possible hierarchisation of constitutional norms regarding human rights and other matters.[4]

Acclimatisation

Finally, it might be worth noticing that the importance of the phenomenon of "fertilisation" is likely to be over-evaluated compared to what would be well

---

[2] Cf. E. Lambert, *Le gouvernement des juges et la lutte contre la législation sociale aux Etats-Unis* (Paris, M. Giard & Cie, 1921).

[3] In Scandinavia, maybe the most vigorous, critical presentation is to be found in E. Andersen, *Forfatning og sædvane* (Copenhagen, G. E. C. Gads Forlag, 1947).

[4] From Norway, see namely some remarks in an article published in 1975 in the law review *Lov og Rett* by the now Chief Justice Carsten Smith ("Domstolene og rettsutviklingen", 292 ff. at. 300–2) and the account of Supreme Court practice in E. Smith, "Judicial Review in Norway—Characteristics and Recent Trends", in *The Role of the Constitution in a Changing Society* (Oslo, The Norwegian Academy of Science and Letters, 1992) 179 ff. at 190 ff.

founded when transposed from the field of biology to that of culture. Solid evidence tells us that children are far from being exact social replicas of their parents. As a matter of fact, even when cultural "fertilisation" or "transplant" actually entails changes in the receiving system the changes will not necessarily be dramatic (or merit to be perceived as such). Whereas national systems will evaluate over time—but more slowly—even if left alone (an assumption that is highly unlikely) systems that adopt "foreign" institutions or concepts will have a tendency to adapt them for their own purposes.

My conviction is that in the field of law the tendency to acclimatise "imported" institutions and concepts to local conditions will invariably be strong. If this is true, it may have a profound impact on paramount questions like the extent to which judicial review of enactments by the political majorities can be reconciled with fundamental principles of democratic government.

The legitimacy question inevitably comes up in every system where one form or another of such review exists. But it may take two main forms: it may focus on the very existence of judicial review, or it may focus on the degree of judicial freedom or self-restraint in cases where such power is exercised. The latter version of the question is more likely to come up in depth in countries where a minimum of practical experience with a system of constitutional justice is available (such as the USA or Germany), than in countries where some sort of constitutional justice comes up for the first time or where the existing system appears to be quite passive (such as Denmark or Japan). In both cases, however, we are faced with closely connected versions of a question which is basically the same: if the control really exercised by the constitutional judge is close to fiction, its legitimacy will not easily attract much attention, and vice versa. But the degree of "activism" will largely be the product of local conditions, not only of the "system" itself.

Another example, well suited for illustrating the need not to dramatise the impact that "fertilisation" may have in cultural fields like the constitutional one, may be found in the absence of clear criteria for distinguishing between mechanisms of "interpreting" and "setting aside" statutes that the judge finds unconstitutional. I will return to this example.

Administrative and constitutional law: the way further

Among numerous others available throughout the world, the current British debate over judicial review and other matters of constitutional significance offers eloquent examples of arguments which seek to show both why foreign or international examples should be imitated and why they should not.[5]

In the United Kingdom, much of this debate focuses not on judicial review of legislation but on acts of the government and other administrative authorities.

---

[5] In the latter sense, see for instance Lord Irvine of Lairg, "Judges and Decision-Makers: The Theory and Practise of *Wednesbury* Review" [1996] PL 59, at 75 ff.

At least to the very large extent that the jurisdiction of the executive (or of the "Crown") is based upon statutory law, the two levels are closely connected: overruling acts of administrative bodies means saying that, according to the judge, the act could not be justified by referring to what Parliament has decided. In the next instance, it means defining what Parliament actually meant to say, even if the message is far from being clear, or frankly giving meaning to the message even in regard to points that the legislator most certainly did not take into account. In many cases it even means overruling decisions taken under the authority of people trusted by the majority in Parliament.

On the other hand, one had better not exaggerate the similarities between judicial review of administrative and legislative enactments. Seen from abroad it is sometimes striking to note the extent to which British debate over the first-mentioned institution has a tendency to move along lines very similar to the debate in other European countries about the legitimacy of judicial review of Acts of Parliament. It sometimes looks as if judicial review at the administrative level should be regarded as almost as doubtful or "dangerous" in a democratic system of government as review of parliamentary enactments.[6]

To the extent that such impressions are correct, it seems as if the profound difference between the two that lies in the far easier access to the correction of judicial choices in administrative than in legislative matters has got lost (see further in the last part of this paper). In my view, the fact that no such thing as a *lex superior* to acts of Parliament is presently known in the United Kingdom gives no convincing argument in the opposite sense: it simply confirms the point that judicial review of administrative enactments (including lending senses to statutory law that Parliament did not necessarily intend) is by no means able to invalidate the majority's attempts to correcting judicial choices through statutory enactment.

On the following pages, I will mainly stick to *constitutional* institutions and concepts such as the judicial review of legislation. I nevertheless believe that the links with parallel issues concerning "fertilisation" or "transplantation" in administrative law that are addressed by the majority of other contributors to this Conference are tighter than they may appear at first glance. I also believe that in neither of these two fields, arguments as to the appropriateness of foreign or international examples can be met by referring to the positive character *per se* of "fertilisation" or "transplant". No cultural change should be supposed to be positive unless the debate is able to demonstrate that the revised institutional set-up would probably be better than the existing one.[7] We thus have to turn to consider some of the key concepts of our subject.[8]

---

[6] For an eloquent example among others, see Lord Irvine of Lairg, *supra* n. 5, 65.

[7] For the occasion, we may forget that only experience will show whether the outcome of the debate corresponds to "reality".

[8] To some extent, the following developments are leaning towards my own contributions in E. Smith (ed.), *Constitutional Justice under Old Constitutions* (The Hague/London/Boston, Kluwer Law International, 1995).

LA LOI, EXPRESSION DE LA VOLONTE GENERALE

Even if under different forms of attack, the British constitutional fundamental still seems to be the so-called sovereignty of Parliament. In continental Europe, the parallel figure may be said to date back to the tradition expressed in article 6 of the French *Déclaration des droits de l'homme et du citoyen* of 1789, according to which *la Loi* is the expression of the general will (*la volonté générale*). The basic effect of these two approaches is the same: the freedom of action of those designated to act on behalf of the political majority is—or should be—unfettered, at least in principle.

At first glance, both of these approaches fit well with the basic constitutional idea that the sovereignty of the people is the basis of every legitimate government. This idea tends to be linked to more or less express assumptions that "democracy" and "majority rule" are one and the same thing. And it is easily taken for granted that rule by the majority of the people is actually realised only if if the majority of the elected representatives are free to act at their own convenience.[9]

For a number of reasons—including obvious, practical ones—majority rule must be admitted as an important part of the everyday life of our governments. But it tends to be forgotten that, originally, *la volonté générale* was not meant simply to be the same thing as any formal expression of the will of the majority. The fact that the majority should have a certain latitude to decide in cases where consensus has not been reached gives no convincing argument for making "rule of the majority" the highest value.

More generally, the idea that some means of restraining majorities, at least temporarily, might be useful even for the changing majorities themselves seems to be quite rarely understood. While countries like Germany, Italy and Spain quite recently have known dictatorship exercised by their own political leaders, this century's dictators in countries like Belgium, France and Norway came from abroad (i.e. Germany), and efforts to establish national regimes of a similar character, like those of Pétain or Quisling, can only be understood in the light of such events.

The setting up of constitutional courts in the former group of countries should be explained as part of global efforts to design constitutional mechanisms aimed at avoiding future, authoritarian derivatives like those which these countries have recently known. In the latter group of countries, on the other hand, historical experience makes it far easier to maintain the traditional view that national, democratically elected assemblies ought not to be kept within constitutional boundaries upheld by non-elected, independent

---

[9] The fact that statistically the majority in Parliament does not necessarily reflect the majority among the voters got a new illustration by the May 1997 Parliamentary elections in the UK: due to the electoral system, the "landslide" victory of the Labour Party was the product of some 45% of the electorate. Other illustrations are very easy to find.

judges. Under such conditions, the main point has been perceived to be the need to avoid dictatorship which, in one way or another, is foreign to domestic, constitutional traditions. The point has *not* been to prevent certain ways of exercising the power conferred upon the genuinely national legislator.

Even less has it been so in countries—such as the United Kingdom—where classical forms of "dictatorship" have been avoided for centuries. Sceptical or frankly hostile attitudes towards imposing effective constitutional limits to the majority's freedom of action have been reinforced partly by changing attitudes in society as a whole towards the role of state intervention in the field of economics, but primarily by the fact that the majoritarian ideology is—or at least seems to be—shared even by many members of the judiciary itself, in Scandinavia as well as in the United Kingdom.

During recent decades, events likely to limit the majoritarian hegemony have nevertheless made themselves felt even in such countries, as in most countries of Western Europe. Among them, the growing influence of the *human rights ideology* should first be mentioned.

It seems to have become more and more clear that a need for certain bonds on political freedom of action necessarily underlies every serious version of the human rights ideology. In the long run, this ideology is not relevant only under Nazi or Communist regimes, nor can the Good Tides credibly be addressed to Third World regimes without provoking some questioning of the relationship between human rights and the political majority's unfettered freedom of action in ordinary, more or less democratic countries in Western Europe.

From this point, there is only a short way to go before admitting that some judicial guarantees of fundamental rights and freedoms might be useful or necessary even under constitutions commonly admitted as democratic. The way is also short to the realisation that if judicial review should of course be seen as some sort of conservative guarantee, it is not bound to be so in the most limited, right-wing political sense (or not merely in this sense). A system of judicial review may well make judges the guardians also of more "progressive" values than property rights, such as freedom of speech or the rights of the defendant in criminal proceedings.[10]

Reference to the current British debate over the need to introduce a domestic "Bill of Rights" is in itself sufficient to illustrate the way in which the rise in common acceptance of some Human Rights ideology has led to sometimes painful doubts about the benefits of unconditional support for the simplest versions of majoritarian principles of government.

Another mainstream in mental development in Europe throughout the last decades has been the growing force of ideas about *federalism* or *regionalism*. This has become an important means in the struggle for combining social

---

[10] In this respect, it is worth noting that France did not open up the way for individual petitions under Art. 25 of the European Convention on Human Rights until the victory of the socialist party in the 1981 elections for the Presidency and for the National Assembly.

peace and regional differences within a number of States that were formerly more centralised. But such constructions are often complicated and fragile because they are based upon compromises between the groups and regions concerned. As such, they usually need mechanisms to help regulate and maintain the basic states of equilibrium. Whereas responsibility of this kind in Europe would traditionally be conferred upon elected assemblies, countries such as Germany, Italy, Spain and Belgium have now followed the path laid by the USA two centuries ago in conferring similar tasks upon constitutional texts and judges.

Thirdly, the emergence and growth of the *European Communities* should not be under-estimated even in this respect. The strongly hierarchical structure of EC law and the important role played by the European Court of justice have certainly influenced not only adjudication but even—if sometimes *a contrario*—constitutional reasoning in the member states. To some extent, this seems to be so even in the United Kingdom, thus inevitably weakening the hegemonic doctrine of Parliamentary sovereignty.

To this should be added the growing weight of the examples furnished by such well-established systems of judicial review of legislation in continental Europe as that of Federal Germany. And to the extent that it is known in Western Europe, the United States Supreme Court's citizen's rights activism in parts of the post-war period has certainly tended to show that even constitutional judges may be able to move society in a direction widely perceived as sympathetic by liberals (and probably by a majority of informed Europeans).[11]

Against this background, the breathtaking growth in systems of constitutional justice in post-war Western Europe[12] and in the former Communist world is far less surprising than it would have been if the strongly established majoritarian way of thinking had been the single point of departure. But "constitutional bonds" and "constitutional justice" are not the same: the former may actually exist without the latter, whereas the opposite scenario may not be conceived. For this reason, it is now time to turn to the key concept of "constitution".

CONSTITUTION

One of the central features of the great bourgeois revolutions was the encapsulation of the more or less absolute monarch into governmental systems based on written constitutions. All texts that are today designated as

---

[11] It is quite another matter whether such activism well beyond the text of the written constitution could be defended as a legitimate part of a constitutional system. For a firm opinion on this point, see A. Scalia, "Modernity and the Constitution" in E. Smith (ed.), *supra* n. 8, 313 ff.

[12] For an outline of the *status quo*, see e.g. L. Favoreu, *Les cours constitutionnelles* (3rd edn., Paris, PUF, Coll. "Que sais-je?", 1996).

constitutions or similar (form of government, basic law . . .) have their roots in this period.

The idea of judicial review of statutory provisions, however, does not have any prominent place in this tradition.[13] In the fundamental debates in Philadelphia and Paris the feeling was rather that the constitution could *not* bind the legislative power. It had to be left to the legislative authority itself to determine the more detailed content of the constitution. It would be better if those elements of checks and balances that were nevertheless felt to be necessary were established through arrangements for the institutional division of the other powers of state.

Institutional arrangements for the division of power between different parts of the legislative and executive branches of government are however often used to serve the players' own purposes. It is difficult for such arrangements to ensure any effective counter-balance in a situation in which the powers of State involved are in agreement about the result, and they provide no guarantee that the interests of others—e.g. the citizens—will be heard.

These features become particularly striking because most constitutions also take up questions other than the institutional ones. The usual thing is that the constitution also contains provisions that—according to their wording—set limits to the freedom of action of political bodies in respect of the citizens. However, constitutional proclamations are not in themselves sufficient to ensure that freedoms and rights carry weight with the legislative power.

The traditional pattern of thought in European history on this point may be illustrated by reference to constitutional development in France. On the one hand the 1789 Declaration on the Rights of Man and the Citizen is undoubtedly one of the most influential documents in the history of human rights. It was also intended to serve as the preamble to the constitution that was to be devised, and in 1791 that was precisely the result. On the other hand a *declaration* is as a starting point indicative, not necessarily normative.[14] Nor is the legal status of a preamble easy to determine. The declaration was at any rate not included in the "actual" *corpus* of the constitution, nor under any circumstances did the constitution itself have any place in the positive law that the courts could apply. Moreover, finally the place that the Declaration of 1789 may nevertheless be assumed to have had in French constitutional law disappeared with the early demise of the Constitution of 1791.

The declaration owes its historical and ideological significance to the fact that it nevertheless did not fall right out of constitutional history. Thus the court for the judicial review of the administration that gradually came into being (the *Conseil d'Etat*) developed a set of judicial *principes généraux* which

---

[13] On alternatives to judicial review in the revolutionary epoch, see J. Elster in E. Smith, *supra* n. 8, 3–21.

[14] See for instance M. Troper, "Qu'est-ce que la déclaration des droits de l'homme" in E. Smith (ed.), *Les droits de l'homme dans le droit national en France et en Norvège* (Paris, Economica, 1990), 23–34.

for a large part were inspired precisely by that declaration. Indeed it happened that Parliament decided that the declaration should be displayed in all schools. However, this is undeniably pretty thin in relation to the question of limits to the freedom of action of the political majority with the power to legislate.

The Constitution of the Third Republic (1875)—which to this day represents the most long-lasting regime in France since the Revolution—did not even provide for any preamble on the rights of man. This was put right after the Second World War, the preamble to the constitution of 1946 "solemnly" declaring that it "confirms . . . the rights and freedoms for mankind and for the citizen that have been laid down through the Declaration of rights in 1789". In the preamble to the present (1958) constitution the French people "declare" in a corresponding manner "solemnly . . . their adherence to human rights . . . as they are laid down in the Declaration of 1789", supplemented through the preamble of 1946. Yet the relevant constitutions themselves still lack clear status as part of positive law: in the line drawn from the struggle against regional "parliaments" of the revolutionary period, it was still not seen as the task of the judiciary to ensure that legislation remained within the limits of the Constitution.

On this point the situation in French law is still the same today. In principle this applies even when the courts are asked to base their judgments upon statutory provisions that most people would regard as unconstitutional. Neither in ordinary nor in administrative courts are constitutional norms in fact a relevant source of argument about the validity of such provisions.[15] The tradition of cultivating "*la loi*" as the expression of the "*volonté générale*" (see above) is still too strong. The willingness to impose on the system of majority rule those bonds that ostensibly follow from the constitution—and particularly from those norms to which the preamble of 1958 refers—is still too weak.

On this point, French law was representative of the situation in most countries in Europe right up to the years after the end of the Second World War. Among the democratic regimes that were in principle based on written constitutions, there were for a long time only two exceptions. The one—as everybody who is interested in these questions knows—was the USA. The other example—which is undeniably much more discreet—was Norway.[16]

THE CONSTITUTION AS POSITIVE LAW

There has often been insistence on the fact that judicial review of legislation is not a "logical necessity" in a legal system that is based on a written

---

[15] When it comes to the judicial review of administrative enactments, on the other hand, the Constitution counts as a norm of reference by which the administration is bound.
[16] For an outline of the Norwegian system, see E. Smith, *supra* n. 4.

constitution.[17] it is not in itself necessary that the competence to decide whether a statute is unconstitutional should lie with the courts. Logically, it might also lie with the legislators themselves, so that the latter, at the same time as they issue an enactment, have finally decided the question of its validity.

This point of view is undoubtedly correct. It also corresponds with historical evidence. As we have seen, the normal solution—even in countries with a written constitution—has *not* been to make judges watch over the limits of the constitution with respect to legislators. The normal practice has been to let the legislative authority be its own judge in such questions.

However, the scope of this point of view is not so great as one might at first imagine, because the problem is posed in the wrong way: it is actually not very meaningful to ask about the "logically necessary" in allowing the courts to set aside enactments that they deem to be unconstitutional. The question does not become meaningful until another question has been answered: have the courts the right (and duty) to apply the constitution when deciding legal questions that are put before them? If the answer to this latter question is in the negative, the question of judicial review of the relationship of statutory provisions to the constitution does not arise at all. This question does not arise unless the courts *can* take into account the superior norms against which the enactment shall be measured.

Let us then return to the question to what extent judicial review of legislation is "logically necessary". If we take as our premise that those courts which might be called upon to exercise such review have the competence to include constitutional norms among those upon which they can base their decisions, there is a lot to suggest that the answer must be in the affirmative. Once the constitution counts as part of the positive law that the courts (too) apply, it is not easy to get away from the fact that it must take precedence over norms of lower rank with which in the opinion of the courts it comes in conflict. A presumption of the constitution as part of positive law must of course mean that the logic that springs from the rules relating to how legal provisions change through any change in their wording comes in with full force.

As already noted, written constitutions are as a rule more difficult to change than other provisions. In most countries, for example, a greater majority is necessary for amending constitutional provisions than is the case with ordinary statutory provisions. The difference in the amendment rules lies at the heart of the hierarchical organisation of legal provisions that we find in all developed legal systems. This hierarchy is only meaningful if norms that it is easier to change must give way to norms it is more difficult to change. Then— and only then—can the constitution become *lex superior* in the judicial universe of the judge.

---

[17] In a Scandinavian context, the most influential example is offered by the well-known Danish "realist" legal philosopher Alf Ross (see for instance his *Dansk Statsforfatningsret* [The Constitution of Denmark] 2nd edn., Copenhagen, Nyt Nordisk Forlag, 1966 I, 182–3).

Thus we are at the core of the type of reasoning that lies behind the growth of judicial review of legislation in both the USA and Norway. In Chief Justice Marshall's famous opinion in *Marbury* v. *Madison* (1803)[18] we find for example:

"It is emphatically the province and duty of the judicial department to say what the law is. Those who apply the rules to particular cases, must of necessity expound and interpret that rule. If two laws conflict with each other, the courts must decide on the operation of each.

So if a law be in opposition to the constitution; if both the law and the constitution apply to a particular case, so that the court must either decide that case conformably to the law, disregarding the constitution; or conformably to the constitution, disregarding the law; the court must determine which of these conflicting rules govern the case. This is the very essence of judicial duty."

According to Chief Justice Lasson the decision of a case before the Norwegian Supreme Court in 1866[19] rested "solely upon the question of constitutional law: what has the Supreme Court to decide when it is presented with the constitution and ordinary law?" Lasson gave the following answer:

"In such a situation, as far as I am familiar with the doctrine of constitutional law, it has been generally accepted that since one cannot require the courts to pass judgement in accordance with both laws at the same time, they must of necessity accord preference to the constitution."

This was the first occasion on which the Norwegian Supreme Court publicly justified its right to review the relationship of legislation to the constitution. We may perhaps say that Peder Lasson is the Norwegian John Marshall. But we can *not* say that the case from 1866 is the Norwegian equivalent of *Marbury* v. *Madison*. As a matter of fact, it has been shown that the Norwegian Constitution at least from the 1820s counted as positive law in the practice of the Supreme Court. When this step had once been taken, it was—as we have seen—little more than a natural consequence that the Constitution had if necessary to take precedence over statute law.

Those expressions of the significance of the hierarchical structure of the legal system that we find in the opinions mentioned, have often been met with irony. This irony is no doubt related to the fact that the starting point with the constitution as part of positive law has frequently been overlooked. Instead a direct attack has been made on the notions of the constitution as *lex superior* and on the judicial review of legislation as a "logically" natural consequence of this.

On the development of this point in the USA Professor Henry Paul Monaghan says for example:

"The emphasis, I think, should not be on higher but on 'law'—because the great American contribution to 'the universal history of law' was, if not to originate, to

[18] 5 US (1 Cranch) 137 (1803).
[19] UfL VI, 165 (my translation).

implement the idea that the constitution was law within the cognizance of the judges. The idea of a constitution as a 'fundamental' law has been around long before the founding of the American Republic. . . . What gave the concept of fundamental law special relevance in America was the increasingly widespread belief that it would be applied by judges."[20]

This view must be just as right for any other legal system: the courts can only have a role in the implementation of constitutionally prescribed limits to political freedom of action to the extent the constitution can be drawn into the argumentation about and as part of the justification for judicial decisions.

LEGAL HIERARCHY

Even if the idea of a "constitution" as part of positive law is admitted, it remains to be discussed why doubtful decisions on the constitutionality of statutory enactments should be left to unelected officials rather than to the legislative branch itself.

A standard answer to that question lies in the reference to the hierarchical structure of the legal system and to the subordinate position of statutory legislation *vis-à-vis* norms of constitutional rank. Owing its very existence as well as its power to the constitution, the legislator is unable to express the "common will" through enactments of a scope or content exceeding the limits established by the same constitution.

An important task of a written constitution is to establish formal and material conditions for the exercise of supreme state powers like those of the executive and legislative branches of government. Leaving the task of defining and upholding such norms to the branch alone upon which a given amount of power is conferred will easily be equal to the legally unconditional surrender to the will of that branch. If, therefore, it is accepted as legitimate to establish some sort of guarantee in order to ensure that e.g. constitutionalised rights are taken away or amended only in the way prescribed for constitutional amendment, it must also be accepted as legitimate to build into that constitution the institutional means deemed necessary to put such guarantees into effect. It is hardly reasonable to want the end while avoiding the proper means of achieving it.

Many examples could illustrate that this point is not, however, always well understood. One of them can be taken from Article 110a of the Constitution of Norway, adopted as recently as 1988. In my own translation, it says:

[20] H. P. Monaghan, "The Constitution of the United States and American Constitutional Law" in E. Smith (ed.), *supra* n. 8, 178–9.

It may be argued that the historical assumption at the basis of the citation is incorrect. But I believe Professor Monaghan to be perfectly right in his main point, quite simply because historical antecedents of application of "constitutional norms" by English courts when "reviewing" statutory enactments did not entail the establishment of judicial review of legislation under modern law.

"It is incumbent upon the authorities of the State so to arrange matters that the Sami population is able to safeguard and develop its language, its culture and its society."

The basic wording of this provision ("It is incumbent upon . . . ") is borrowed from the Constitution's Article 110, adopted in 1954. This provision deals with the so-called "right to work". In that field, there are obvious reasons *not* to establish "rights" in the literal sense, i.e. positions which could be sanctioned by independent courts in cases in which the protected interests have not been respected.[21] In the context of the more recent Article 110a, on the other hand, the situation is radically different, among other reasons because the Samis count less than one per cent of the global population of Norway. To a large extent, the use of the basic wording just mentioned even in the latter context implies that this tiny minority is left no way of legitimately defending its constitutionally established position other than to trust the overwhelming, ethnical and political majority and to try to convince it to respect the declaration of good will contained in Article 110a.

This possibility may be good enough as long as the majority remains in good faith. But the evaluation of this part of the basic legal situation might become very different in an unknown future: if and when this part of the political setting changes, it will become clear why it is not satisfactory, in the long run, to leave the immediate upholding of constitutional restraints on the majority's freedom of action to that majority itself.[22] In my eyes, the fact that "rights" like those often said to be given to the Sami population in Norway are of a "positive" nature is far from giving a satisfactory answer.

Such considerations may contribute to making it desirable to establish more satisfactory guarantees against the will of succeeding majorities than simple proclamations of constitutional norms as *lex superior* of a given legal system. It may also be that mechanisms of internal checks and balances which are known to most constitutional systems, such as elements of separation of powers, of bicameralism and of federalism, are not found sufficient. If this is so then the way forward is to give access to some sort of control by independent agencies, i.e. courts of a more or less specialised nature.

With *Kelsen*, it should be pointed out that, at least formally, such courts have no power to curtail statutory provisions because the *content* of those provisions is deemed contrary to the constitution (or to the will of the judges themselves). In the last resort, a system of judicial review is about ensuring

---

[21] Theoretically, however, recourse to the Court of Impeachment (*Riksretten*, see Arts. 86–7 of the Constitution) is of course a possible means against transgressions by e.g. a Minister.

[22] See further in E. Smith, "Constitutional protection of minorities: The Rights and Protection of the Sami Population in Norway" in *Scandinavian Studies in Law*, Vol. 34 (Stockholm, 1990), 235–59.

To the remarks in the text it should be added that, according to the *travaux préparatoires* of Art 110a, the access to court might not be entirely closed, and that a number of further complications linked to the character of the protected spheres established by this article (language, culture . . .) have not been dealt with in the preceding remarks.

that proper *procedures* have been chosen for enactments submitted to the judge: if most political decisions may be given legislative clothing, some can only be reached by following the procedure established for amending the constitution itself. Unless such demands are satisfied, it is for the judge to say that another procedure must be chosen in order to make that enactment legally binding. Implicitly, he then also says that properly enacted provisions will be accepted by the judiciary.

Of course I do not pretend that everything should be accepted just because it has been introduced by constitutional amendment. From the Century of Enlightenment and from too many later occasions we have learnt that our duty to obey state orders should have limits—Article 2 of the French 1789 Declaration for example speaks about the right to *"résistance à l'oppression"* as *"naturel et imprescriptible"*. But I leave it open here whether we would then move away from one constitutional system to another, or quite simply move from the province of law towards those of morality or of religion.

By following the path to formal, constitutional amendment, the political branches of government can always secure the last word in case of conflict with the judiciary. As we shall see, this observation is an important element in the further reasoning on the legitimacy of judicial review.

At the same time however, the conditions for amending the constitution are typically more strict than those to be observed when adopting ordinary legislation. For this reason, the need to follow the procedure established for formally amending the constitution often implies that the simple majority of the day is deprived of the possibility of reaching some of its aims.

This observation is likely to trouble those who are attached to the idea of democracy as more or less equal to "majority rule". But a number of answers can be given to such people. First, and rather formally, the power to decide which can be exercised by the legislative assembly, i.e. the majority within it, is derived from the constitution. Thus it can only be exercised according to the forms and within the material limits established by this same instrument: *"la loi n'exprime la volonté générale que dans le respect de la Constitution"* (Vedel).

Secondly, the values inherent in democracy in the simplest sense, i.e. when identified with rule of the majority, are not the only ones to be taken into account. A good society must also ensure respect for a number of values linked e.g. to the distinction between public and private life and to fundamental ideas about equality, tolerance and respect for individuals and for minorities. And even more, the majority of the day should have no right, in a democratic society, to adopt legal measures in order to hinder others in acceding to that same position. Even if it may seem paradoxical to some, it is nevertheless true that protecting freedom of expression from intrusions from the political majority implies protecting important prerequisites for democracy.

To these observations should be added, at least for some countries, the need for some independent arbitrator to ensure a minimum of respect for federal and other institutional requirements prescribed by the constitution. To the extent that Scotland actually accedes to some autonomy, this point might be of some interest even within the United Kingdom.

From the preceding remarks, the conclusion appears to be that the normative legitimacy[23] of judicial review of legislation in a democratic society is not difficult to establish. This way of answering the legitimacy question would have been fully sufficient, had it not been that almost every decision to be taken by judges as to the constitutionality of given, statutory provisions is more or less doubtful: as a matter of fact, litigation in this field is rarely about simple, more or less automatic deductions from constitutional texts. Quite the contrary, judicial decisions will easily imply choices of a more or less clear, political character.

We thus still have to ask why non-elected judges are more competent to operate such choices than elected officials bound to present themselves to the electorate on regular occasions.

JUDICIAL REVIEW

Much debate over the desirability of introducing systems of judicial review of legislation seems to be based upon the assumption that such a reform will attribute to judges a power they do not already have to "set aside" statutory provisions as unconstitutional. In a formal sense, this assumption is certainly correct.

In practice however, the difference will often be less colourful: within the common law tradition, for instance, I get the firm impression that self-confident judges of the English type will frequently be able to construe statutory enactments in a way they find just without ever having to invite speaking about "setting them aside" or "not giving them effect".[24] A similar observation seems to be valid, by the way, when it comes to judicial review of administrative enactments.

In the Federal Republic of Germany, the European Convention of Human Rights enjoys a rank similar to statutory enactments but not superior to them. In principle, this means accepting that legislation adopted after the entering into force of the Convention as part of domestic law has priority to norms laid down by the latter. But in several decisions, the Constitutional Court has

---

[23] The way I use of the concept of "normative legitimacy", it focuses upon the question whether one version or another of a system of judicial review can be *justified* as part of a democratic system of government. With Habermas, we might talk of the "Anerkennungswürdigkeit" of systems of judicial review. See further in E. Smith (ed.), *supra* n. 8, 369 ff.

[24] British courts often have to use this technique. Perhaps the high water mark is the influential decision of the House of Lords in *Anisminic* v. *Foreign Compensation Commission* [1969] 2 AC 147. Sir William Wade says of this case that it interpreted the Act of Parliament "to mean the exact opposite of what it appeared to say" (*Wade & Forsyth:* Administrative Law, 7th edn., Oxford, Clarendon Press, 1994), 32).

almost neutralised the *lex posterior* principle by saying that the legislator could normally not be supposed to have intentionally violated international obligations of this nature.[25]

To the extent that similar attitudes are adopted by the judiciary in countries in which no system of "judicial review" has been formally introduced, it is likely to resolve the bulk of possible conflicts between domestic legislation subsequent to the country's entering into the treaty system, and obligations flowing from the treaty. In this way, international norms may operate in domestic law independently of their adoption at a supra-legislative level as well as independently of the establishment of systems of judicial review to look after their effective application.

On the other hand, the impact of the "interpretation" approach to judicial review *de facto* and *de jure* should not be overestimated. In any case, the difference remains that the judge—in a system where a conflicting norm has not been given a formal rank superior to that of ordinary legislation—could not easily get around statutory enactments that are clearly meant to be applied even if contrary to the "superior" norm. In Western societies, there is a tendency to suppose that the probability of such violations is close to zero. But such a supposition reflects a view of our future that may easily reveal itself as being over-optimistic and that—in any case—does not take care of the fundamental function of constitutions, that is to prevent problems in the unknown future.

The fact that the interpretative approach is not necessarily enough even under more peaceful conditions than we have the right to anticipate for the future, has recently been illustrated by a decision of the Norwegian Supreme Court on a question relating to the right to strike.[26] After having concluded that the Royal decree forbidding a strike that was announced for petroleum installations in the North Sea was not contrary to the country's international obligations, the Court took care to state that the ban on the strike had been based upon the government's intention to intervene even if the measure was contrary to the relevant ILO engagements. In such circumstances, the Court stated that the Royal decree would have been valid "even if violating international law provisions on the protection of the right to strike".

Legally, this *obiter dictum* of the Supreme Court is no doubt correct. It also has the merit of highlighting this particular feature of the "incorporation at ordinary statutory level" option (which seems to be parallel to the "entrenched Bill of Rights" option eagerly advocated in current British debate). In doing so, the Supreme Court of Norway has forcefully contributed an illustration of the difficulties inherent in agreeing to be "bound" by norms on fundamental human rights only to the extent that the competent national authorities—and first of all the legislator—accept.[27] As a matter of fact, such

[25] See for instance the 1974 decision in BVerfGE 74, 358, 370.
[26] Judgemnt of 10 Apr. 1997 (lnr. 24/1997, nr 351/1995), not yet published.
[27] On this occasion I take the liberty of avoiding the question of the distinction between international and domestic legal bonds.

a position, which it would not be completely misleading to qualify as hypo-critical, is largely dominnant today in the Western World.

We thus see that as a matter of principle the final choice is between a sys-tem where no legal means can really oppose legislation adopted by the major-ity of elected representatives of the nation, and a system where respect for the written constitution can be *imposed* upon political majorities hostile to or—more likely—ignorant of the constitutional framework by which they are bound. But in practice more or less well settled constitutional systems are of course unlikely to enter into *either/or* situations of this nature very often.

If neither the possible censorship exercised by the voters at regular intervals nor other institutional means are found sufficient to ensure a satisfactory degree of respect for the written constitution, some sort of a constitutional judge is to be called for. And when such a judge has been installed, there is a constant need to define and redefine his role in constitutional matters, namely when his way of reading the constitution differs from that adopted by the democratically elected legislator.

As a matter of fact, there are no sharp distinctions between questions relat-ing to the very existence of a system of judicial review of legislation and ques-tions related to the way such a system is operated. And it is worthwhile underlining that even in constitutional settings—as in the USA—where the institution of judicial review of legislation itself is hardly questioned, lively debates are almost constantly going on as to the *intensity* of the control actu-ally operated and—respectively—as to the relative freedom of action of the judge compared to that of the lawmaker.

POPULAR SOVEREIGNTY *VS.* RIGHTS

We have already noted the doubtful character of most constitutional questions presented to constitutional judges, whereas the path to constitutional amend-ment tends to be complicated (see further below). Consequently, satisfactory answers to the legitimacy question can only be given if some elements of *posi-tive* justification for conferring a decisive role in constitutional affairs upon unelected officials such as judges can be added to the hierarchical and other criteria that have already been touched upon. In my view, this part of the answer should mainly emphasise the different tasks of the judicial and polit-ical channels and, thus, the need to *supplement* the political one.

In the present context, two main arguments should briefly be explored. The first is the need for decision-makers that enjoy *independence* from the legisla-tive branch of government: the legitimacy question has no sense if it is not deemed preferable to establish some institutional guarantee for ensuring that the constitution is respected even when a constitutional norm is conceived by the judge in a way that contravenes the will of the legislator. In other words, it must be looked upon as desirable to see at least some constitutional provisions as more than declarations of intent at the mercy of changing political majorities.

From this presupposition, it follows that a part of the task of upholding such provisions must be conferred upon bodies independent of the political majorities themselves. In this necessity lies the very core of the dilemma of legitimacy of judicial review of legislation in democratic societies. But this dilemma cannot be avoided. If the reviewing bodies do not enjoy a high degree of independence,[28] the institution of constitutional justice itself loses its sense. Somewhat paradoxically, we could say that the presence of the legitimacy dilemma created by the independence of the constitutional judge is a *conditio sine qua non* for the legitimacy of judicial review of statutory provisions.

The second positive argument in favour of judicial review of legislation, as a supplement to the political channel of decision-making to be evoked here, lies in the different *procedural* needs when constitutionally relevant matters are dealt with by the legislative and judicial branches of government. The point is *not* that the typical judicial way of reaching decisions is necessarily better than the typical political one. The point is simply that these two ways are *different* and that for *certain* purposes, the former is better than the latter.

The main elements in the typical procedure to be followed before a court gives the legal answer to a particular question could briefly be described by words like *contradiction* and *formal justification*. The procedure, whether written or oral, will have to respect a certain number of fundamental principles, such as those meant to ensure equal access for the parties to the decision-maker, who—in his turn—is bound to explain why he found one set of arguments more convincing than the other.

These principles are no doubt fundamental even if the parties in fact often or almost always differ, for example as far as their ability to expose the facts and arguments most suitable for serving their own case is concerned. Rather is it better to state that they are fundamental *because* the parties are generally unequal.

On the other hand, judicial procedures are not necessarily able to provide for the broad illumination of an issue needed for fulfilling typical legislative purposes. This is so for example because the arguments likely to be advanced by a broader audience are not likely to be represented in a proper manner by individual litigants in specific cases. This is one—if not the only—reason why a judge should be reluctant to invent answers to constitutional questions which are at the same time doubtful and of a rather pronounced, political character.

Quite obviously the borderline between constitutional questions which could reasonably be said to be legal ones and questions which are rather

---

[28] It goes without saying that judicial independence *vis-à-vis* legislators (as *vis-à-vis* political authorities at large) can never be complete. However, this point will not be further developed here.

political in the sense of demanding legislative rather than judicial action, is not sharp. The fact that the typical judicial procedure does not fit well into the resolution of questions of the latter type does not, however, expose a real weakness in this procedure. These characteristics should rather be looked upon as proper parts of typical legal procedures well suited for proceedings of a typical legal character, but of course less well suited to the needs of typical decision-making in the political field.

Seen from this angle, judicial decision-making is particularly able to ensure equal access to the judge and to impose upon him a duty to take careful account of the arguments advanced by each of the parties before making up his mind. This ability is certainly superior to the ability of the legislature systematically to listen to and carefully consider the arguments and interests of those who are most directly concerned by legislative enactments.

The freedom of expression and debate, as protected by the constitution, is fundamental in democratic societies. But even when this mechanism is properly taken care of, strong or well organised interests will usually be far more able than weaker or less well organised interests to make use of it by making themselves heard by important decision-makers. And even when such a public debate takes place, the quality of the argument will often be quite poor, and a lot of questions which are to be decided by legislative action will not be submitted at all to such debate.

In another direction, it should be noted that legislative decisions will often be marked by the need for political compromises rather than by the need carefully to consider more specific interests at stake in each case.

No society of any importance could possibly cover every common, political decision by proper public debate, and it is certainly not illegitimate for a political system to search for compromises when needed for gathering majorities necessary for governing. It should be stressed that typical political procedures are best—or at least necessary—for accomplishing an important number of fundamental tasks in society.

At the same time, however, typical judicial procedures are the superior ones for other categories of societal decisions. The task of defining major guidelines for society should normally not be conferred upon unelected judges. But judges acting under fundamental legal principles of contradiction, etc., are no doubt often to be preferred for ensuring proper consideration of particular interests presuppossedly harmed by legislative enactments.

When constantly searching for the proper delimitations between judicial and legislative tasks in the constitutional sphere, one should take into account that most often judicial review *and* legislation could be described not as conflicting, but rather as useful, complementary means among others to achieve better societies. Too often, debates regarding the role of courts in society leave us with the impression that the judiciary is a major, if not *the* major threat against majority rule and the pre-eminent role of parliaments. As a matter of fact, numerous other competitors (like international organisations, multinational enterprises and social movements of different kinds) are more powerful *vis à vis* the governmental systems of modern Nation-States. I firmly believe it to be true that in the long run the judiciary is by far the least dangerous branch of government.

Equal access to the court does not necessarily ensure equal success as to the *outcome* of the proceedings. But opportunities to expose facts and arguments to decision-makers bound to listen, to try to understand, and to justify their decisions, are useful in themselves. This is so both for the party who does not win and for society as such.

Against this background, it is crucial for the legitimacy of each system of judicial review of legislation to respond properly to those fundamental principles of legal procedure which make it possible to distinguish between judicial and political decision-making and which—in certain contexts—make the former path to authoritative decisions superior to the latter.

CORRECTING JUDICIAL CHOICES

The last and most fundamental criterion for the legitimacy of judicial review of legislation resides in the power of the constituent power to correct, for the future, constitutional choices made by judges. Of course this criterion is closely linked to the role of the constitution at the top of hierarchical legal structures.

In a French context, this point has recently been stressed by Georges Vedel in the following words:

> "It is [the] completeness of the power of constitutional revision that gives legitimacy to the review of constitutionality of statutory enactments. To any person who complains that the law enacted by the vote of the representatives of the Nation is not sovereign like the Nation itself, the answer is that 'the law gives expression to the general will only in respecting the Constitution'.
>
>   This formulation justifies the review of constitutionality, but it has this virtue only because it implies that the barrier the law meets in the Constitution may be raised by the people as sovereign or their representatives, if they have recourse to the supreme mode of expression: constitutional revision. If judges do not govern, it is because at any given moment the sovereign, on condition that he appears in majesty as the Constituent, may . . . quash their judgments."[29]

This way of reasoning is valid even for other countries with democratically elected legislatures. That is why doubtful, constitutional choices by unelected officials like judges are difficult to admit as prevailing over choices by representative bodies unless those choices could be corrected for the future by the supreme—i.e. the constituent—power of the land.

---

[29] G. Vedel, "Schengen et Maastricht" 1992–2 *Revue française de Droit administratif* 173 ff. (at 179–80). English translation by Patrick N. Chaffey.

Formally—and to the extent that we disregard norms of supra-constitutional rank[30]—the way to constitutional amendment is no doubt open in every country. The fact that such amendments are more difficult to obtain than statutory enactments is not in itself an argument against the legitimacy of judicial review. On the contrary, this fact carries one of the basic features in systems of government where a written constitution has been adopted in order precisely to frame and condition day-to-day political decisions. In a more outspoken manner, Justice Scalia of the United States Supreme Court has put it this way:

> "The very objective of a basic law, it seems to me, is to place certain matters beyond risk of change, except through the extraordinary democratic majorities that consti-tutional amendment requires. Thus it seems to me no more valid a criticism of old constitutions to say that they 'obstruct modernity' than it would be a valid criticism of artillery pieces, for example, to say that they kill people, or of airplanes to say that they get high off the ground. The whole *purpose* of a constitution—old or new—is to impede change, or, pejoratively put, to 'obstruct modernity'."[31]

On the other hand, the debate on the legitimacy of judicial review should probably not satisfy itself with considering the formal rules concerning con-stitutional amendment. It should also take into account *how* difficult it is in practice to obtain constitutional amendments found necessary to correct judi-cial choices (or for any reason whatsoever). If this path is literally never open—due to traditions or for some other reason—even for qualified politi-cal majorities, judicial review becomes more difficult to defend.

In most European countries with written constitutions, it appears enough to indicate that recent history shows beyond doubt that the way to constitu-tional amendment is not at all inaccessible when desired by a sufficient polit-ical majority. For this reason, no particular problem regarding the legitimacy of judicial review of legislation can arise on this point.

In the United States of America, the federal Constitution has also been amended on several occasions throughout history. Some of these modifica-tions have even been connected more or less directly with controversial choices which the Supreme Court has made.[32]

On the other hand, the need for ratification by at least three fourths of the States has apparently contributed to rendering it almost impossible to pass even constitutional amendments adopted by two thirds of both Houses in Congress.[33] Because the formal possibility of correcting judicial choices by

---

[30] Of course this word is misleading when designating norms laid down by the constitutional text itself. But the point is of course that such norms are intended to block the way to constitu-tional amendment of a certain content, for instance the re-introduction of monarchy (France), the introduction of unequal representation of the federated states in the US Senate without their own consent, the modification of the "spirit" or the "principles" of the Constitution (Norway) or of the core of some fundamental rights (Germany).

[31] A. Scalia, "Modernity and the Constitution" in E. Smith (ed.), *supra* n. 8, 315.

[32] This was the case e.g. with Amendment XVI (1913) on federal income taxes.

[33] See US Constitution art. V.

amending even the United States Constitution remains open, this situation is not susceptible to completely undermine the legitimacy of judicial review of federal legislation. But at the same time, far-reaching judicial activism in the constitutional field is not easy to reconcile with the overwhelming practical difficulties that have to be overcome even when massive political majorities strive to obtain such amendment.

It is worthwhile noticing that in some countries particular questions are raised by the almost sacred character of some of their ancient constitutional texts. To what extent would it be practically or politically possible, for instance, to amend or abolish the French Declaration of Rights of 1789 or the first ten Amendments to the United States Constitution?[34] To the extent that provisions the constitutional judge is asked to uphold are untouchable *de facto*, if not *de jure*, the fundamental argument concerning the possibility of correcting judicial choices by way of constitutional amendment ineluctably fails: how can the activity of unelected guardians of some venerable stone tablets, worded in a general and rather vague manner as they usually are, be reconciled with modern concerns about democracy?

Luckily enough, most of us may feel free to treat the legitimacy question in our own constitutional systems in much more pragmatic terms. This is true in the constitutional field to which most of the preceding remarks have been devoted. It is even more so when it comes to judicial review of administrative enactments: to the extent that the public administration, as is generally the case, is submitted to ordinary legislation, it is even easier to correct doubtful judicial choices by amending statutes adopted by the simple majority of the day.

---

[34] Such texts could of course be supplemented by more recent ones, such as the Preambles to the 1946 and 1958 Constitutions in France. But this solution leaves it to the judge at least to reconcile provisions from different periods and of largely different ideological inspiration.

9

The Constitution and the Justification of Judicial Power

Professor Smith's paper contains a number of statements which are likely to provoke little opposition from those familiar with the debate over the constitutional status of human rights in the United Kingdom.[1] His acknowledgement of the layers of confusion which have surrounded a number of previous attempts to analyse the public law systems of foreign countries[2] and his recognition of the open-textured nature of many issues which require constitutional adjudication[3] are both likely to command widespread approbation. This paper focuses on one particular aspect of his analysis: that which seeks to justify the judicial review of primary legislation under a written constitution.[4] Professor Smith advances two principal arguments which I propose to address in turn.[5] They are that:

---

* Fellow of Trinity College, Cambridge.

[1] Recent discussions include M. Hunt, *Using Human Rights Law in English Courts* (Oxford, Hart, 1997) and R. Gordon and R. Wilmot-Smith (eds.), *Human Rights in the United Kingdom* (Oxford, OUP, 1996).

[2] E. Smith, 101, 104, 106 Montesquieu, *The Spirit of Laws* (Berkeley, Cal., 1977), Book XI, ch. 6; de Lolme, *Constitution de l'Angleterre* (Paris, 1792) on the nature of English constitutionalism, and Dicey, *Introduction to the Study of the Law of the Constitution* (8th edn., Macmillan, London, 1915), ch. XII on French *droit administratif*. A further stratum of debate surrounds the extent to which writers on political philosophy have been misrepresented by subsequent interpreters. For example, "[i]t may be historically interesting that Montesquieu and later the American founders took him [Locke] up in a sense which he cannot be said to have contemplated . . . " (Locke, *Two Treatises of Government* (2nd edn., by Laslett, Cambridge, Cambridge University Press, 1967), 119 and J. Dunn, *The Political Thought of John Locke* (Cambridge, Cambridge University Press, 1969), 6–8; cf M. C. Vile, *Constitutionalism and the Separation of Powers* (Oxford, Clarendon Press, 1967), ch. III, and H. Aarsleff, "Locke's Influence" in V. Chappell (ed.), *The Cambridge Companion to Locke* (Cambridge, CUP, 1994).

[3] *Ibid.*, 120–121.

[4] Given this focus and the examples cited by Professor Smith, this chapter draws more on American than European illustrations.

[5] Professor Smith also argues that judicial review may provide an alternative and complementary form of political participation (*supra* 121) and that the process of constitutional amendment further legitimises constitutional review (*supra* 122). These points are addressed briefly at ns. 31 and 33, below.

i. judicial review flows of necessity from the existence of a constitution which has the status of law;[6] and

ii. a good society is not one in which the will of the majority is considered to be the only value which is worth advancing; equality, tolerance and respect for individuals and minorities are also important interests which should in some cases be insulated from the will of the majority. Such insulation can best be provided by the judiciary which is independent of the legislature and, to a substantial extent, of the need to follow popular opinion.[7]

The first is a familiar argument. As Professor Smith notes, it is one which was used in the most famous of all cases on judicial review: *Marbury* v. *Madison*.[8] It is also an argument that appealed to at least some of those responsible for the drafting, and then for the defence, of the United States Constitution. As Hamilton wrote

"By a limited Constitution, I understand one which contains certain specified exceptions to the legislative authority; such, for instance, as that it shall pass no bills of attainder, no ex post facto laws, and the like. Limitations of this kind can be preserved in practice no other way than through the medium of courts of justice, whose duty it must be to declare all acts contrary to the manifest tenor of the Constitution void. Without this, all the reservations of particular rights or privileges would amount to nothing."[9]

Even in the context of English law, this line of reasoning has proved persuasive in determining the limits of the jurisdiction of decision-making bodies which derive their authority from Acts of Parliament. The judgment of Farwell LJ in *R.* v. *Shoreditch Assessment Committee, ex parte Morgan* provides the most familiar form of this argument from legal logic:[10]

"Subjection in this respect to the High Court['s supervisory jurisdiction] is a necessary and inseparable incident to all tribunals of limited jurisdiction; for the existence of the limit necessitates an authority to determine and enforce it: it is a contradiction in terms to create a tribunal with limited jurisdiction and unlimited power to determine such limits at its own will and pleasure . . . "[11]

Professor Smith is also keen to emphasise that it is only if the constitution has the status of law that the argument from logical necessity will apply. Yet even

[6] *Supra* 111–112.

[7] *Supra* 116. A similar argument (positing a distinction between statistical and communal democracy) is advanced by R. Dworkin, *Freedom's Law* (Oxford, OUP, 1997), ch. 18.

[8] 5 US (1 Cranch) 137 (1803). For discussion of Marshall CJ's reasoning, see Van Alstyne, "A Critical Guide to *Marbury* v. *Madison*" [1969] Duke LJ 1; O'Fallon, "Marbury" 44 *Stan.LRev.* 219 (1992) and *Eakin* v. *Raub*, 12 S. & R. 330 (Pa. 1825) (*per* Justice Gibson in dissent).

[9] Madison, Hamilton and Jay, *The Federalist Papers* (Harmondsworth, Penguin, 1987), No. LXXVIII. The illustrations cited by Hamilton are relatively uncontroversial as they are all examples in which judical intervention would require the exercise of little or no discretion.

[10] The term "legal logic" is from H. W. R. Wade and C. F. Forsyth, *Administrative Law* (7th edn., Oxford, OUP, 1994), 301.

[11] [1910] 2 KB 859, 880.

when qualified in this manner, this thesis does not make it inevitable that it is the judicial view on the question of constitutionality which should prevail. As Tribe has written of the reasoning in *Marbury v. Madison*:

> "Marshall's justification for his assertion of federal judicial power to interpret and apply the Constitution is not conclusive. The premise of a written Constitution would not be disserved, and legislative power would not necessarily be unbounded, if Congress itself judged the constitutionality of its enactments. Under such a system, courts would not ignore the Constitution; rather, they would simply treat the legislative interpretation as definitive, and thus leave to Congress the task of resolving apparent conflicts between statute and Constitution."[12]

Thus a number of legal systems possess written constitutions with the status of law and yet have not adopted the United States mode of judicial review. In some systems an internal sub-committee of the legislature ensures the constitutionality of proposed or actual legislation; in others a specialist body outside the legislature, but other than the courts, will perform this function.[13] Thus, however well the notion of judicial review of primary legislation fits with the history of the United States Constitution,[14] or review of the legality of the decisions of inferior bodies accommodates the High Court's traditional supervisory jurisdiction,[15] neither justification can be based on this ground alone. Indeed, this explains why the argument from necessity was supplemented by a number of others in the reasoning of Marshall CJ in *Marbury* and why Professor Smith proceeds to adduce policy-based justifications for judicial review in addition to his appeal to pure reason.

Turning to these arguments, Professor Smith next advances a normative conception of the good society which, he argues, should respect certain values such as the distinction between public and private life and fundamental ideas about equality, tolerance and respect for individuals and minorities. This is not an unusual catalogue of interests in a liberal state but, as with all prescriptive statements of what constitutes a good society, it is not a vision which will be shared by all.[16] Nevertheless, the idea that the judicial branch of government has a legitimate role in preserving certain values from legislative encroachment has achieved widespread currency.[17] The great advantage of

---

[12] L. H. Tribe, *American Constitutional Law* (Foundation, 1988), 25.

[13] For examples, see A. R. Brewer-Carias, *Judicial Review in Comparative Law* (Cambridge, 1989), and R. R. Ludwikowski, *Constitution-Making in the Region of Former Soviet Dominance* (Duke, 1996), ch. 5.

[14] It is difficult to form a conclusive view of the Framers' intentions from the available materials (Bickel, *The Least Dangerous Branch* (Indianapolis, 1962) 15–16).

[15] The argument from legal logic has been refuted in this context too (D.M. Gordon: "The Relation of Facts to Jurisdiction" (1929) 45 *LQR* 459).

[16] Some feminist scholars have in particular criticised the liberal focus on the separate spheres of public and private life (K. O'Donovan, *Sexual Divisions in Law* (London, Weidenfeld, 1985)). For a discussion of cultural relativism in the context of rights, see A. A. An-Na'im (ed.), *Human Rights in Cross-Cultural Perspectives* (Pennsylvania, 1992).

[17] M. Cappelletti, *Judicial Review in Comparative Perspective* (Oxford, OUP, 1989), 40–6 and 204–11.

this mode of analysis is that it directly addresses the so-called counter-majoritarian difficulty at the core of judicial review of the constitutionality of primary legislation. The counter-majoritarian difficulty arises because at first sight it appears anti-democratic that a small, unrepresentative and unaccountable minority of the population which happens to hold judicial office should be able to overrule the expression of legislative will which represents (however imperfectly) a much larger group of the population. The counter-majoritarian difficulty has never been better expressed than it was by Bickel:

> "[W]hen the Supreme Court declares unconstitutional a legislative act or the action of an elected executive, it thwarts the will of representatives of the actual here and now; it exercises control, not in behalf of the prevailing majority, but against it . . . [This] is the reason the charge can be made that judicial review is undemocratic."[18]

This difficulty may be addressed in a number of ways. The first is to undermine the democratic credentials of the legislative and executive branches of government.[19] This might be thought to be a particularly fruitful mechanism in the United Kingdom as the democratic profile of the legislature is questionable. The first reason for this lies in the composition of the sovereign body which is validly constituted for legislative purposes only when acting as both Houses of Parliament and the monarch.[20] Although the House of Lords does contain a substantial number of members who have been appointed by the government, its composition (if not its active membership) is still dominated by the principle of heredity and not popular representation. The monarch can, manifestly, claim no majoritarian legitimacy. Of course, it is true that as a result of law and convention, real legislative power is exercised by the House of Commons which has a superior claim to represent the will of the governed.[21] However, the combination of the first-past-the-post electoral system and executive domination of the House of Commons means that the legislative will is at best the expression of the intention of those elected by the largest single minority of the electorate, and this will rarely be a majority even of those entitled to vote.[22]

[18] A. Bickel, *supra* n. 14, 16–17. See Wright, "Professor Bickel, The Scholarly Tradition and the Supreme Court", 84 *Harv.LRev.* 769 (1971).

[19] Smith, *supra* 107. A further strand of this line of reasoning is to emphasise that judicial appointments are not entirely removed from the political process and hence possess some form of accountability (Dahl, "Decision-Making in a Democracy: The Supreme Court as a National Policy-Maker" 6 *JPub.L* 279 (1957) on the US Supreme Court). In the UK although appointments to the senior judiciary are nominally made by the Crown, the latter habitually acts on the advice of the Prime Minister or the Lord Chancellor, both of whom are members of the executive (R. D. Brazier, *Constitutional Practice* (Oxford, OUP, 1994), ch. 12).

[20] In this sense the UK constitution can be seen to reflect theories of mixed government (that is, representing the monarchical, aristocratic and democratic interests in society) rather than popular representation (M. C. Vile, *supra* n.2, ch. II).

[21] C. Turpin, *British Government and the Constitution* (London, Butterworths, 1995), ch. 1.

[22] The question whether it is meaningful to speak of the will of a collective body like the legislature is not addressed here.

This argument is not very persuasive when one realises that what is in issue is a question of the *relative* institutional capacity of legislature, executive and judiciary to reflect the will of the majority of those governed. However imperfect the system of popular representation at Westminster, it will invariably be vastly superior to that of the judiciary which still represents a small, and overwhelmingly male, socio-economic group drawn from the most successful practitioners at the English Bar.

Professor Smith therefore rightly addresses most of his argument to those theories of review which deal directly with the counter-majoritarian difficulty. Attempts to defend judicial intervention in the context of constitutional review have usually taken an approached based on either the substantive or the procedural limitations of majoritarianism. An example of the former is often associated with the name of Alexander Bickel who famously defended judicial review on the ground that:

> "[G]overnment should serve not only what we conceive from time to time to be our immediate material needs but also certain enduring values . . . [and] courts have certain capacities for dealing with matters of principle that legislatures and executives do not possess. Judges have, or should have, the leisure, the training, and the insulation to follow the ways of the scholar in pursuing the ends of government."[23]

This position is plainly problematic. It is not clear that courts (even the United States Supreme Court) are, or ever were, staffed by the kind of judicial figures Bickel describes or that the process of litigation does lend itself to the form of reflection he advances. Indeed, the judiciary has revealed itself to be as susceptible as the other branches of government to the temporary pressures of extreme circumstance. For example, the United States Supreme Court upheld the compulsory internment in California of all those of Japanese descent during the Second World War[24] and the United Kingdom courts have repeatedly held that judicial control of administrative power must be tempered by deference to the executive in times of public emergency.[25]

Further difficulties arise when one considers the limitations by which Bickel himself circumscribed the judicial power to impose its conception of society's enduring values. Bickel accepted that judicial discretion could not be unlimited and stated that it would be constrained by the need to ensure that the values imposed by the courts did not diverge too much (either temporally or substantively) from those which would receive widespread acceptance from

---

[23] Bickel, *supra* n. 14, 24–6.

[24] *Korematsu* v. *United States*, 323 US 214 (1944) and *Hirabayashi* v. *United States*, 320 US 81 (1943).

[25] *Liversidge* v. *Anderson* [1942] AC 206; *R.* v. *Secretary of State for the Home Department, ex parte Cheblak* [1991] 1 WLR 890. A similar point is made in K. D. Ewing, "The Bill of Rights Debate: Democracy or Juristocracy in Britain?" in K. D. Ewing, C. A. Gearty and B. A. Hepple, *Human Rights and Labour Law—Essays for Paul O'Higgins* (London, Mansell, 1994). See also the decision of the European Court of Human Rights in *Branningan and McBride* v. *United Kingdom* (Publ. Eur. Ct.HR, Ser. A No. 258B).

the population at large.[26] Once this limitation is acknowledged, much of the power of Bickel's initial statement is lost. It is not clear why the judges should have the coercive power to impose their view of the enduring values of society when these values are to be discerned by the judiciary on the basis of its necessarily imperfect perception of what the people really want. In other words, once the relationship between the judicial function and the articulation of the people's views is acknowledged, the explanatory force of this justification is almost entirely undermined.

Perhaps a more fruitful mode of analysis is to address the procedural aspects of the problem of majoritarianism. The most famous attempt to do so in these terms is John Hart Ely's *Democracy and Distrust*.[27] The relevant part of Ely's theory for our purposes argues that legislatures operate in an essentially majoritarian manner and as such consistently fail to serve the interests of certain groups which do not exercise sufficient influence over the law-making process. Since these groups are failed by the political process, it is necessary that judges should subject legislation which affects them to a more searching form of constitutional scrutiny. This part of Ely's theory is based on the famous footnote 4 in the opinion of Justice Stone in the Supreme Court case of *United States* v. *Carolene Products Co.* in which the Justice refers to the:

> "prejudice against discrete and insular minorities . . . which tends seriously to curtail the operation of those political processes ordinarily to be relied upon to protect minorities, and which may call for a correspondingly more searching judicial inquiry."[28]

This position has been accepted by some leading constitutional courts which have acknowledged that the purpose of entrenched fundamental rights *is* to preserve certain issues from resolution in accordance with the wishes of majorities in the interests of minority protection. For example, Justice Jackson made the following statement in the United States Supreme Court in 1943:

> "The very purpose of a Bill of Rights was to withdraw certain subjects from the vicissitudes of political controversy, to place them beyond the reach of majorities and officials and to establish them as legal principles to be applied by the courts. One's right to life, liberty and property, to free speech, a free press, freedom of worship and assembly and other fundamental rights may not be submitted to vote; they depend on the outcome of no elections."[29]

---

[26] Bickel, *supra* n. 14, chs. 5 and 6. The distinction between judicial law-making which is "activist" (keeping the law up-to-date with the changing popular consensus) and "dynamic" (which seeks to use law to generate a change in popular consensus) is also drawn in P. Devlin, *The Judge* (Oxford, OUP, 1981), ch. 1.

[27] *Democracy and Distrust—A Theory of Judicial Review* (Harvard, Harvard University Press, 1980).

[28] 304 US 144, 152–3 (1938). See Justice Lewis Powell, "Carolene Products Revisited", 82 *Colum.LRev.* 1087 (1982); J. Balkin, "The Footnote", 83 *Nw.ULRev.* 275 (1989); B. Ackerman, "Beyond Carolene Products", 98 *Harv.LRev.* 713 (1985) and T. Sandalow, "Judicial Protection of Minorities", 75 *Mich.LRev.* 1162 (1977).

[29] *West Virginia State Board of Education* v. *Barnette*, 319 US 624, 638 (1943).

Perhaps more interestingly, the Constitutional Court in South Africa has explicitly adopted a counter-majoritarian justification for its decision in the case of *Makwanyane* which held that the death penalty violated the South African interim Constitution notwithstanding widespread public support for its continuance. As Chaskalson P stated:

> "Public opinion may have some relevance to the enquiry, but, in itself, it is no sub-stitute for the duty vested in the Courts to interpret the Constitution without fear or favour. If public opinion were to be decisive, there would be no need for consti-tutional adjudication. The protection of rights would then be left to Parliament, which has a mandate from the public, and is answerable to the public for the way its mandate is exercised . . . The very reason for establishing the new legal order, and for vesting the power of judicial review of all legislation in the courts, was to protect the rights of minorities and others who cannot protect their rights ade-quately through the democratic process."[30]

The argument appears persuasive but encounters some grave difficulties, perhaps the most serious of which is that it cannot be used as a justification for most examples of the review of the constitutionality of legislative action. In most cases, judicial intervention is not based on the protection of minori-ties but is founded on the preservation of certain values from legislative encroachment irrespective of whether the impact of such laws would fall dis-proportionately on certain groups. Hence, the protection of minorities cannot justify the edifice of judicial review but only one, admittedly significant, aspect of it. In addition some commentators reject the contention that the judiciary in fact advances countermajoritarian principles at all and cite illustrations in which the judges have shown themselves to be unsympathetic to the interests of minorities.[31]

A third problem is that identifying enhanced judicial scrutiny with legisla-tion which affects minorities may be a rather crude reflection of their likely importance as not all minorities have disproportionately low levels of influ-ence over the legislature. Some minorities (such as those which represent the interests of large financial concerns) exercise an influence disproportionate to

---

[30] *S.* v. *Makwanyane and Another*, 1995 (3) SA 391, 431B–E; M. Zlotnick, "The Death Penalty and Public Opinion" (1996) 12 *SAJHR* 70.

[31] The school desegregation decision of the US Supreme Court in *Brown* v. *Board of Education of Topeka*, 347 US 483 (1954) is often advanced as an example of the judiciary advancing a counter-majoritarian position, but this interpretation is far from inevitable (D. Bell, "Brown and the Interest-Convergence Dilemma" in D. Bell (ed.), *Shades of Brown* (1980) and G. A. Spann, "Pure Politics", 88 *Mich.LRev.* 1971 (1990)). Moreover, many would reject the argument that judicial review does or can provide a distinct and complementary form of participation for those who are excluded by the mechanism of parliamentary law-making and that the process of adju-dication is as likely as that of legislation to be dominated by sectional interests (M. Shapiro, *Freedom of Speech: The Supreme Court and Judicial Review* (Englewood Cliffs, Prentice Hall, 1966); P. Railton, "Judicial Review, Elites and Liberal Democracy" in *Nomos XXV: Liberal Democracy* (New York, New York University Press, 1983). For an analysis of those who invoke the judicial review jurisdiction in England and Wales, see L. Bridges, G. Meszaros and M. Sunkin, *Judicial Review in Perspective* (London, Cavendish, 1995).

their numerical size. This leads to a fourth difficulty. Many laws disadvantage minority groups but in some cases most people accept that this is a legitimate aim for the legislature to seek to achieve. Ely gives the example of a law which disadvantages burglars as a group. One can assume that this group is not well-represented in the legislature (or is, at least, unlikely to attract much overt support there), yet most would accept that such a law would not be subject to stricter judicial scrutiny for this reason alone. This result fits easily with our intuitions about the protection of minorities but requires a court to engage in a form of reasoning about the purposes of the constitution and of those who drafted the law in question which forces them to make substantive choices about the proper scope of governmental activity.[32] Once it is accepted that the theory will involve the court in drawing what are essentially public policy lines when it comes to consider whether or not the minority affected by a piece of legislation is one which deserves additional judicial protection, the exercise loses the objectivity one would expect from the argument's ostensible emphasis on procedure.[33]

However, recent criticisms of judicial review have taken a different line: one which places the dispute directly in the arena of the rights debate.[34] The starting-point of this argument is to challenge the traditional opposition of rights and democracy which one encounters in many of the counter-majoritarian justifications for review. It is relatively easy to argue that rights should triumph if the fundamental interests of the individual are juxtaposed with the more nebulous collective interests of the majority.[35] However, one can argue that this is a skewed comparison and that it is equally possible to break down this collective interest into constituent parts which are rights-based. The point here is that traditional theory has consistently undermined the extent to which individuals have a fundamental right to participate fully in the democratic running of the country. This must include participation in the debate over conflicts between different rights. Yet in a nation with a fundamental set of constitutional rights protected against the ordinary processes of legislative amendment, citizens are confined to participation in debates concerning issues of social and economic policy. Not only are individuals thus deprived, but political debate becomes limited to the same range of issues and the constant

---

[32] R. H. Bork, *The Tempting of America* (Touchstone, 1990), ch. 9.

[33] The justification for constitutional review which is based on the protection of minorities also sits uneasily with the notion that the Constitution itself and judicial decisions interpreting it can be overturned by the process of constitutional amendment. Most constitutions provide that amendment is legitimate by a super-majority (perhaps two-thirds of those voting in a referendum) and Professor Smith suggests that this provides a further mitigation of the "anti-democratic" nature of judicial review (*supra* 123). Yet if the legitimacy of review is based on the protection of minorities, it is unclear why the fact that *more* people are persuaded to oppress a minority should require judicial deference.

[34] The following section draws heavily on J. Waldron, "A Rights-Based Critique of Constitutional Rights" (1993) 13 *OJLS* 18. Some similar points are made in J. Allan, "Bills of Rights and Judicial Power—A Liberal's Quandary" (1996) 16 *OJLS* 337.

[35] R. M. Dworkin, *Taking Rights Seriously* (London, Duckworth, 1977).

dialectic of rights is shifted out of the political arena and into that of law where it will be dominated by expert and sectional interests.[36]

There is much to this argument. It is unquestionably the function of entrenched constitutional provisions to remove certain issues from the arena of political resolution. This demonstrates a singular and perhaps self-contradictory set of values. Those who decide to entrench the protection of certain rights are revealing a remarkable level of self-confidence in their own ability to determine how the balance between competing values should be struck. Yet they are simultaneously expressing a high degree of distrust for those who will form the political majority of future generations. This distrust sits ill with the idea of entrenching certain fundamental rights which most regard as justified by respect for the autonomy of the beneficiaries (including future beneficiaries) of human rights. Thus by entrenching certain interests, the present majority is saying two incompatible things: first, that future generations are entitled as autonomous human beings to exercise certain rights; yet, secondly, that our respect for their autonomy is not sufficient for us to grant to them the same range of decision-making power which we possessed and exercised in drafting or approving our entrenched constitution.

This argument may be illustrated by the position taken in the High Court of Australia in recent years. In *Nationwide News Pty. Ltd* v. *Wills*[37] and *Australian Capital Television Pty. Ltd* v. *The Commonwealth*[38] the High Court developed the principle that, although the Australian Constitution contained no explicit bill of rights, it was based upon certain premises which were entitled to judicial protection from legislative infringement. One such premise, as inferred by the Court, was that the Constitution is based upon a concept of representative democracy and responsible government.[39] From this, the High Court deduced that freedom of political expression is a fundamental right under Australian constitutional law and that the Court had the power to hold Acts passed by the Commonwealth legislature to be invalid for violating this norm. For example, in the *Australian Capital Television* case, the High Court struck down amendments introduced into the Broadcasting Act 1942 which sought to regulate the transmission of political matters in the run-up to elections.[40] More recent pronouncements of the Court suggest that it is

---

[36] See *supra* n. 31.

[37] (1992) 177 CLR 1.

[38] (1992) 177 CLR 106. The other leading cases are *Theophanous* v. *Herald & Weekly Times Ltd* (1994) 182 CLR 104 and *Stephens* v. *Western Australian Newspapers Ltd* (1994) 182 CLR 211.

[39] This inference was based in particular on ss. 7 (members to the Senate to be "chosen by the people of the State"), 24 (members of the House of Representatives to be "chosen by the people of the Commonwealth") and 128 of the Constitution (requiring the support of a majority of electors in a majority of states as well as the support of an overall majority of all electors voting to amend the Constitution).

[40] The amendments were contained in the Political Broadcasts and Political Disclosures Act 1991.

becoming more cautious in its approach to implied constitutional rights.[41] Nevertheless, these cases reveal the extreme difficulties encountered by a court which decides to privilege one set of rights (here to political expression) over another (to participate fully in the balancing of rights through the political process).[42] The great irony remains that the Court, in purported furtherance of a concept of representative democracy, overruled the legislative judgment of the representatives of the people in passing the Political Broadcasts and Political Disclosures Act 1991.[43]

This position, which places the dispute firmly in the arena of the clash between competing rights, is a more formidable one. One response is to state that the concept of ensuring full political participation is self-contradictory, in that if its adherents believe that political participation by all citizens is so important, then surely even they would accept that *this* right should be provided with fundamental constitutional status. It is important not to overstate this argument. It would not provide a justification for the many civil and political rights which are regarded by many as essential to the functioning of a mature democracy such as rights to freedom of expression or association. These could, consistently with the above position, be limited by the majority as an exercise of its political will. However, what if the majority decided to disenfranchise a significant minority of the population, let us say, all those who were (or who have at least one parent who was) born in the Indian subcontinent. One could argue that this would amount to a more tangible violation of the right to democratic participation than a law which prevented the majority of citizens from voting to, say, re-introduce slavery. In other words, is a society really more democratic and a better respecter of all rights (including those of political participation) if it places no legal limitations at all on the ability of the legislative majority to exercise its will?

Perhaps the difficulty with conducting the debate in this manner is that the juxtaposition of the opposing constitutional orders is too extreme to allow a rational compromise to be reached between them. Individuals do need to guard their fundamental rights to participate in the resolution of the grand issues regarding the extent of our freedoms and when their curtailment is legitimate. It probably is the case that the notion of political participation has been accorded insufficient priority in the canon of constitutional fundamentals.[44] Yet, as Professor Smith's paper demonstrates, the most valuable lesson

---

[41] *Lange* v. *Australian Broadcasting Corporation* (High Court decision of 8 July 1997 available at http://www.austlii.edu.au/cases/cth/high_ct/recentcases.html).

[42] Six members of the Court in the *ACT case* accepted that the framers of the Constitution had rejected the idea of including a bill of rights in the Constitution, preferring to leave the protection of fundamental rights to the political process.

[43] In the *Nationwide* case, Brennan J held that " . . . the representative democracy ordained by our Constitution carried with it a comparable freedom for the Australian people and that freedom circumscribes the legislative powers conferred on the Parliament by the Constitution", *supra* n. 37, 50.

[44] Rights to some form of political participation are contained in Art. 21 of the Universal Declaration of Human Rights, Art. 25 of the International Covenant of Civil and Political Rights

we can draw from the study of comparative public law is an awareness of the flexibility with which regimes have rationalised their constitutional orders. Even in recent years the different responses to the difficulties outlined above which have been adopted in Canada,[45] New Zealand,[46] Australia,[47] South Africa[48] and those states emerging from Soviet dominance[49] provide a diversity of paradigms which can inform the debate in this country without entailing the extremism of either British legislative or United States judicial supremacism.[50]

and in Art. 3 of Protocol 1 of the European Convention on Human Rights. See H. J. Steiner, "Political Participation as a Human Right", 1 *Harv. Hum. Rts. Y'bk* 77 (1988) and T. Franck, "The Emerging Right to Democratic Governance", 86 *Am. J Int. L* 46 (1992)

[45] D. Beatty, "The Canadian Charter of Rights: Lessons and Laments (1997) 60 *MLR* 481 and T. G. Ison, "A Constitutional Bill of Rights—The Canadian Experience" (1997) 60 *MLR* 499.

[46] A. S. Butler, "The Bill of Rights Debate: Why the New Zealand Bill of Rights Act 1990 is a Bad Model for Britain" (1997) 17 *OJLS* 323.

[47] See the special issue of the Sydney Law Review for 1994 on the High Court's Freedom of Speech Cases.

[48] S. Kentridge, "Bills of Rights—The South African Experiment" (1996) 112 *LQR* 237 and "Parliamentary Supremacy and the Judiciary under a Bill of Rights: Some Commonwealth Lessons" [1997] PL 96 and A. Cockrell, "The South African Bill of Rights and the 'Duck/Rabbit' " (1997) 60 *MLR* 513.

[49] R. R. Ludwikowski, *supra* n. 13.

[50] The term judicial supremacy is used in C. G. Haines, *The American Doctrine of Judicial Supremacy* (California, 1932) and R. H. Jackson, *The Struggle for Judicial Supremacy* (New York, 1941).

10

Developments in Italian Administrative Law through Cross-fertilisation

LUISA TORCHIA

1. INTRODUCTION

The influence of Community law on Italian administrative law was ignored for a long time, for two main reasons. First, the European Community was conceived as a public power without an administrative apparatus. European policies were implemented by and through national administrations and, as a consequence, developments of the national administrative system were perceived as endogenous phenomena and not linked nor referred to the operation of the European Community.[1] Secondly, the very close link between administrative law and the State, in Italy as in other continental countries, fostered the opinion that administrative law could not allow even a comparative analysis of the different systems and *a fortiori* the influence of laws, which like Community law, do not originate in and from the State.

Furthermore, the Constitutional Court does not recognise that the two systems are fully integrated. Although it recognises the judges' power/duty to disapply national law in favour of Community law, its decisions postulate a mere co-ordination between two autonomous orders.[2]

In the last few years, though, and especially since the adoption of the Single European Act, the process of integration (and cross-fertilisation) has acquired momentum and there is a more widespread perception in legal doctrine of the relevance and dimension of the European developments: it is not still

---

[1] S. Cassese, "La Costituzione europea", 1991 *Quaderni costituzionali* 901; S. Cassese, "Il sistema amministrativo europeo e la sua evoluzione", 1991 *Riv. trim. dir. pubbl.* 769; G. Falcon, "Dal diritto amministrativo nazionale al diritto amministrativo comunitario", 1991 *Riv. it. dir. pubbl. com.* 351; A. Massera, "Una nozione comunitaria, di pubblica amministrazione" in *El desenvolupament del dret administratiu europeu* (Barcelona, 1993); J. Schwarze (ed.), *Administrative Law under European Influence* (London, Sweet and Maxwell/Nomos, 1996).

[2] Corte costituzionale, judgments nos. 113/1985 and 389/1989; M. P. Chiti, "I signori del diritto comunitario: la Corte di giustizia e lo sviluppo del diritto amministrativo europeo", 1991 *Riv. trim. dir. pubbl.* 796.

conventional wisdom, but it is no longer an extravagance. This new con sciousness has led to a new wave of comparative studies and, more to the point, of studies focused on interaction between Italian administrative law and Community law.[3]

There are two different relevant phenomena. First, there is the direct influence of Community law on Italian administrative law, when a Community legal instrument supersedes a national legal instrument. An example of this is that a single licence has substituted the national authorisation for banks and other financial intermediaries.

In this case, we have a Community legal instrument—i.e. the licence— which is now used by national administrative law in different countries as a substitute for former national legal instruments. The result is that the legal regime in a given field, in our example financial markets, is common to all national legal orders, at least in its crucial features.

Another interesting effect of this phenomenon is the circulation of national administrative acts, for example the licence issued by the Bank of Italy, in other countries, beyond the boundaries of the issuing authority's jurisdiction. Thus, there is a division of administrative power between the authority issuing the licence (home country control) and the relevant authority in the country in which the licenced firm actually operates (host country control).

Secondly, there is the indirect influence of Community law on Italian administrative law, described by scholars in terms of "convergence" of the different national systems. An example is the new Italian law on access to the bar for lawyers: the new law was not a juridical obligation, but it was necessary to warrant effectiveness of the principle of free movement and non-discriminatory practices.[4] In fact the control of discriminatory practices is one of the most effective instruments of change in national administrative law in general and in Italian administrative law specifically, because it requires the elimination of exactly those specific and peculiar rules which are rooted in national history.[5]

Both the direct and indirect influence of Community law produce developments through cross-fertilisation in different domains of administrative law, and in each domain the speed, breadth and relevance of the changes can differ.[6]

---

[3] S. Cassese, "L'influenza del diritto amministrativo comunitario sui diritti amministrativi nazionali", 1993 Riv.it.dir.pubbl.com. 329; M. P. Chiti, "Tendencies towards European Standards in national Administrative Law, Italian Report", in Schwartze, (ed.), *supra* n. 1; E. Picozza, "L'incidenza del diritto comunitario (e del diritto internazionale) sui concetti fondamentali del diritto pubblico dell'economia", 1996 Riv.it.dir.pubbl.com. 239 and by the same author "Alcune riflessioni circa la rilevanza del diritto comunitario sui principi del diritto amministrativo italiano", in *Studi in memoria di F. Piga* (Milan, Giuffrè, 1992), vol. I.

[4] S. Case C–55/94, *Reinard Gebhard* v. *Ordine degli Avvocati e dei procuratori di Milano*, 30 Nov. 1995, not yet reported.

[5] P. Legrand, "European Legal Systems are not converging" (1996) 45 *ICLQ* 52.

[6] S. Cassese, "Stato-nazione e funzione pubblica" [1997] 1 *Giornale di diritto amministrativo*, 88; M. P. Chiti, "La meta della integrazione europea: Stato, Unione internazionale o 'Monstro simile'?", 1996 Riv.it.dir.pubbl.com. 591.

In this paper I do not give a full and complete picture of these developments. I shall point out, as significant examples, three domains where developments are especially conspicuous: the development of the concepts of State and public administration, the development of market regulation, and the developments concerning the legal protection of individual rights (although, in this last case, we have an occurrence of aborted cross-fertilisation, on compensation in respect of legitimate interests).

For each case I shall point out, briefly, the traditional concept, the developments induced by Community law and, when possible, the effects of cross-fertilisation. As sometimes happens with cross fertilisation, the results are not always established and the hybrid could revert to the original species.

2. THE CONCEPTS OF STATE AND OF PUBLIC ADMINISTRATION

The concept of State is central for Italian administrative law and traditionally is one of the concepts most analysed and discussed. As a result of this analysis and discussion, extending over many decades of legal studies, the conventional concept of State as a legal entity, with its own personality, all encompassing (law, statutes, rights, public bodies, private citizens), has been abandoned and replaced by an array of different concepts. The State as *a* legal entity is a subject and not any longer *the* subject of the internal legal order, and here are other public bodies with a high degree of autonomy (for example regions and municipalities). Further, public and "statal" are no longer synonymous; the term State can be used to identify the society as a whole (*Stato-comunità*) or the legal order (*Stato-ordinamento*) or the government (*Stato-apparato*).

The concept of public administration has been expanded as well, and the strict version including only central departments has been replaced by longer and longer lists, until the perception of variety and multiplicity of public administration models has become commonplace. In many recent statutes, such as Law no. 241/1990, on administrative procedure and Decreto legislativo no. 29/1993, on the reform of the civil service, rules are established for many different public bodies and there is no attempt to use or identify a unitary concept of public administration.[7] These new concepts of State and public administration have been changing, through cross-fertilisation due to Community law, in a threefold way.

The first issue is the indifference of Community law to the concept of State, even if this concept is so relevant in continental Europe legal systems. Community law is completely indifferent to the State as a legal entity, its organisation, its position as a special subject in the legal order, the provision

---

[7] The D.Lgs. no. 29/1993, art.1, lists the following public bodies subjected to new rules on civil service: State central departments, schools, regions, provinces, municipalities, universities, housing authorities, chambers of commerce, health service.

ot special rules and special judges. This indifference is very clear in the Maastricht Treaty, but it also appears from the decisions of the European Court of Justice (ECJ). Singling out, as an example, the decisions on state liability, the Court has established that liability can be imputed to the State whatever is the public authority or body responsible for the wrongful action (or inaction), including the Parliament and the judiciary.[8] The indifference of the Community to the concept of State has interacted with the revision of the concept within Italian administrative law and has contributed to diminish further the scientific and operational value of this concept.

The concept of administrative organisation has undergone a cross-fertilisation process as well. Organisation is relevant in Italian administrative law because relationships both within and between organisations are legally relevant and explained with different legal models.

The main instrument of change, here, is that European policies are not implemented through a European public apparatus, but through national administration. That means you can have a central department in a member of the Community operating not for the State, but for the Community. This phenomenon has been described as co-administration.[9] When the Community has the decision-making power and the national administration has the power of implementation, they are necessary one to the other, implying that organisations and procedures depend on and are governed by two different subjects. Here, too, we have a weakening of the concept of State as the main and most relevant subject in the national legal order: the subject to which, at the end of the day, everything goes back.

A third point will be analysed in greater detail. In Community law and in the judgments of the ECJ there are several different legal concepts of public administration. Although these legal concepts can be different in some respects, they have a very important element in common: at the core of the concept there is a functional, not a structural definition.[10] This is true for at least three cases. First, the rules in the Maastricht Treaty on public enterprise are inspired by the irrelevance of the public or private control of firms (Article 222). Secondly, the rules on public procurement introduce a concept of "public body" based on the nature of the activity and not on structural elements. Thirdly, the enforcement by the ECJ of the principle of free movement in the domain of employment with national public administrations uses such an approach. This functional concept of public administration is the core of an important process of cross-fertilisation.

---

[8] See Joined Cases C–6 and 9/90 *Francovich and Others* [1991] ECR I–5357; Joined Cases C–43 and 48/93 *Brasserie du Pêcheur* v. *Germany* and *The Queen* v. *Secretary of State for Transport, ex parte Factortame Ltd* [1996] ECR I–1029.

[9] C. Franchini, *Amministrazione italiana e amministrazione comunitaria* (Padova, Cedam, 1992).

[10] D. Sorace, "L'ente pubblico fra diritto comunitario e diritto nazionale", 1992 *Riv. it. dir. pubbl. com.* 357.

As far as legal doctrine is concerned, the functional concept has made possible the transposition of the so called "objective concept"[11] of public service to administrative activity as a whole. When some functional elements recur—for example, the industrial nature of activity, the activity's links with the satisfaction of needs and interests which are not of an industrial or commercial nature, direct or indirect participation in the exercise of public power—specific rules are applied, independently of the structural nature or organisational form of the subject concerned.[12]

These rules are applied, then, not because of the nature of the subject, but because of the nature of the activity. This confirms an important new postulate of the most modern Italian legal doctrine: Italian administrative law is not so much a part of public law, but it is more and more a mix of public law and private law elements.

The introduction of a functional definition of public administration has also been registered by the national parliament and by the administrative judge.

For instance, as far as public procurements are concerned, the Italian law (no. 109/1994) is largely inspired by Community law, which affirms the general rule that competitive tendering is necessary with exceptions accepted only in terms of strict interpretation. But in Italian law this general principle has interacted with traditional Italian unwillingness to resort to competitive tendering, resulting, in the domain of local public services, in a mixed construction. Local authorities can promote the constitution of companies in which they hold less than 50 per cent of the shares, and competitive tendering is used to choose the partner(s) in the company, while public service is attributed to the company directly, at the moment of incorporation (supplementary provisions can be defined with agreement acts between the local authority and the company).[13]

The Italian administrative judge has also incorporated the functional notion of public administration in his decisions, using it, for instance, to confirm his jurisdiction over public enterprises even after their privatisation. Through a skilful use of Community directives on public procurements, the Council of State (*Consiglio di Stato*), has stated, for instance, that the State Railway Company, even after being privatised, is a public enterprise in a "substantial" (as opposed to "formal") way, as it provides not only the transportation service, but is also responsible for other duties which have a public nature. As a consequence, it operates as a substitute for public administration and it must follow the same procedures, for instance for public procurements, as the Transportation Department.[14]

In this case too, then, rules referring to the structure of the subject and rules referring to its activity can be differentiated, undermining a correspondence

---

[11] U. Pototschnig, *I pubblici servizi* (Padova, Cedam, 1964).
[12] A. Massera, *Una nozione comunitaria di pubblica amministrazione*.
[13] Dpr n. 533/1996.
[14] Cons. Stato, Sez. VI, 20 May 1995, no. 498.

which has for a long time been a traditional feature of Italian administrative law.

3. LEGAL PROTECTION OF INDIVIDUAL RIGHTS

Community law provides instruments for both direct and indirect legal protection of individual rights. An example of direct legal protection is the Directive on protection of consumers, which has been introduced into the Italian system with a renovation of the Civil Code.[15] The Directive has, however, also had an effect on Italian administrative law, because it requires the establishment of an independent authority, empowered to adjudicate, decide and impose sanctions.

The spread of independent regulatory commissions in Italy is fostered by the inadequacy of central departments and other long-established public authorities, for carrying out regulation and adjudication duties, and by the growing inadequacy of overloaded judges to settle ever new questions and conflicts in old and new domains of public law.

We have a cross-fertilisation, here, between the Italian preference for independent authorities and the Community preference for remedies of non judicial nature.

More relevant for Italian administrative law has been the empowering of national judges to guarantee enforcement of Community law and the right of free movement.[16] The duty of national judges to enforce Community law has granted, first, the possibility of suspension of the national act in contrast with Community law and, later, the power to grant interim relief measures.[17] The effect is the enlargement of legal protection through interim relief measures and a narrowing of the difference between interim and final decisions. This trend has also been manifested in a recent Italian statute, which provides special rules for judgment in the public procurement domain, requiring the judge to guarantee the interim relief measure in a very short time and shortening the time allowed for the final decision.

The protection of the right of free movement requires a strict and accurate motivation of administrative acts restricting its enforcement, so that the non-discriminatory nature of the decision is evident and can be fully disclosed by judicial review. The duty to give motivation, which is, after the enactement

[15] Council Directive 93/13/EEC on unfair terms in consumer contracts ([1993] OJ L95/29) was implemented through l.n. 52/1996, art. 25, which adds 5 new arts. to the Italian Civil Code.
[16] G. Cocco, "L'insostenibile leggerezza del diritto italiano", 1996 Riv.it.dir.pubbl.com. 629 and G. Greco, "L'effettività della giustizia amministrativa italiana nel quadro del diritto europeo", *ibid.*, 797; R. Caranta, *Giustizia amministrativa e Comunità europea* (Naples, Jovene, 1992).
[17] European Court of Justice, Nota informativa riguardante la proposizione di domande di pronuncia pregiudiziale da parte dei giudici nazionali (ottobre 1996), *Giornale di diritto amministrativo*, n. 11, 1996, 1083, comment by G. P. Manzella.

of Law no 241/1990, a general principle in Italian system, finds, in this way, a specific cause.

Lastly, I shall cite a case of aborted cross-fertilisation. Compensation in respect of legitimate expectations has always been denied by the Italian judges, on the formal ground (to cut a long story short) that legitimate interests exist only insofar as administrative activity brings them into existence and for a further, never stated, but always present ground, the belief that the State cannot afford to pay for this kind of damage.

As a consequence of Directive 89/665, a new statute has been adopted, providing compensation for legitimate expectations in the domain of public procurement. Italian judges have, however, been quick to deny any general relevance to this statutory provision. On the contrary, they have stated that, by introducing a specific provision, the parliament was actually confirming a general principle of non-compensation, which could be removed, one supposes, only with several, specific and sectorial provisions.

4. MARKET REGULATION: LIBERALISATION AND PRIVATISATION

The effects of cross-fertilisation in this domain are especially prominent, for three reasons. First, in Italy the public sector was very large and public intervention in the economy extensive. Secondly, market regulation was established by public law statutes and the array of controls on the private sector was very large. Thirdly, public services and utilities were actually public monopolies. This situation has changed dramatically in the last ten years.

The public sector has been trimmed through privatisation, although the effect more often has been the the privatisation of the organisation (a public body transformed into a company, with the State as the only or the main shareholder) than a real "rolling back" of the State. Public property and public command have been replaced, more and more often, with regulation: the State entrepreneur has evolved into the regulating State. This has brought a change in policies, which were no longer directed to "governing" the market, but to guaranteeing the rules of the game, the game being one of fairness, competition, free access, transparency and information.[18] The enforcement of these new policies require a new organisational model, the independent regulatory commissions, which have become a common and standing feature in Italian legal order.

Public services and public utilities are also undergoing important changes. At the end of the process, it is likely that the public monopoly model will be abandoned and free access to private entrepreneurs will be assured, even in sectors in which the network property or management will remain in public hands (telecommunications and railway being prominent examples).

[18] S. Cassese, "Poteri indipendenti, Stati, relazioni ultrastatali" [1996] V *Foro italiano* col. 7; L. Torchia, *Il controllo pubblico della finanza privata* (Padua, Cedam, 1992).

Given the breadth of change, the cross-fertilisation process has important dimensions, but is still in progress. I shall examine, as examples, only two concepts which have undergone a significant change and I shall try to point out the consequences of this change in relation to a specific segment of the financial markets.

The first concept is "public control", evolving both in content and in the nature of the controller. The content of the concept has been changing because public control is no longer aimed at guaranteeing the conformity or, at least, the compatibility between private enterprise and public interest.

Article 41 of the Italian Constitution provides for a so-called "mixed system": the freedom of private enterprise is guaranteed as a constitutional right, but it can be limited by State intervention for social aims. Since the 1950s this provision has accomodated a very pervasive and thorough system of public intervention. In may fields a private firm was able to operate only if it was granted a licence, and public authorities had wide discretion in granting such licences and carrying out the connected control duties.

"Control" was indeed a discretionary activity, and private enterprises had to conform to general and specific rules and standards set up by public authorities. Control, nowadays, is aimed instead at guaranteeing that each and every subject, private or public, complies with the rules of the game. These rules are introduced by statutes and are specified by independent regulatory commissions, which are also in charge of enforcement and the imposition of sanctions for unlawful conduct.

The main difference with the tradition of Italian administrative law is that, in this case, there is no bilateral relation between the public administration in charge of control and the private subject who must comply. Such bilateral relations reflected the (public) power/(private) freedom relationship which has been at the core of the historical ambivalence of Italian administrative law. This enabled public authorities to encroach upon private freedom in order to pursue public interest and it guaranteed that private freedom could be restricted or otherwise limited by public authorities only if there was a statute allowing the intervention and within legally established limits.

The changing nature of public control has led to a trilateral relationship, between the independent regulatory commission responsible for control, the private subject responsible for complying and the other private subjects whose interests are protected through public control. Rules of conduct are aimed not at the pursuing of public interest, but to garantee specific private interests.[19]

Let us consider, for instance, financial markets regulation. Markets must be competitive, information asymmetry must be corrected, and access must be free. Public controls pursuing these goals are established to protect the rights of consumers, investors, and private entrepreneurs. The result is public

[19] L. Torchia, "Gli interessi affidati alla cura delle autorità indipendenti" in Cassese and Franchini (eds.), *I garanti delle regole* (Bologna, Il Mulino, 1996).

controls on private activities to protect private rights (these last assume more frequently a collective, rather than an individual dimension).

Thus, two relationships are relevant in the legal order: the relationship between private subjects (for example, between competing entrepreneurs, and between financial firms and investors) and the relationship between the public authority in charge of control and private subjects. The public authority must assume in this case neutral and impartial conduct of strict enforcement of the law, with an enhancement of adjudicatory powers, while little room remains for discretionary powers.

The second concept undergoing an important change is that of the regulated market, especially again in the financial sector. Financial markets have been, for a long time, forums where public control was exercised and the management of the market was, legally, a public service. But nowadays they are in the process of becoming self-regulated institutions. As an example, let us consider the new securities market law, enacted in compliance with Directives 93/22 and 93/6. With this new law the single licence was introduced, abandoning the old rule of incorporation condemned by the ECJ. The new law has also provided for the division of regulatory powers between the independent authority (Consob) and private professional companies.

It is important to identify the main features of the new institutional arrangement, to measure the difference by comparison with the past. First, organisation and management of regulated financial markets are defined as a business (and not a public service) activity. Secondly, this business activity can be carried out by public limited companies. Minimum capital requirements and activities of these companies are defined by Consob regulation. Thirdly, the organisation and the management of the market are regulated by an act of the assembly of the public limited company and, thus, by a private law act.

Regulation, control and inspection duties are split between the Consob and companies. The Consob must authorise the setting up of the regulated market, must verify company requirements and their regulations' conformity to Community law. The Consob also has a general power to inspect regulated markets and companies and can supersede their decisions when expediency and need arise. The companies have regulation powers, enacted in a general way with the assembly deliberation and case by case with specific acts, e.g. on such matters as which financial intermediaries and which financial instruments can operate in the market.

The main effect of this new institutional arrangement is the transformation of the legal notion of market, nowadays resulting from a complex mix of private law and public law elements. The regulated market is no longer an instrument of public service, nor is it "governed" by a public body, but neither is it completely self-regulated. It has become an institution, managed by private bodies and with a more distant public control, that can be identified as a sort of "second degree" control: the role of the public authority is mainly directed to verify how well the private bodies carry out their duties.

5. CONCLUSIONS

A new legal language is spreading through European countries. This new language, as the hellenistic *koinè* (common speech) is a simplified version of local dialects, enriched with new terms and new words. The hellenistic *koinè* was not only, though, a universal language, but also a common set of beliefs and attitudes: a Greek was a man of Greek culture more than a man of Greek origin. It is not by chance that the dominant philosophical school in that period—marked by the interaction between East and West after the conquests of Alexander the Great—was Stoicism, with its stress on cosmopolitan citizenship and on common elements between Greek and non-Greek, man and woman, slave and not slave.

This new legal language is, by definition, as often happens with hybrids, impure and is still evolving. But if it is true that, as has been pointed out in the classical work on legal transplants by A. Watson,[20] lawyers and legal scholars prefer to think that there is more to law than their reasoning and that what they call law is based on authority and precedent, law originating from cross-fertilisation stands a good chance of becoming ever more encompassing and to become the parameter for evaluation and interpretation of legal problems and cases in a particular internal legal order.

[20] *Legal Transplants* (1984).

11

Mechanisms for Cross-fertilisation of Administrative Law in Europe

JOHN BELL

Legal systems have internal dynamics which give them their special character, and it is important to understand these in order to appreciate what makes a legal tradition distinctive. But legal systems are not immutable. They change through national and international pressures. Cross-fertilisation (often in the form of convergence) is an important facet of legal evolution. Different authors adopt diverging positions on the extent to which legal traditions and systems are self-contained and self-reproducing (in Teubner's term, *auto-poietic*).[1] My own view would be that, at the moment, European administrative law traditions remain very national, but that international interaction and collaboration at a practical and an academic level has and will continue to shape the development of specific national traditions.

I would draw a distinction between *transplants* and *cross-fertilisation*. Transplants involve the transposition of a doctrine from one legal system into another. There are doubts about the effectiveness of this process, and John Allison has rightly raised concerns about the way in which the notion of a distinction between public and private law can simply be transplanted into the English legal system from countries such as France.[2] Cross-fertilisation implies a different, more indirect process. It implies that an external stimulus promotes an evolution within the receiving legal system. The evolution involves an internal adaptation by the receiving legal system in its own way. The new development is a distinctive but organic product of that system rather than a bolt-on. This process often gives rise to greater convergence between the receiving legal system and the external stimulus, but this need not be the case. (The notion of the 'rule of law' offers an illustration of divergent conceptions,

---

[1] G. Teubner, *Law as an Autopoietic System* (Oxford, Blackwell, 1993). In Teubner's view, "Autopoietic closure does not mean that the [legal] system is independent of its environment. Evolution's relation to the environment is not brought about, however, by direct, causal, external influence on legal developments. Rather, it evolves through processes of co-evolution in which the co-evolving systems exert an indirect influence on each other" (*ibid.*, 61).

[2] *A Continental Distinction in the Common Law* (Oxford, Clarendon Press, 1996). See more generally, A. Watson, *Legal Transplants* (Edinburgh, 1984), ch. 3.

if not concepts, emerging from a common, liberal political agenda.³) Given this indirect character of legal development, we cannot expect to identify evidence of its occurrence with ease.

This paper will try to do four things:

(a) provide an overview of the different European administrative law traditions and the extent to which there are common views on the scope of administrative law;
(b) identify the principal features of convergence within contemporary European administrative law systems;
(c) sketch significant features in the dynamics of any legal system which make it distinctive; and
(d) identify the mechanisms which are leading to a greater *rapprochement* between legal systems.

Throughout the paper, I will make reference to Jürgen Schwarze's new edited collections *Administrative Law under European Influence*.⁴ This collection offers very useful insights into the way thirteen of the fifteen Member States of the EU perceive European influences on their administrative law.

A. INTRODUCTION: THE EUROPEAN ADMINISTRATIVE LAW TRADITIONS

Before embarking on my three main areas, I want to say why I think that administrative law is interesting as an area of comparative law research, and I want to sketch the basic features of European administrative law systems. Sabino Cassese argues that there are two distinct emphases within European traditions of administrative law.⁵ The first treats administrative law as about the control of the administration and thus focuses particularly upon judicial review (*le contentieux administratif* or *Verwaltungsgerichtsbarkeit*). The second focuses upon mechanisms for achieving social goals through collective action, upon legislation and institutions which realise these social aspirations. From this we get a law about the administration and administrative action (*le droit administratif* or *Verwaltungsrecht*). These emphases and the balance between them radically shape national administrative law traditions and affect the way ideas from other systems can be incorporated.

The study of "legal families" in the seminal works of Zweigert and Kötz and David⁶ focuses on private law. Zweigert and Kötz recognise that legal sys-

³ See J. Rivero in *L'État de droit. Mélanges Braibant* (Paris, 1996), 609 ff. and cf. J. Bell in *ibid.*, 15 ff.

⁴ London, 1996.

⁵ *Le Basi del Diritto Amministrativo* (2nd revised edn., Bologna 1995), sect. 4.7. See also J. Bell, "Convergences and Divergences in European Administrative Law" [1992] 1 *Riv. Ital. Dir. Pubbl. Communitario* 3.

⁶ K. Zweigert and H. Kötz, *An Introduction to Comparative Law* (2nd edn. trans. T. Weir, Oxford, Clarendon Press, 1987), ch. 5; R. David and J. Brierly, *The Major Legal Systems in the World Today* (3rd edn., London, Butterworth, 1985), 17–20.

tems are not monolithic and that, for example, German constitutional law has more resemblance to American constitutional law than to French constitutional law, though German private law would resemble French private law more than American private law.[7] But the bulk of the International Encyclopedia and works on comparative law have focused on the divisions of western private law into the Germanic, Franco-Roman, and common law traditions. One would also wish to argue that Scandinavian systems are distinctive.

The administrative law traditions have a different configuration, because the influences do not depend on Roman law, but on state traditions developed in the medieval period and particularly in the nineteenth century. I would identify at least four different groupings.

The French-influenced systems (France, Belgium, Greece, Luxembourg, Italy, Portugal, Spain) have a number of common features. For them, public law is the law governing administrative activity in the broadest sense and is not necessarily limited to public bodies. This activity is done in the public interest as opposed to the private interest, and it leads to a distinction between public law and private law (though there are degrees of intensity in this distinction) which affects both substantive law and procedure.[8] Responses to Schwarze's questionnaire demonstrate a pre-occupation with refined concepts of "the administration", "public service", "public property" and "administrative acts". The first three define the subjects and subject-matter of administrative law, whilst the fourth focuses on the conditions for the validity of administrative action, as well as publicity and access to them. The broad nature of the activity encompassed by this conception of administrative law is captured by the emphasis on public service, rather than just public order, an activity based approach rather than an organic approach to the definition of administrative law.

The Germanic systems: the Germans share the separation of public and private law in terms of law and the courts, but there is greater overlap between the two branches of law. Administrative judges are part of the same corps as other judges, but with a special assignment. Liability rules are more common between public and private law. There is not the same conception of "public service" which identifies administrative law in France—it is more concerned with an institutional "administration" and its acts, an organic conception of administrative law. Administrative law is the law governing the administration.

The common law systems and the Netherlands: the common law countries, Britain and Ireland, and the Netherlands focus very little on the organic or

---

[7] *Supra* n. 6, 75.

[8] The importance of the distinction between the public and private interest in shaping administrative law is not a product of the 1789 Revolution, but is well formulated in the 16th and 17th centuries: J.-L. Mestre, *Introduction historique au droit administratif français* (Paris, 1985), 99–103. Thus the separation between the courts handling administrative and civil matters was already being developed through the Edict of St Germain-en-Laye of 1641 in terms not dissimilar to the *loi* of 16–24 Aug. 1790.

public service aspects. Indeed, neither group has a legal concept of "public service". They have also been used to very little distinction between the administrative judge and the private law judge.[9] They lead a third tendency which focuses on the judicial control of administrative action—administrative law as the law operated by the administrative judge. The control of discretionary power and standards of administrative procedure, as well as judicial remedies, are the dominant issues in the British, Dutch and Irish contributions to Schwarze's book. These systems have also had the tradition of administrative tribunals which provide a kind of administrative justice outside the ordinary court system. Indeed, one could argue that these systems have a strong tradition of administrative *non-law*, rather than administrative law, of which the *Citizen's Charter* is but a recent manifestation.[10]

The Scandinavians: In Schwarze's book , the Danish report treats administrative law as being about the redress of grievances against the state. As a result, much of the discussion is neither about administrative organisation nor courts, but about the role of the Ombudsman and how he does not fit well into the European law structures.[11] The Ombudsman also has an important role in Norway and Sweden, more so than in other European countries. All the same, in other respects, Norway has a well developed administrative law on judicial review, and its conceptual structure has great similarity to German law, though without a jurisdictional division between public and private courts.[12] Like German law, its discussion of public services is more institutional than conceptual.[13] On the other hand, the Norwegians have a significant number of tribunals within the administration to provide redress in a way not dissimilar to English administrative tribunals. The Swedes and Finns have distinct administrative structures, so it would not be correct to consider the Scandinavian countries as a homogeneous bloc.[14] Nevertheless, the relative importance of the Ombudsman is one feature which makes a significant impact on the role of the judicial review aspect of administrative law.

Schwarze's analysis proceeds on the assumption that there is agreement on what counts as administrative law. His respondents reveal that this is not

---

[9] For a detailed analysis see J. Allison, *supra* n. 2, ch 5.

[10] See J. Bell, "De la nécessité d'un droit administratif", *AJDA*, special number 20 June 1995, 99 at 106–7. I have in mind here the fact that *ex gratia* payments, administrative guidance and other extra-legal means are frequently used to deal with issues which the French tradition would certainly use law to handle.

[11] See Schwarze, *supra* n. 4, 377 at 385 ff.; also J. A. Jensen, "Basic Features of Danish Public Law" [1995] 1 *EPL* 149, 153 argues that judicial review in courts is not important, but that review by the Ombudsman is very important.

[12] I am indebted to Eivind Smith for his comments. A full treatment of the subject is found in T. Eckhoff and E. Smith, *Forvaltningsrett* (6th edn., Oslo, 1997) and a briefer overview in E. Smith, "Norvège: La justice administrative" [1988] *Rfda* 248.

[13] See Eckhoff and Smith, *supra* n. 12, 366–8.

[14] See e.g. S. Strömholm, *An Introduction to Swedish Law* (Stockholm, 1981), ch. 3; F. Sejersted, "Introduction to Norwegian Public Law" [1995] 1 *EPL* 177, esp. 183;. M. Suski, "Finland: General Features of Public Law" [1996] 2 *EPL* 182; H.-H. Vogel, "Swedish Administrative Law in a State of Change" [1997] 3 *EPL* 26.

altogether the case. We do not share a common focus of attention when talking about administrative law. Schwarze's book is a good illustration in that, when asked to talk about the way in which European law has influenced domestic law, the respondents end up talking about very different things: some about public employment, others about judicial review, others about government liability. As Dubois has pointed out,[15] European Community developments have proceeded on the basis of a narrower conception of public law than the French and Germans have been used to relying on. Thus in developing European Community administrative law, there is a further conception of administrative law which we have to take into account, but it is not one which other systems have adopted. At most, some legal systems have adapted their conception of administrative law to comply with EC law, e.g. in the scope of public employment. The European Convention has focused more laterally across the different branches of law by concentrating on fair procedures and the rights of citizens. This offers a partial contribution to common standards in administrative law. But the underlying divergence of perception in national traditions remains significant.

While there are overlaps with concepts of "legal families" discussed in private law, the groupings of legal systems in administrative law are different. For a start, Roman law is not a major influence. By contrast, conceptions of the State developed in the nineteenth century are more influential.[16] (It is significant that the common law and Dutch systems are (or were) monarchical with institutional continuity from before the French Revolution.) Scandinavian systems are distinctive in administrative law because they developed distinctive institutional practices both for decision-making and remedies.

The divergence of conceptions of administrative law and the institutional structures out of which it grows provides the context for understanding the extent of any convergence between the legal systems in Europe and the scope for cross-fertilisation. I would like to approach the issue of cross-fertilisation by setting it in the context of the pressures for convergence and those for divergence which affect legal systems. Cross-fertilisation negotiates these pressures by accepting appropriate cases for convergence, but accepting also that the solutions adopted will be divergent in some respects between legal systems.

B. THE SCOPE OF CONVERGENCE

I would identify four principal areas for convergence at the present time in Europe. In the first place, there is convergence in values. The signing of the European Convention on Human Rights symbolises the extent to which the different countries agree on important values which should regulate the

---

[15] In *AJDA*, special issue 20 June 1996, 108.
[16] K. Dyson, *The State Tradition in Western Europe* (Oxford, 1980).

exercise of administrative power. The common values go back a long way. Medieval customary law recognised duties to indemnify citizens for expropriation or for the effects of civil disturbances.[17] It is argued by Mestre that the grounds of review recognised by English administrative law have much in common with pre-Revolutionary France.[18] The suggestion is that there is a stock of common values which has served to influence the proper control exercised by the law over the state since medieval times. The nineteenth century witnessed a growing agreement on fundamental rights of the citizen and the need to subject the administration to judicial control. But, if liberal political principles had some influence, then radically distinct political agendas produced institutional arrangements which were governed by distinct principles. The convergence in recent years on policies such as privatisation has dismantled many state monopolies and blurred the public and private divide, as well as reducing the importance of public sector employment.[19] We are left with many institutional arrangements which are similar because there is an agreed political agenda. The distinctive organisations of the State have become similar through this process. (All the same, we should not be deceived into thinking that fundamental attachments to "the public service", "collaboration with social partners" and to the distinctiveness of public employment do not still create divisions between legal systems.) Luisa Torchia talks about concerns for open government, the access of the public to administrative reasons and documents.[20] There are also concerns to develop citizens' charters in a number of countries to change the culture of public servants. The commonality of the political and administrative agenda provides scope for collaboration.

The second area of convergence is in the pressure exerted by EC law and European Convention on Human Rights (ECHR) case law. Both supranational systems set a common agenda to which each legal system has to adapt. Areas such as prisoners' rights, delay in litigation, protection against telephone tapping have been important. But the setting of a basic agenda in Sweden and the Netherlands in terms of basic standards of redress against the administration have also been significant.[21] European Community law has been significant in defining civil servants, defining areas in which there is a state interest to protect which justifies restricting competition, and in setting up competition in public procurement. The destruction of telecom and postal monopolies, as well as freedom of broadcasting all help to harmonise the institutions and practices of the administration across the European Union. The basic subject-matter regulated by public law has changed. In addition, the

[17] Mestre, *supra* n. 8, 99–101.
[18] J. Mestre in E. V. Heylen (ed.), *Verwaltung und Verwaltungsrecht* (1996) 8 JEV 37.
[19] A good example is the development of Italian public employment from a classical state bureaucracy to more private law models outside a narrow core of governmental functions: see M. Rusciano and L. Zoppoli, *L'impiego pubblico nel diritto del lavoro* (Turin, 1993), esp. ch. 6.
[20] L. Torchia, *Il procedimento amministrativo: profili comparati* (Milan, 1993).
[21] See *Benthem* v. *Netherlands* (1985) 8 EHRR 1; *Pudas* v. *Sweden* (1987) ECHR, ser. A, vol. 125 and A. W. Bradley, "Administrative Justice: A Developing Human Right?" [1995] 1 *EPL* 347.

development of EU law and the ECHR is a common enterprise in which lawyers from different jurisdictions are engaged. In trying to solve problems together, there is a natural pressure for convergence. In developing the rules of administrative law to govern EU institutions, there is an inevitable need to produce a solution with which individuals from different jurisdictions can work.

The third aspect of convergence resulting from the above is an increased legalisation of administrative relations. The German report in Schwarze's collection notes that informal administrative interpretation cannot be relied upon as sufficient implementation of EC norms.[22] The whole area of public procurement is far more regulated than it was in order to secure competition. The ECHR has had similar effects on the rights of prisoners and concepts of legitimate expectation, the giving of reasons and access to government information have the result of greater formalisation. The changes which the Swedes and Dutch have introduced into their administrative law systems as a reaction to decisions of the European Court of Human Rights are more legalistic than what was there before. Quite a number of countries have moved to developing codes of administrative procedure which then give rights in law. There is a cultural shift away from informal regulation (which typically benefits the administration) to more formal legal rights which can be enforced by citizens in the courts. The increase in administrative litigation in many countries reflects how the situation has changed.

Fourthly, there is convergence on terminology and even on concepts. A prerequisite for any working together is an agreement on the language within which to discuss issues. Whatever national terminology one uses, a common agenda encourages an understanding of others' terminology and the use of a common vocabulary. In Schwarze's work, it is interesting that most national reporters mention the concept of "proportionality" as evidence of Europeanisation of domestic administrative law. It is as if this term crystallises existing understandings developed under different labels in national law. There is less emphasis in the national reports that the recognition of "proportionality" as a ground of judicial review of administrative action represents a greater intensity of review from what was there before.[23] The concept of "legitimate expectation" provides a different outcome. For some systems, the case law of the ECJ in this area offers a new standard which is adopted, for others it offers no advance on the past and is even resisted as being less progressive.[24] Have we learnt a new language, or are we learning new values which will subject the administration to a different level of scrutiny?

---

[22] *Supra* n. 4, 128.

[23] The point can be reinforced by examining further jurisdictions. Thus Norwegian writing makes use of proportionality (*forholdsmessighet*) to bring together various aspects of law and judicial decision-making over a long period of time, but questions whether this constitutes a general principle (*proporsjonalitetsprinsipp*): Eckhoff and Smith, *supra* n. 12, 301–4 and 375–6.

[24] Compare Schwarze *supra* n. 4, 415 (Greece) and 723 (Spain) with 568, 572–4 (Netherlands).

The last question represents a serious issue for any analysis of Europeanisation. New values, new (common) activities are the basis for real change, real development. The use of new concepts or new (common) terminology may just be a matter of repackaging what we have been doing for years. The fact that we all use the same label "proportionality" does not necessarily denote a change in policy or action.

C. THE DYNAMICS OF DISTINCTIVENESS

"Notre droit administratif, plus que tout autre branche du droit français, apparaissait commun un droit strictement franco-français, pratiquement un gallicisme juridique de bon aloi. Or l'européanisation' va conduire de façon plus ou moins forcée à un certain métissage du droit administratif français."[25]

The sense that administrative law is special is not confined to the French. Martin Loughlin has argued:

"The journey of finding effective, enlightened and liberating conditions of government is a journey through history and on tracks formed within specific cultural traditions. The maps drawn by societies other than our own are undoubtedly of innate interest. . . . But as guides on the journey they must be treated with great circumspection."[26]

Zweigert and Kötz identify certain features as central to the distinctiveness of a legal family. These are basically: history, style of legal thought, ideology, sources and legal concepts.[27] Each of these builds towards a distinctive style of a legal system. The Roman origins of French law, a strongly conceptual and deductive style of legal reasoning, and distinctive legal concepts make it different from the English common law despite the common liberal political ideology. The core of this analysis is that law is not just a set of rules or norms, but a way of thinking. Although law involves a tradition of handing on texts, the central element of the tradition is the approach which is adopted to the texts and the process of interpretation.[28] Zweigert and Kötz, and more recently Samuel and Legrand, have argued that *mentalité* is a defining feature of a legal culture and legal tradition.[29] To take an analogy, it is not just that France and England simply eat different kinds of bread; the *boulangerie* and its bread play a different part in social life. It is the difference in legal culture

[25] Flauss, in Schwarze, *supra* n. 4, 113.
[26] "The Importance of Elsewhere" (1993) 4 *Pub. Law Rev.* 44 at 57.
[27] *Supra* n. 6, 69.
[28] M. Krygier, "Law as Tradition" (1986) 5 *Law and Philosophy* 237; see also J. Bell, "The Acceptability of Legal Arguments" in N. MacCormick and P. Birks (eds.), *The Legal Mind* (Oxford, Clarendon Press, 1986) 45 at 53–6.
[29] Zweigert and Kötz, *supra* n. 6, 71; G. Samuel, *The Foundations of Legal Reasoning* (Antwerp, 1995), 28; P. Legrand, "European Legal Systems are not Converging" (1996) 45 *ICLQ* 52.

and not just the content or procedure of law which the various authors have highlighted.

Legrand has made much of the idea that differences in *mentalité* are actually an obstacle to genuine Europeanisation. He argues that legal systems are not really converging because of common rules, since there is no growing together of legal cultures.[30] The idea of a *mentalité* expresses a difference in world view:

> "The essential key for an appreciation of legal culture lies in an unravelling of the cognitive structure that characterises that culture. The aim must be to try to define the frame of perception and understanding of a legal community so as to explicate how a community thinks about the law and why it thinks about the law in the way it does. The comparatist must, therefore, focus on the cognitive structure of a given legal culture and more specifically on the epistemological foundations of that cognitive structure. it is this epistemological substratum which best epitomises what I wish to refer to as the legal *mentalité* (the collective mental programme) or the interiorised legal culture, within a given legal culture."[31]

His point is that you must go beyond rules to examine the symbolic and perceptual features which bring the law in a particular system together. When examined in this way, there is "a primordial cleavage" between civil and common law.[32] This is demonstrated in legal reasoning, the importance of systematisation, the character of rules, the role of facts, the meaning of rights and the relationship of present law to the past.

More recently, he has argued that the nature of legal cultures is such that a European civil code is a forlorn and useless project.[33] It is interesting to note that, alone of the contributors to his book, Jürgen Schwarze thinks that there is something to be gained from having a European code of administrative law. The objections are primarily that it would add nothing, but there is a certain similarity of others in approach to Legrand.

I would accept that there is something in this analysis. The suggestion is that a French lawyer will approach a problem differently from an English lawyer. To take an example of whether a beneficiary can sue a lawyer for a negligently drafted will, the French lawyer starts with a different conceptual grid in which distinctive concepts of "contract" and "delict" play a significant part, and for which privity is understood in a special way. The reasoning process focuses on the framework of the civil code and the strong influence of doctrinal legal writing, as well as case law. Ideas of rights and adherence to principle will be important. These aspects of doctrinal coherence and acceptability of the legal arguments are not just historical, but shape the approach of current lawyers. You only have to read *White* v. *Jones*[34] to see

---

[30] *Supra* n. 29.
[31] *Ibid.*, 60.
[32] *Ibid.*, 63.
[33] P. Legrand, "Against a European Civil Code" (1997) 60 *MLR* 44.
[34] [1995] 2 AC 207.

the force of these aspects of a legal tradition. The way you have learnt your law, its conceptual map, the conceptions of doctrinal coherence and acceptable legal argument, the authoritative sources which must be used are all part of a legal culture. For this reason, Zweigert and Kötz suggest that "legal institutions", as I describe them legal concepts, are much more important features in distinguishing legal mentalities and legal families than the sources from which the law is drawn.[35]

I would depart from Legrand's pessimistic stance in two respects: first, there is a difference between a system's self-presentation and what goes on and, secondly, legal cultures are neither homogeneous nor unchanging.

My first point is that the way legal systems present themselves to the outside world, particularly in academic writing, often exaggerates what actually goes on. I have made this point at length elsewhere[36] and will rehearse only part of the argument. Having spent some months sitting in on cases decided in French administrative courts, notably in the Conseil d'Etat, I think I detected a strong similarity in reasoning between French and English administrative judges.[37] Almost all the forms of legal argument which are described in Neil MacCormick's *Legal Reasoning and Legal Theory*[38] can be found in the way French judges and *commissaires du gouvernement* argue, either in public or in private sessions. Now this may just be that French administrative law is not codified and is, in reality, a kind of common law system. The authorities in French administrative law are judicial and doctrinal legal writing features only as prominently as in English law (if that). But a similar exercise conducted by Mitchel Lasser[39] in relation to French private law has yielded very similar results to my own. The pragmatics of judicial decision-making make legal reasoning rather similar. The judgment published may be of a different style, but it serves a different function. As Lasser suggests, there are reasons why the self-presentation in case law, supported by academic introductions to the French legal system, perpetuate a myth. What is presented in introductions to law is a doctrinal paradigm of legal reasoning which is fed by the exiguous nature of the reasons given in judicial judgments. But there is a different perception on legal reasoning if you look at how judges work, which is the paradigm used in the common law. One must, I think, be wary of suggesting that *mentalité* is a great barrier. The ECJ, like other international courts, is a good example of how *mentalité* does not seem to get in the way. It may well be that the operational context is critical to behaviour

---

[35] *Supra* n. 6, 71.

[36] J. Bell, "English Law and French Law—Not so Different?" [1995] *CLP* 63, 80–90.

[37] See J. Bell, "Reflections on the Procedure of the Conseil d'État" in G. Hand and J. McBride (eds.), *Droit sans Frontières* (1991), 211

[38] Oxford, 1978. See also, D. N.MacCormick and R. S. Summers, *Interpreting Precedents. A Comparative Study*, ch. 18.

[39] M. Lasser, "Judicial (Self-)Portraits: Judicial Discourse in the French Legal System", 104 *Yale LJ* 1325 (1995).

and approaches to law, at least as much as inherited culture and conceptual maps.[40]

Basil Markesinis has suggested that this argument perhaps underestimates the influence of the self-presentation of a legal system in terms of legal education and advocacy in court.[41] He certainly has a point but, in terms of mechanisms for cross-fertilisation, the importance of the operational context and the ability of judges (or practising lawyers) to transcend differences of legal culture provide an important qualification to the arguments of Legrand.

The discussion of French administrative law indicates that the French legal system is not homogeneous. French private law is codified, but public law and, to a lesser extent, commercial law is not. The French legal system is made up of a number of legal cultures. The administrative law culture differs from the private law culture, the culture of criminal law differs from that in constitutional law. Other systems are more or less unified. The different cultures demonstrate that there is a spectrum within which we all have to work. There is not a monolith. The other feature is that the cultures are not unchanging. To take a simple example, the modern textbook. The French private law textbook owes its format and origin in German treatises of the mid-nineteenth century. The English textbook owes its origin to the French and its casebooks owe their origins to the Americans. Not only texts, but also doctrines have proved possible to move, such as frustration and mistake in contract law.[42] The doctrine of proportionality seems to be a similar migrant concept.

In summary, the notion of distinct *mentalités* is a significant feature of legal systems, but it is not determinative. This feature of a culture is not a barrier to either collaboration or the migration of ideas. It may, however, identify limits to homogenisation. Pierre Legrand talks of different *govern-mentalités* between different legal systems.[43] There are different ideas about how the State should function which underpin administrative law. There are also differences in whether powers are inherent in the State or not. But here, the difference is not between common law and civil law, but between French-influenced systems and the rest. The common values of liberal democracy and the collaboration involved in the EU project ensure that there is scope for change within individual legal systems. Recent developments in the Netherlands are perhaps the clearest indication of the way the ECHR has been able to influence a national administrative law.

---

[40] I am grateful to Prof. Alan Dashwood for this point.
[41] B. Markesinis, *Foreign Law and Comparative Methodology* (Oxford, Hart, 1997), 23.
[42] A. W. B. Simpson, "Innovation in Nineteenth Century Contract Law" (1975) 91 *LQR* 247.
[43] 45 *ICLQ* 75.

D. THE DYNAMICS OF EUROPEANISATION

Rob Widdershoven and Roel de Lange suggest that chasing European influences in national law is like chasing the Abominable Snowman.[44] Though not sharing the despair of those authors, we need to recognise that the task is not easy. It is therefore appropriate to start with thoughts from private law.

In discussing the Europeanisation of private law, Basil Markesinis[45] identifies five features encouraging convergence:

(1) legal education, especially the SOCRATES programme, develops young lawyers who are aware of and interested in other legal systems;

(2) judges and practitioners are involved in a practice of law which is more European in terms of the norms applied and working with other lawyers or judges in resolving legal problems;

(3) there are international conventions which provide common standards across all countries in matters such as sales, transport of goods and persons, child abduction, etc., but they also create an "atmosphere" in which the national lawyer is used to comparing national solutions with those of the wider international community;

(4) EC directives and ECJ/ECHR case law provide common points of reference outside the national tradition and create a common dynamic of policy development and the creation of standards. These create a process of common judicial development;

(5) there are at root common social problems which all legal systems have to deal with and which are not specific to a particular country. Issues such as consumer protection, the weakening of traditional family ties, the growing awareness of entitlements, pornography transcend national boundaries and require solutions which are not dependent on traditional legal classifications.

In brief, he argues that "as a result of multiple influences, one can argue that a new corpus of law, a kind of European *jus commune*, is gradually developing and, indeed, it may be developing faster than one is prepared to acknowledge".[46] This analysis is equally applicable to the migration of conceptions.

At its core, this analysis depends on a view of what makes up a legal culture. I have argued elsewhere that a legal tradition "is not just rules and processes, but is essentially the practice of people who operate and perpetuate the tradition. . . . The existence of institutions brings us to the heart of a legal tradition. A tradition is a set of practices among a caste of lawyers."[47]

---

[44] In J. Schwarze, *supra* n. 4, 540.

[45] *The Gradual Convergence* (Oxford, 1994), 21.

[46] *Supra* n. 41, 20.

[47] J. Bell, "Comparative Law and Legal Theory" in W. Krawietz *et al.*, *Prescriptive Formality and Normative Rationality in Modern Legal Systems. Festschrift for Robert S. Summers* (Berlin, 1994), 19 at 29.

Just as Legrand focuses on the *mentalité* which is developed by that legal community, so Markesinis concentrates on the institutional structures and practices which shape legal thinking. Van Caenegem has identified professors, judges and law givers as the three main institutional actors in legal development, but he sees political history as important in shaping the respective roles of each in that process.[48] His emphasis is on both the key players shaping a legal culture and the way the law fits into the political climate of the day.

Legrand is heavily influenced by the way separate legal education, reinforced by constant use of certain forms of legal argument and legal sources, helps to define a distinctive outlook as a lawyer. But, for Markesinis, a broader focus of academic education (for a minority) and the constant requirement in certain aspects of practice to go beyond national norms and national approaches to interpretation help to encourage a broader outlook. There is a political climate into which this fits. The collaborative venture of the European courts, international treaties and resolving common problems offer a common sense of direction which help to produce a different self-perception: not as just an English or a French lawyer, but as also a European lawyer. Hein Kötz makes a similar point. He argues[49] that unification of law is not achieved primarily through common legislation, but rather through the development of a common legal culture:

> "The emphasis should be on encouraging the growth of a common European legal culture. Comparative lawyers should seek opportunities to support that shared culture by common training, building a common legal literature, creating occasions for the exchange and transfer of common experience. This emphasis is likely to result in less attention to the technicalities of uniform legislation and more attention to the substance both in European legal science and in the training of European lawyers. This movement must aim at the identification and teaching of common legal principles and institutions which the European nations have in common, in other words: of a European common law, a European *ius commune*."[50]

Kötz is clear that there needs to be common legislation, but that this is not enough. It creates the occasion for collaboration, but does not produce a common result or change a legal outlook. After all, norms have to be interpreted and can be interpreted in different ways. In addition, the purpose of norms may not be appreciated. The old joke among Catholic canon lawyers is that canon law is made in Rome to be kept the other side of the Alps! There are cultural approaches to law and its place in society which have to be factored into an analysis of legal evolution.

As I have suggested, we need to view the work of lawyers not only in terms of a legal culture, but also in terms of an operational setting. The institutional setting (of lawyers, courts and processes) is only part of the institutional

---

[48] R. C. Van Caenegem, *Judges, Legislators and Professors* (Cambridge, 1987), 108.
[49] "Comparative Legal Research and its Function in the Development of Harmonized Law. The European Perspective" in N. Jareborg, *Towards Universal Law* (Uppsala, 1995), 20.
[50] *Ibid.*, 27–8.

context; there is also the wider non-institutional context of the community which the law serves.[51] We need to understand legal development in this complex setting, rather than just to trace legal rules and their implementation in other legal systems.

In summary, we can say that to identify the influences of harmonisation, we need to look at common rules and concepts, and the influence of common courts interpreting these, but also the "atmosphere" which this creates of looking beyond national rules and ways of approaching questions. We also need to look for the indicators of an emerging common culture in legal education, legal practice, and legal thinking, notably in the development of collaborative projects to deal with common of novel issues.

The form of current European influence

The most frequently noted items of influence on national laws in the reports in Schwarze and elsewhere[52] focus on the protection of legitimate interests, the regime of government liability for non-implementation of EC rules or for restitution of unlawfully paid monies, and proportionality. The second is clearly a European influence since it requires national implementation of EC rules. This process of direct incorporation of foreign concepts because they are part of domestic law is significant.[53] Koopmans has argued that there is a European administrative law in the making as the European Convention and EC law combine together to set standards both for Community institutions and for Member States.[54] Each is directly effective in most EU States, so that national judges are applying common norms as interpreted by common courts as an integral part of national law. National judges have to apply ideas which are not native to their own legal system

The fact of this process of direct application of external norms provokes a review of existing national norms, even where EC law or the ECHR is not directly relevant. There is then the question of how far national legal systems are prepared to have a two-speed justice—one set of standards when EC or ECHR law applies and one for purely domestic cases. No legal system seems willing to tolerate this, unless it believes the external norm to be fundamentally wrong. In a classic case like *M v. Home Office*,[55] national law is brought

---

[51] See further V. Gessner, A. Hoeland and C. Varga, *European Legal Cultures* (Aldershot, Gower 1996), 245–50.

[52] See *Actualité Juridique—Droit Administratif*, special issue, 20 June 1996, 110–55.

[53] E.g. *R. v. Chief Constable of Sussex, ex parte International Trader's Ferry Ltd* [1997] 2 All ER 65 using proportionality to interpret art. 36 EEC. This is the process described by Koopmans as external rules operating as internal norms: *infra* n. 54, 61.

[54] T. Koopmans, "European Public Law: Reality and Prospects" [1991] *PL* 53. Both he and Galmot, *infra* n. 62, refer to Case 222/84 *Johnston v. Chief Constable of Northern Ireland* [1987] QB 129 as an illustration of this movement.

[55] [1993] 3 All ER 537; [1994] 1 AC 277.

into line with EC law, even where no EC issue is at stake. This is the "atmospheric" effect of international treaties well identified by Markesinis. The fact of having to work together in implementing a common legal system and administrative structure though distinct national laws inevitably encourages comparison between the approaches of different legal systems. From English law, one can note the way in which ECJ decisions on remedies have influenced the House of Lords to develop domestic remedies against the administration in *M* v. *Home Office* and *Woolwich BS* v. *IRC*.[56] A similar development can be seen in other jurisdictions.[57] But such national developments illustrate the way in which cross-fertilisation takes place. The confrontation with another system or an international legal order provides the propitious moment for a development in national law. The national legal order tries to find the most appropriate way to accommodate the new insight into its own conceptual structure and legal culture. As a result, the national solutions are not identical in form, even if they may be broadly similar in result.[58]

The source of such change is less clear when a doctrinal label is borrowed from EC law, though is also prevalent in other Member States. Thus the Dutch would argue that their use of proportionality owes as much to the influence of German legal writing as to the influence of EC and ECHR law.[59] Indeed, though the modern use of the term has its origins in Prussian administrative law, the idea can be found operating in fourteenth century French law.[60] What we have is a judicial and doctrinal debate which crystallises around certain terms. These terms are then used to rationalise existing national concepts and to produce a new impetus within national administrative law.[61] The operation of EC or ECHR law may be the catalyst for comparative reflection, but it does not mean that those legal systems are the source from which the change is drawn.

The European systems themselves have to develop an administrative law for EC institutions or to put flesh on the ECHR. These are developed by selecting ideas from the different national legal systems. Although the judges of the ECJ do not want any "levelling down" it is clear that the selection of the "most advanced" legal approach to problems forms part of the Court's role

---

[56] [1993] 3 All ER 537; [1993] AC 70.

[57] For France see CE Ass. 28 Feb. 1992, *Soc. Arizona Tabacco Products*, AJDA 1992, 210. The concept of "legitimate expectation" has a similar impact on national legal systems, e.g. TA Strasbourg, 8 Dec. 1994, Rfda 1995, 963.

[58] Paul Craig's proposals for developing English tort liability after *Brasserie du Pêcheur* are a good illustration of how cross-fertilisation of this kind occurs: "Once More Unto the Breach: The Community, the State and Damages Liability" (1997) 113 *LQR* 67 and Chapter 6 *supra*.

[59] Schwarze, *supra* n. 4, 555.

[60] See PrOVG, 10 Apr. 1886, Sammlung PrOVGE 13, 424 (control of police powers concerning the sale of alcohol); Mestre, *supra* n. 8, 136–7 concerning the enlargement of the square of the church of St. Agricola in Avignon.

[61] A good illustration is the work of Jowell in "Proportionality: Neither Novel nor Dangerous" in *New Directions in Judicial Review* (London, 1988), 51.

and that comparative law is an essential tool in this process.[62] The various "general principles of law recognised by the constitutions of Member States" are an explicit recognition of this process of influence and selection. Once set as a "Eurostandard", it serves as a point of reference to be accepted or rejected by national legal systems. But the "Eurostandard" is equally applicable to EC institutions and in that way there is a mutual influence.

The comments in Schwarze and elsewhere suggest that this process of comparison and influence has some way to go before it becomes a major feature of national legal systems. Most commentators recognise that, in terms of the procedure of administrative justice, the ECHR is having a major influence, securing adequate remedies, access to the courts and reduction in delay.[63] EC law is seen as involving rather specific sectoral rules. Indeed, the German report suggests that the ECJ produces a set of individual decisions without an overall set of principles.[64] Jean-Bernard Auby remarks:

> "Since Community law increasingly impregnates administrative law, a European administrative law is well and truly in the process of developing, but without administrative law becoming totally European."[65]

This remark corresponds with that of Flauss in the Schwarze collection that European administrative law principles remain primarily accessory aspects of domestic administrative law: to fill gaps and to act as a corrective.[66] The dominant influences are national, but the European legal standards, derived from a selection from national administrative laws, provide a vehicle for cross-fertilisation.

What mechanisms are in place?

If we examine these forces for cross-fertilisation, we can notice a number of sources of influence.

Informal mechanisms

Academic writing and education: Van Caenegem writes that: "In contrast with the judge and the lawgiver the jurist has no direct power, cannot send anyone to prison, or proclaim laws. The best he can do is to try and influence those in power, or simply to serve them."[67] The process of influence involves

[62] See Y. Galmot, "Réflexions sur le recours au droit comparé" [1990] *RFDA* 255. For an analysis of the often implicit value-judgments involved in such use of comparative law see J. Hill, "Comparative Law, Law Reform and Legal Theory" (1989) 9 *OJLS* 101.
[63] See A. W. Bradley, *supra* n. 21, for a fuller analysis.
[64] Schwarze, *supra* n. 4, 207.
[65] "Le droit administratif européen: entre l'observation et l'hypothèse", *AJDA* special issue 20 June 1996, 189 at 192.
[66] Schwarze, *supra* n. 4, 101.
[67] *Supra* n. 48, 155.

creating a climate and even an agenda into which judges and law-givers are drawn. Comparison of other systems has long been a trait of academic writing. Dicey's long discussion of French administrative law was influential in shaping domestic legal thinking and in encouraging detailed study of how the French system works. More recent writing on the United States and Canada has offered the British different models of public law development. In part, as with Dicey, the process is one of self-definition: we define ourselves by reference to other countries and note our distinctiveness. The study of proportionality, open government and judicial review procedure has served to offer ideas for reform which are then picked up as the opportunity presents. In more recent times, the study of United Kingdom privatisation has provided challenges to domestic conceptions of administrative law in other European countries. It is often where legal traditions consider themselves to be underdeveloped that they look outside for ideas and benchmarks. English administrative law scholarship certainly looked to France in the 1950s and 1960s; Danish and Dutch legal scholarship looked especially to Germany. But the Danes note that in recent years their system has been more self-contained as the system has developed.[68]

The use of EC law and ECHR law as major elements of the domestic legal education of future lawyers (or as part of continuing education) provides a further opportunity for the study of the different ideas. SOCRATES provides a cross-fertilisation within the student body, such that those learning law in a particular university will not all plan to practise in that jurisdiction. Furthermore, it becomes accepted that the qualification in private international law required to become a lawyer in Belgium can be acquired by studying that subject in Spain. This mutual recognition, plus more specifically designed common courses, help foster an idea that the activity of learning the law is not narrowly confined to what is done by a national group of students in order to qualify in a national legal profession.

Judges and practitioners: practice requires lawyers of different jurisdictions to work together on deals and in courts. This has been less true of administrative lawyers since they have tended to work for or in relation to their own governments. Privatisation and developments such as the regulation of public procurement has broken down this national perspective to some extent. It is said that the idea of "proportionality" gained currency among judges in Europe who worked together on the internal tribunal of the ILO dealing with discipline in staff cases, although they were each making use of concepts which were current in their own countries.[69] Ideas about what is "the most advanced" set of principles on remedies etc. are also supported by the

---

[68] Schwarze *supra* n. 4, 401.

[69] See X. Phillipe, *Le contrôle de proportionnalité dans les jurisprudences constitutionnelles et administratives françaises* (Paris, 1990), 52–3 commenting on the ILO court's decisions of 14 May 1973, *Ferrechia* and *Khelifati* in which the judges were Letourneur (France), Lord Devlin (UK), and Grisel (Switzerland). Letourneur was the judge who introduced proportionality into French law.

common understandings developed from working together in the same court. The need to collaborate in the implementation of decisions and in operating the same law has encouraged more exchanges of an informal kind among judges. Visits between senior judges in France and England are now institutionalised.

GROTIUS for practitioners, like SOCRATES for students, is designed to foster this process of mutual understanding. What is sought is a way of influencing the opinion-formers, creating intellectual leadership among key actors to move away from attachment to national conceptions of what is right and to seek better solutions if they can be found elsewhere. In some European countries, the key elites are academic. In other administrative law systems, such as France and Britain, the elites are judges. The parentage of ideas such as proportionality in different legal systems is interesting. The key actors in France in promoting the idea of proportionality have been initially judicial, influenced by their experience in other judicial discussions.[70] By contrast, the running in Britain has been made by academics who have gradually won round a number of key judges. But the acceptability of the idea in both systems has depended on judicial pronouncements. As Van Caenegem points out, intellectual leadership has to be performed by persuading key actors within the legal system, whether by collaboration or by standing out with distinct views.[71]

Formal mechanisms

In many areas, as Aldo Sandulli has suggested, there is not only a *spontaneous* development of a national legal system under the influence of ideas from professors or judges, but there may be more formal *guided* development as a result of legislation, especially at EU and ECHR levels.[72]

1. *Lawgivers*: the legislative process is frequently preceded by comparative studies. Legislation at the European level certainly involves this. Among the major examples, one can point to the creation of Ombudsmen in different European countries in the 1960s and 1970s, or to privatisation in the 1980s and 1990s. Solutions to problems were adopted and adapted to national requirements such that the British and French ombudsmen are different from the Scandinavian, and French privatisation has different aspects from the English system. The Dutch reform of its administrative justice is a good example of the development of an indigenous model under a European impetus. The creation of a formal administrative court structure has retained much of what was previously involved in tribunals, but these are now linked to the judicial system in a formal way. This indigenous process of fertilisation

[70] See X. Phillipe, *supra* n. 69, 62–79. See also A. Sandulli, "Eccesso di potere e controllo di proporzionalità. Profili comparati" [1995] *Rivista trimestrale di diritto pubblico* 329 at 330–5.
[71] *Supra* n. 48, 157.
[72] *Supra* n. 70, 354.

reflects the particular historical and political contexts in which decisions were taken. Vincent Wright has demonstrated this in his analysis of the French and Italian Councils of State.[73] The Italian was influenced by the French, but is different in some significant ways, notably in terms of the influence of the *corps* of their Councilors in government. This is the result of different historical and political conditions in Piedmont and Paris which shaped their evolution.

2. *Judges*: the judicial input arises from the acceptance that judges do make rules in any legal system, though the authority attached varies in its binding-ness.[74] In developing national law, there is a general process of comparison and, as has been mentioned, one of paralleling of developments which have been imposed on the national law by EC and ECHR law. This is a process of internal harmonisation to prevent a kind of two-speed legal system with one set of ideas and values being applied to implement an international treaty and another to implement national law.

Within a legal family, there has long been comparison, e.g. English courts looking at common law developments and French courts looking to Italy and Germany. The phenomenon of inter-family comparison has been rarer, though it is not unknown.[75] The discussion of economic loss and privity by Lord Goff in *White* v. *Jones*[76] is a rarer example of inter-family comparison. In administrative law, I know of fewer examples of this process. I think administrative law has been seen as a relationship between individuals and their own State defined by the particular political conditions of that State, and so comparisons made across legal families in court are rarer, though they are frequent in academic writing.

The extent of cross-fertilisation

This last point on the sources for comparison brings into focus the extent of any real comparison. I would suggest that there are four aspects of adminis-trative law which merit consideration: administrative institutions, administra-tive procedures, procedures for judicial review and basic values governing the administration. I do not believe developments and cross-fertilisation are likely to be the same in each.

Administrative institutions change under European and national political pressure. For example, the civil service has been redefined in continental legal

---

[73] V. Wright, "Conseil d'Etat" e Consiglio di Stato: le radici storiche della loro diversità" in Y. Mény, *Il Consiglio di Stato in Francia e in Italia* (Bologna, 1994) 23 at pp. 48–50.

[74] See D. N. MacCormick and R.S. Summers (eds.), *Interpreting Precedent* (Aldershot, 1997), ch. 14.

[75] See e.g. the discussion with counsel in *Thomas* v. *Thomas* (1842) 2 QB 851 and the wide ranging review of motor car reform by le Marc'hadour in his *rapport* to Cass. ch. réun. 13 Feb. 1930, *Jand'heur c. Les Galéries Belfortaises*, D. 1930.1. 57.

[76] *Supra* n. 34.

systems to comply with requirements of free movement of labour. It was unacceptable that posts as train drivers could be reserved to nationals simply because they were civil service posts. Privatisation of telecommunications has gathered pace as a result of EC directives ensuring freedom of competition. In other areas, privatisation in Britain was copied because it seemed to offer non-governmental sources for investment and offer potential for greater efficiency in the long run and capital for other government projects in the short term. This is not to suggest that there has not been a great deal of national tailoring of how privatisation operates.[77] But it is a good example of cross-fertilisation across the divide between common law and civil law systems.

Administrative procedures are also subject to common influences. The recent decisions of the ECJ requiring access to documents in EU affairs[78] reflect the broader movement of open government within Europe and outside. It is in the area of administrative procedure that the ECHR has been significant. Duties to give reasons and to allow access to information have been introduced in various countries.[79] Other countries in Europe have gone further and enacted codes of administrative procedure which enshrine some of these ideas. Again there is a sense that the liberal political agenda and contemporary values help to shape administrative procedure. But the evidence is that the appropriate moment is dictated by domestic political circumstances much more than by formal external pressure. The example of other countries is useful, especially where the ECHR has taken some lead e.g. on prisoners' rights, but on the whole, it has not been the driving force for political change in this area.

Judicial review procedures are perhaps the most nationally idiosyncratic aspects of administrative law. The explanations for the structure of any one country owe as much to history and chance as they do to any deep-seated rationale. There have been various reforms in recent years where countries have taken ideas from other systems, e.g. procedures for limiting access, for widening standing, or for establishing a reference on a point of law. But the form these have taken represent as much a distinctive national development as they do a borrowing from another system. In particular, the connection between administrative and ordinary civil procedures is distinctive from system to system for a whole variety of reasons.[80]

It is in the area of values that there has been perhaps the clearest common development. Human rights protection is only one aspect. Changes in the conception of public services have resulted in "customer friendly" approaches in a number of countries—you get paid if trains are late in a large number of

---

[77] C. Graham and T. Prosser, *Privatizing Public Enterprise* (Oxford, 1991); S. Cassese, *La nuova costituzione economica* (Rome, 1995), Part VI.

[78] Case T–194/94, *Carvel* v. *EU Council* [1996] All ER (EC) 53.

[79] See L. Torchia, *supra* n. 20.

[80] For an analysis, see CERAP, *Le contrôle juridictionnel de l'administration* (Paris, 1991), chs. 2 and 3.

countries now. The role of the State seems common ground between Spanish socialists and German conservatives. Sometimes these ideas are enshrined in EU or ECHR legislation, but often they are just the common currency of political debate.

CONCLUSION

My conclusion is that to evaluate the processes of cross-fertilisation which are taking place in Europe, we need to appreciate the nature of a legal system. A legal system is not just a set of rules (or even principles), but is a set of traditions and practices which shape and sustain an attitude to law and its role in society (Legrand's notion of a *mentalité*). The legal system, in the last analysis, depends on the operation of a legal community. If the legal system and its tradition are to change, it is necessary that key actors, law givers, judges and academics exert influence. As Van Caenegem points out, whatever the good ideas among academics and judges, there needs to be a political climate and will in favour of change.

Administrative law is traditionally more nationally specific than private law. Whereas private commercial relationships are relatively common between different countries, relations of individuals to specific forms of government are quite distinct. Institutions of government are very divergent. For example, forms of local government, structures of ministries and the organisation of the civil service are quite different between France, Italy, Sweden and the United Kingdom. How an individual is affected by government is different in consequence. As has been stated, procedures for judicial review are also very different. These differences set a framework within which any changes have to fit. Thus even if there is commonness of values and a willingness to change, the form in which change will take place is likely to vary from country to country. Even if there is agreement on the policy outcome, there will not be uniformity in application. Cross-fertilisation will involve careful selection and adaptation of ideas from other legal systems to develop indigenous concepts and rules which can fit into the domestic tradition. On the whole, administrative law, linked as it is to political processes, will remain stronger ground for cross-fertilisation than for transplants.

12

Transplantation and Cross-fertilisation

JOHN W. F. ALLISON*

In a recent article, Alan Watson emphasises the "obvious fact of massive borrowing" by and within legal systems and the hesitancy of scholars "to consider its implications".[1] Extensive interaction between legal systems is certainly obvious in European public law. While the European Court of Justice (ECJ) is required to determine the non-contractual liability of the Community "in accordance with the general principles common to the laws of the Member States",[2] national courts are required to apply and, so, become familiar with principles of Community law developed elsewhere. Even in purely domestic law, that is, in cases lacking a Community law component, remedial shortcomings exposed by developments to achieve the effective protection of Community law rights are pressures for change.[3]

How to assess European influences in purely English law is the subject of this Chapter. I will first place them in the context of the long-standing debate on transplantation. I will then elaborate on John Bell's distinction between transplantation and cross-fertilisation[4] and suggest that a process of cross-fertilisation, which takes account of various considerations, such as legal culture and institutional differences, will help avoid the hazards of transplantation. Finally, I will apply the requirements of that process to the potential influence of the ECJ's test for state liability in *Brasserie du Pêcheur*.[5] In particular, I will consider Paul Craig's advocacy of that test as a model to be

---

* This chapter is developed from my comments on the conference papers of John Bell and Paul Craig, *supra* Chaps. 11 and 6 above.

[1] "Aspects of Reception of Law" (1996) 44 *AJCL* 335 at 335.

[2] Art. 215 of the EEC Treaty.

[3] See, e.g., *Woolwich Equitable Building Society* v. *Inland Revenue Commissioners* [1993] AC 70 at 177E; *M* v. *Home Office* [1992] 2 WLR 73 at 99H–100B, 101CD, [1993] 3 WLR 433 at 448F, 463E. See generally W. van Gerven, "Bridging the Gap between Community and National Laws: Towards a Principle of Homogeneity in the Field of Legal Remedies?" (1995) 32 *CML Rev.* 679.

[4] See *supra* Chap. 11 above.

[5] Joined Cases C–46 and 48/93 *Brasserie du Pêcheur* v. *Germany, R.* v. *Transport Secretary, ex parte Factortame Ltd* [1996] All ER (EC) 301.

followed by the English courts in purely domestic law.[6] His advocacy deserves special attention because of its quality and prominence.

About twenty years ago, in a famous article, Otto Kahn-Freund drew attention to the hazards of legal transplantation.[7] He presented his analysis as a development from Montesquieu who had described successful transplantation as extremely uncertain (*"un très grand hasard"*[8]) because laws should conform to the variety of factors—governmental, social and environmental—that together constitute "the spirit of the laws".[9] Kahn-Freund updated Montesquieu's analysis and spelt out its implications for using comparative law in law reform. Whereas Montesquieu had stressed the importance of social and environmental obstacles to transplantation, Kahn-Freund argued that, because of a process of "political differentiation" and "economic, social, cultural assimilation", the political—the proximity of relationship between transplant and power structure—had become more important than the social and environmental.[10] Kahn-Freund stressed that transplantation is more difficult the closer the transplant is to the foreign power structure. He therefore concluded that successful transplantation requires "a knowledge not only of the foreign law, but also of its social, and above all its political context".[11]

Alan Watson[12] took issue with Kahn-Freund and Montesquieu. He denied the hazards of legal transplantation. With particular reference to the reception of Roman law he stressed the frequency of successful borrowing which he attributed, in part, to the judicial need for authority.[13] He depicted transplantation as a source of ideas and an opportunity for reforming the transplant.[14] He argued that political, social and economic differences are not obstacles to transplantation and therefore that "the recipient system does not require any real knowledge of the social, economic, geographical and

---

[6] P. P. Craig, "Once More unto the Breach: The Community, the State and Damages Liability" (1997) 113 *LQR* 67 and Chapter 6 *supra*.

[7] O. Kahn-Freund, "On Uses and Misuses of Comparative Law" (1974) 37 *MLR* 1. See also *id.*, "Common Law and Civil Law—Imaginary and Real Obstacles to Assimilation" in M. Cappelletti (ed.), *New Perspectives for a Common Law of Europe* (Leyden, 1978), 137–68.

[8] Baron Montesquieu, *De l'esprit des loix* (J. Brèthe de la Gressaye (ed.)) (Paris, 1950), i, bk. 1, ch. 3, 26.

[9] Montesquieu, *The Spirit of the Laws* (A. M. Cohler, B. C. Miller and H. S. Stone (trs. and eds.)) (Cambridge, 1989), bk. 1, ch. 3, 8–9.

[10] Kahn-Freund, *supra* n. 7, 8.

[11] *Ibid.*, 27.

[12] A. Watson, "Legal Transplants and Law Reform" (1976) 92 *LQR* 79. See also *id.*, *Legal Transplants: An Approach to Comparative Law* (Edinburgh, 1974); *id.*, "Aspects of Reception", *supra* n. 1.

[13] *Legal Transplants, supra* n. 12, 88–94, 99. In "Aspects of Reception", *supra* n. 1. Watson also emphasises reasons of economic efficiency and the role of sheer chance.

[14] *Legal Transplants, supra* n. 12, 97, 99.

political context of the origin and growth of the original rule".[15] Generally, Watson presented transplantation as an extremely common and normal feature of legal evolution.

Choosing between the positions of Kahn-Freund and Watson was rendered difficult by the good deal of common sense expressed by both. On the one hand, the transplantation of abortion or divorce laws, for example, to a different social and religious context would surely be hazardous or of limited effectiveness.[16] On the other hand, transplantation does seem to have been common in the evolution of legal systems.

A significant conceptual advance has, however, now provided the beginnings of an answer to the dilemma. In Chapter 11 of this volume, John Bell carefully distinguishes between transplantation and cross-fertilisation. He describes transplantation as the direct "transposition of a doctrine from one legal system into another".[17] It may also be described as "mechanical transposition"[18] or, to use Carol Harlow's characteristically vivid turn of phrase, the buying of "fashionable offerings in the cultural bazaar".[19] In contrast, cross-fertilisation, according to Bell, is the indirect promotion, through an external impetus, of careful internal legal evolution fitted to a domestic tradition. The distinction between transplantation and cross-fertilisation, as drawn by Bell, provides a useful synthesis, a useful method of accommodating the views of both Kahn-Freund and Watson. As emphasised by Kahn-Freund, *transplantation*—direct and mechanical—is often of questionable effectiveness. But, as emphasised by Watson, *cross-fertilisation*—indirectly promoted and evolving to suit context—can be both common and desirable.

DISTINGUISHING BETWEEN TRANSPLANTATION AND CROSS-FERTILISATION

The residual difficulty concerns application of the distinction to particular instances of interaction between legal systems. Two prominent examples illustrate the difficulty. First, the concept of proportionality appears from one perspective as a proposed transplant unsuited to the English legal system[20] and, from another, as the object of cross-fertilisation, evolving under the rubric of

---

[15] "Legal Transplants and Law Reform", *supra* n. 12, 81.

[16] See also, e.g., the transplantation of the separation of powers: J. W. F. Allison, *A Continental Distinction in the Common Law: A Historical and Comparative Perspective on English Public Law* (Oxford, 1996), 16–18; J. H. Merryman, "The French Deviation" (1996) 44 *AJCL* 109 at 116–17.

[17] *Supra* 147.

[18] R. Dehousse, "Comparing National and EC Law: The Problem of the Level of Analysis" (1994) 42 *AJCL* 761 at 777.

[19] "Europe, Convergence and Administrative Procedures", Conference Paper, Cambridge, 3 May 1997.

[20] See S. Boyron, "Proportionality in English Administrative Law: A Faulty Transplant?" (1992) 12 *OJLS* 237.

Wednesbury unreasonableness.[21] Secondly, the English public–private divide might seem, at first glance, to be both a questionable transplant[22] and the object of cross-fertilisation because of its home-grown features—its remedial character[23] and increasingly pragmatic application by the English courts.[24] Cross-fertilisation therefore requires further elaboration.

The distinctness of legal systems

As described by John Bell, cross-fertilisation involves a careful response to external influences and internal evolution suited to the distinctness of a legal system. What makes a legal system distinct has been viewed in different ways at different times. Montesquieu originally emphasised the role of environmental factors, such as "the climate, be it freezing, torrid or temperate" and "the properties of the terrain, its location and extent".[25] Then, Kahn-Freund in the 1970s argued that political factors had become more important than the environmental ones. His reason was the process of "political differentiation" resulting in the "gulf between the communist and the non-communist world . . . and that between dictatorships and democracies . . . and a seemingly endless series of variations on the democratic theme".[26] Since Kahn-Freund wrote, the changes in Africa and Eastern Europe and in socialist attitudes to the private sector have considerably reduced the sense of political difference. John Bell points out that the "role of the State seems common ground between Spanish socialists and German conservatives".[27] This political convergence is partly[28] responsible for the current emphasis on the cultural, rather than the political. John Bell, Carol Harlow and Pierre Legrand all[29] describe the distinctness of legal systems by reference to culture or tradition.

---

[21] See J. Jowell and A. Lester, "Proportionality: Neither Novel nor Dangerous" in J. Jowell and D. Oliver (eds.), *New Directions in Judicial Review* (London, 1988), 51–72.

[22] See *Davy* v. *Spelthorne Borough Council* [1983] 3 All ER 278 at 285H; Lord Denning, *The Closing Chapter* (London, 1983), 119; Allison, *supra* n. 16.

[23] See S. A. de Smith, Lord Woolf and J. Jowell, *Judicial Review of Administrative Action* (5th edn., London, 1995), 159–60; Lord Woolf, *Protection of the Public—A New Challenge* (London, 1990), 25–6.

[24] See e.g. *Roy* v. *Kensington and Chelsea and Westminster Family Practitioner Committee* [1992] 2 WLR 239; *Mercury Communications Ltd.* v. *Telecommunications Director* [1996] 1 WLR 48.

[25] *Supra* n. 9, 8–9.

[26] "Uses and Misuses", *supra* n. 7, 11–12.

[27] *Supra* 167.

[28] It has also served as a means of escape from the distinction between base and superstructure in Marxist thinking: G. Samuel, *The Foundations of Legal Reasoning* (Antwerp, 1995), 62–3.

[29] See Bell, *supra* Chap. 11; P. Legrand, "European Legal Systems Are Not Converging" (1996) 45 *ICLQ* 52; *id.*, "Against a European Civil Code" (1997) 60 *MLR* 44.

The difficult concept of legal culture

Culture or tradition is variously characterised. John Bell, for example, argues that a legal tradition "is not just rules and processes, but is essentially the practice of people who operate and perpetuate the tradition. . . . The existence of institutions brings us to the heart of a legal tradition. A tradition is a set of practices among a caste of lawyers".[30] In contrast, Pierre Legrand argues that the "essential key for an appreciation of a legal culture lies in an unravelling of the cognitive structure that characterises that culture".[31] Elsewhere, he states that:

> "The notion of 'legal tradition' implies, among other features, an idiosyncratic cognitive approach to law. In other words, there have developed, and there exist, both a civil law and a common law mentalité—two different ways of thinking about the law, about what it is to have knowledge of law and about the role of law in society."[32]

He explains the difference in cognitive structure by reference to differences in legal reasoning and in approaches to rules, facts and rights *inter alia.*[33]

How legal culture is characterised matters because it affects the view of obstacles in the way of transplantation, the adaptations necessary in cross-fertilisation, and the potential for consequent convergence. For example, on the one hand, Legrand's emphasis on culture as a world view exposes an insurmountable obstacle, an irreducible "epistemological chasm":

> "A common law lawyer, trained in England, in the context of a particular cognitive approach to systems, rules, facts, rights and the presence of the past, will simply never be able to appreciate a system, a rule, a fact, a right or the past as her Continental counterpart understands them."[34]

For Legrand, "unity can only arise from a commonality of experience, which assumes a commonality of meaning, which presupposes in turn a symbolic community",[35] all of which he suggests are rendered unattainable by the epistemological chasm between the civil law and the common law. On the other hand, Bell's characterisation of legal culture as practice highlights indicators of an emerging common European legal culture in legal education, collaborative projects, and the work of courts and practitioners.[36] A certain convergence through cross-fertilisation is then feasible.

---

[30] "Comparative Law and Legal Theory" in W. Krawietz *et al., Prescriptive Formality and Normative Rationality in Modern Legal Systems. Festschrift for Robert S. Summers* (Berlin, 1994), 19 at 29.
[31] "European Legal Systems", *supra* n. 29, 60.
[32] "Against a European Civil Code", *supra* n. 29, 45.
[33] "European Legal Systems", *supra* n. 29, 64 ff.
[34] *Ibid.,* 79.
[35] "Against a European Civil Code", *supra* n. 29, 60. See Samuel, *supra* n. 28, especially at 294.
[36] See 158–160 above.

Bell advances various good reasons for not characterising culture in terms of world view and for not adopting Legrand's pessimistic stance on convergence. He rightly warns that a system's self-presentation may misrepresent real practices[37] and stresses that "legal cultures are neither homogeneous nor unchanging".[38] His telling points, however, raise general doubts about the use of a concept of culture or tradition in dealing with issues of transplantation, cross-fertilisation and convergence. When we apply the concept of culture, we are required to grasp a multiplicity of cultures in any one system, their changing character and some reality behind a system's self-presentation. If we look beyond that self-presentation, we see a range of practices, institutions and procedures, but face the difficult question, what makes any particular practice cultural or traditional, what makes it expressive of culture or tradition? Furthermore, we can expect culture or tradition often to be most influential when unnoticed and not in issue.[39] According to Legrand, " 'culture' concerns frameworks of intangibles within which interpretive communities operate" and as "culture shapes legal culture, legal culture fashions culture".[40] We are then, by implication, required to look at both the intangibles of legal culture and those of culture at large in society. In the face of such daunting tasks, an understandable tendency is indeed to treat culture as homogeneous and unchanging, to speak in general terms of the culture of "the civil law" and that of "the common law".[41] The concept of legal culture has then become a great grey soup into which anything and everything may be put.

A concept of legal culture is nonetheless difficult to dispense with. Traditional attitudes affect cross-fertilisation profoundly. Two famous and far-reaching examples illustrate their effect. In France, distrust of *gouvernement des juges* transformed Montesquieu's separation of powers, derived from his study of the rough English separation, into a radical prohibition of judicial interference with executive and legislature.[42] And, in England, the aversion to *droit administratif* expressed and perpetuated by Dicey's *Law of the Constitution* for successive generations obstructed the development of an English public law comparable to the French.[43] Some concept of legal culture

[37] See, e.g., the misleading traditional view of the role of case law on the Continent. On this, see generally J. P. Dawson, *The Oracles of the Law* (Ann Arbor, 1968), chap. 5; A. Watson, *The Making of the Civil Law* (London, 1981), 39 ff.; M. Shapiro, *Courts: A Comparative and Political Analysis* (Chicago, 1981), chap. 3.

[38] *Supra* 156. See also Legrand, "European Legal Systems", *supra* n. 29, 63–4; *id.*, "Against a European Civil Code", *supra* n. 29, 45, especially n. 7. See, e.g., L. Torchia, Chap. 10 above; P. Birkinshaw, "European Integration and United Kingdom Constitutional Law" (1997) 3 *EPL* 57.

[39] See M. Krygier, "Law as Tradition" (1986) 5 *Law and Philosophy* 237 at 246.

[40] "European Legal Systems", *supra* n. 29, 56; *id.*, "Against a European Civil Code", *supra* n. 29, 48–9, especially n. 30.

[41] See e.g. Legrand, "European Legal Systems", *supra* n. 29, 64–74, 79; *id.*, "Against a European Civil Code", *supra* n. 29, 55–6.

[42] See J. W. F. Allison, "Cultural Divergence, the Separation of Powers and the Public-Private Divide" (1997) 9 *ERPL* 1.

[43] A. V. Dicey, *An Introduction to the Study of the Law of the Constitution*, (10th edn., London, 1959), chap. 12. See, e.g., Lord Hewart, *The New Despotism* (London, 1929), 37–42;

or tradition is required to emphasise the role of historic[44] attitudes and to clarify their continuing relevance to the resilience of established institutions and the receptivity to inspiration from elsewhere.

A concept of legal culture might usefully denote an environment of traditional attitudes but should be elaborated with care and treated with caution. As John Bell reminds us, legal cultures are not homogenous and are open to change. Conceptual elaboration can help explain Bell's caveats. Attitudes that are traditional[45] may be characterised by their origins in experiences of the past, their significance in the present and an interpretive process by which they are transmitted from past to present. Whereas changes occur in transmission, homogeneity is precluded by variation in historical experiences and their histories. An inquiry into legal culture is therefore unavoidably difficult but need not be all-embracing. Understood as an environment of traditional attitudes, legal culture need not subsume the rules, processes, practices and institutions that also characterise a distinct legal system.[46] Although relevant to cross-fertilisation, it is but one consideration amongst others more amenable to analysis.

Other considerations

Adapting or evolving a distinct legal system in response to an external impetus may involve legal doctrines, prevailing theories and judicial institutions and procedures. At least the following considerations therefore require attention if cross-fertilisation is not to degenerate into hazardous transplantation. First, we need to consider doctrinal ramifications—how legal rules and doctrines might adapt to the external impetus and whether or how they might still fulfil the functions[47] we require them to fulfil. In English administrative law, for example, the evolution of legitimate expectation calls into question the doctrinal distinction between review of the procedure and that of the substance of administrative decision-making.[48]

Donoughmore Committee, *Report of the Committee on Ministers' Powers* (London, 1932), Cmnd. 4060, 110–12; Franks Committee, *Report of the Committee on Administrative Tribunals and Enquiries* (London, 1957), Cmnd. 218, paras. 121–3. See generally Allison, *supra* n. 16, 18–23, 157–63.

[44] An appreciation of the continuing significance of history is common to various writings on the distinctness of legal systems. See, e.g., K. Zweigert and H. Kötz, *An Introduction to Comparative Law* (2nd edn., Oxford, 1992), 69; Kahn-Freund, "Obstacles to Assimilation", *supra* n. 7, 158–68; R. C. van Caenegem, *Judges, Legislators and Professors: Chapters in European Legal History* (Cambridge, 1987), especially at 108.

[45] See Krygier's rigorous analysis of the concept of tradition in "Law as Tradition", *supra* n. 39.

[46] Cf. Bell quoted *supra* 173.

[47] In "Comparing National and EC Law", Dehousse elaborates on the significance of functional differences, *supra* n. 18.

[48] See *R. v. Minister of Agriculture, Fisheries and Food, ex parte Hamble Fisheries* [1995] 2 All ER 714; *R. v. Transport Secretary, ex parte Richmond upon Thames London Borough Council* [1994] 1 All ER 577; C. F. Forsyth, "The Provenance and Protection of Legitimate Expectations" (1988) 47 *CLJ* 238.

Secondly, we need to consider how the internal adaptation might be justified in the legal and political theory or theories underpinning the legal system.[49] The development of an English distinction between public and private
law is illustrative. Nigel Simmonds argues that "the distinction . . . depends
on substantive issues of political theory":

> "It is only in the context of a political theory that distinguishes between the area of
> autonomy within which individual transactions may have effect according to the
> will of the parties, and the area of central regulation and public planning, that a
> distinction between public and private law can be maintained."[50]

To avoid the distinction's mechanical transplantation, we have then to consider
whether and how those substantive theoretical issues might be addressed.[51]

Thirdly, we need to consider how domestic judicial institutions and procedures might cope with the proposed doctrinal adaptation. In English administrative law, for example, Lord Lowry found reason to reject the concept of
proportionality beyond the rubric of *Wednesbury* unreasonableness by considering that English judges would not be "equipped by training or experience" to apply it, or "furnished with the requisite knowledge and advice".[52]
Institutions and procedures can be reformed,[53] but existing and continuing
restrictions on judicial competence remain crucial to cross-fertilisation.

THE ECJ'S TEST FOR STATE LIABILITY AS A MODEL FOR ENGLISH
COURTS

The requirements of cross-fertilisation can be applied to Paul Craig's persuasive advocacy of the ECJ's decision in *Brasserie du Pêcheur*.[54] He argues that,
even in English cases in which there is no Community law component, the
ECJ's jurisprudence "shows a way of adding to the existing heads of liability,
without thereby imposing excessive burdens upon public authorities".[55] He
suggests that the English courts would do well to draw on the ECJ's test for
state liability with its criterion of sufficiently serious breach.

---

[49] Cf. P. P. Craig, *Public Law and Democracy in the United Kingdom and Unites States of
America* (Oxford, 1990), 3.

[50] N. E. Simmonds, *The Decline of Juridical Reason: Doctrine and Theory in the Legal Order*
(Manchester, 1984), 130–1.

[51] See generally J. W. F. Allison, "Theoretical and Institutional Underpinnings of a Separate
Administrative Law" in M. Taggart (ed.), *The Province of Administrative Law* (Oxford, 1997),
71–89.

[52] *Brind* v. *Home Secretary* [1991] 1 All ER 720 at 739B.

[53] See, e.g., proposed correctives to adversarial procedures in England: Lord Woolf, *Access to
Justice: Final Report to the Lord Chancellor on the Civil Justice System in England and Wales*
(London, 1996); *id.*, *Protection of the Public*, *supra* n. 23, 109–13; M. Loughlin, "Innovative
Financing in Local Government: The Limits of Legal Instrumentalism—Part II" [1991] *PL* 568; J.
W. F. Allison, "The Procedural Reason for Judicial Restraint" [1994] *PL* 452.

[54] *Supra* n. 6 and Chapter 6.

[55] "Once More unto the Breach", *supra* n. 6, 89–94, especially at 90.

In reaching his far-reaching conclusion, Craig has demonstrated the general caution required in cross-fertilisation. Four years ago, after *Francovich*,[56] he described the difficulty of extending state liability to breach of Community law in general. He fully recognised that an extension could be regarded as "the opening of Pandora's box" with an impact beyond Community law.[57] He concluded: "One thing is clear. If strict liability for an invalid (or illegal) act does become the norm, then the business of government will become risky indeed".[58] Only after *Brasserie du Pêcheur* and further analysis does he express general approval. In contrast to his general caution, however, his regard for the specific considerations crucial to cross-fertilisation is open to question.

Legal culture

Advocacy of the ECJ's test for state liability as a model for English courts encounters at least two traditional attitudes in English legal culture: one, towards the public–private divide; another, towards the judicial activism demonstrated by the ECJ.

First, the ECJ adopted a principle of state liability and must therefore distinguish the state and, in so doing, draw a public–private divide. In English law, a traditional scepticism towards such a divide is evident in the extremely rare use of the concept of the state. That scepticism was powerfully expressed by Dicey in his analysis of the rule of law and persists in the criticism of the procedural distinction established in *O'Reilly* v. *Mackman*.[59] In comparison with Continental traditions, the English legal tradition appears stateless, and the state's identity, peculiarly problematic.[60]

Craig does mention the problem of identifying various bodies, such as fringe organisations and privatised utilities with a *de facto* or *de iure* monopoly, as state bodies for the purpose of imposing liability.[61] He does not, however, attempt to resolve it or rely on the ECJ's own attempts. In *Foster*, the ECJ laid down criteria for applying its own public–private distinction, introduced in *Marshall*, that restricts the direct effect of directives to the vertical plane, that is, to the state and bodies emanating from the state.[62] As pointed

---

[56] Cases C–6/90 and 9/90 *Francovich* v. *Italian Republic* [1991] ECR I–5357.

[57] "*Francovich*, Remedies and the Scope of Damages Liability" (1993) 109 *LQR* 595 at 620.

[58] *Ibid.*, 621.

[59] [1982] 3 All ER 1124; Dicey, *supra* n. 43, chap. 4.

[60] Notions of the Crown and individual officers of the Crown have been preferred to a legal concept of the state. See H. W. R. Wade, "The Crown—Old Platitudes and New Heresies" (1992) 142 *NLJ* 1275, 1315; Allison, *supra* n. 16, chaps. 4–5; *id.*, "Theoretical and Institutional Underpinnings of a Separate Administrative Law", *supra* n. 51, 72–9. On neglect of the "state" in the British intellectual tradition, see K. H. F. Dyson, *The State Tradition in Western Europe: A Study of an Idea and Institution* (Oxford, 1980), chap. 7.

[61] "Once More unto the Breach", *supra* n. 6, 70–1.

[62] Case C–188/89 *Foster* v. *British Gas plc.* [1990] ECR I–3313; Case C–152/84 *Marshall* v. *Southampton and South West Hampshire Area Health Authority (Teaching)* [1986] ECR 723.

out by Craig, however, it may not adopt the same criteria when dealing with liability. And, even if it does so, its criteria are open to a "range of possible meanings"[63] and are difficult to apply.[64]

Furthermore, traditional English scepticism towards distinguishing public from private is confirmed within the very realm of Community law by the strong criticism of the ECJ's public–private distinction in *Marshall*. To those distrustful of the public–private divide, it must appear ironic that, although the public–private distinction restricting the direct effect of directives to the state and its emanations was seriously challenged in *Faccini Dori*,[65] a similar distinction has now been given new significance in the area of liability. In *Francovich*, the ECJ ameliorated the distinction restricting the scope of directives with direct effect by providing for state liability in the event of their non-implementation by a state legislature. In *Brasserie du Pêcheur*, it has aggravated the problem of distinguishing public from private by imposing liability on state bodies generally. How the ECJ's test for state liability can serve as a model nonetheless and in the stateless English legal tradition is unclear.

Secondly, Craig's advocacy of the ECJ's test as a model encounters a traditional distrust of the activism demonstrated by the ECJ. Craig recognises the distrust:

"Some will doubtless view these decisions [on state liability] as another example of unwarranted judicial activism. The judgments will be criticised for reading into the Treaty new obligations which are not explicitly contained therein. The possibility of a Treaty amendment, made pursuant to the 1996 Intergovernmental Conference, to limit the E.C.J.'s powers will be raised once again."[66]

To the distrust, Craig responds as follows:

"Any proper analysis of whether the Court has done so [overstepped its proper bounds] can only be determined in the light of two connected considerations. One is the Treaty itself and the obligations contained therein. The other consideration is the theory of adjudication and interpretation which is brought to bear on this basic document. Critics of the E.C.J. rarely if ever make clear their assumptions concerning the theory of adjudication and interpretation which the Court should adopt."[67]

The ECJ's advocates, however, would more easily allay cultural concerns about activism by elaborating on their own theory of adjudication than by expecting one from its critics. Craig does suggest specific justifications in Community law for the very existence of state liability but does not himself suggest a theory of adjudication, nor one that might justify an activist imitation by national courts in purely national law. Craig's analysis could not be

[63] Craig, *supra* n. 6, 71.
[64] See, e.g., *Doughty* v. *Rolls-Royce plc.* [1992] 1 CMLR 1045.
[65] See the AG's powerful advocacy that directives be given horizontal direct effect in Case C–91/92 *Faccini Dori* v. *Recreb Srl.* [1995] All ER (EC) 1.
[66] *Supra* n. 6, 77.
[67] *Ibid.*, 77–8.

all-inclusive but, in a continuing process of cross-fertilisation, advocates of the ECJ's test for state liability need to address concerns about judicial activism.

Doctrinal adaptation

Craig provides a rigorous analysis of how English courts might draw on the ECJ's test for state liability in developing the torts of negligence and breach of statutory duty. He concludes that the ECJ's "test does encapsulate an appropriate balance between the need to make government financially liable for its actions, and the equally important necessity of not imposing on government a too onerous regime of liability, which could hinder it in the discharge of its responsibilities".[68] His analysis itself does emphasise how the justiciability concerns of the English courts might be accommodated, but his overall conclusion equates Community and domestic governmental needs and neglects functional differences between Community and domestic rules[69] on state liability. In *Brasserie du Pêcheur*, the ECJ was principally concerned with rendering Community law effective: "As appears from the judgment in *Francovich* . . . , the full effectiveness of Community law would be impaired if individuals were unable to obtain redress when their rights were infringed by a breach of Community law."[70] In contrast, the English courts have been preoccupied both with avoiding the non-justiciable and with not dictating financial priorities to government.[71] Whether the balance encapsulated by the ECJ's test can be appropriate in both Community law and English law despite significant functional differences is questionable. In English law, different needs weigh down the balance.

Theoretical implications

If the English courts were generally to apply the ECJ's test for state liability, they would reduce the disparity between the remedial protection afforded to rights in Community law and that afforded to rights in purely English law. On a number of recent occasions, they have viewed such disparity with unease and dissatisfaction. In *M* v. *Home Office*, Lord Donaldson in the Court of Appeal declared that, as a result of *Factortame (No. 2)*, "[i]t is anomalous and wrong in principle that the powers of the courts to 'hold the ring' pending the resolution of a dispute should be limited where central government is a party

---

[68] *Ibid.*, 89–94, especially at 94.
[69] See generally Dehousse, *supra* n. 18.
[70] *Supra* n. 5, para. 20.
[71] See, e.g., *Dorset Yacht Co.* v. *Home Office* [1970] AC 1004, especially at 1067B–8C; *Anns* v. *Merton London Borough Council* [1978] AC 728, especially at 754C–5F; *X (Minors)* v. *Bedfordshire County Council* [1995] 2 AC 633, especially at 736A–40; C. Harlow, "Fault Liability in French and English Public Law" (1976) 39 *MLR* 516.

to the dispute, particularly when these limitations have been removed by
European Community law if the dispute concerns rights under that law".[72]
Then, in the House of Lords, Lord Woolf described the "unhappy situation"
following *Factortame (No. 2)* "that while a citizen is entitled to obtain injunc-
tive relief (including interim relief) against the Crown or an officer of the
Crown to protect his interests under Community law he cannot do so in respect
of his other interests which may be just as important".[73] His Lordship stressed
that it "would be most regrettable if an approach which is inconsistent with
that which exists in Community law should be allowed to persist if this is not
strictly necessary".[74] And, in the *Woolwich* case, Lord Goff commented that,
"at a time when Community law is becoming increasingly important, it would
be strange if the right of the citizen to recover overpaid charges were to be more
restricted under domestic law than it is under European law".[75]

In the light of the judicial statements of dissatisfaction with remedial disparity, Craig is right to suggest that, while "in formal legal terms the E.C.J.s
decisions (on state liability) will have no impact in cases where there is no
Community law component . . . [i]t is equally clear that this formal legal
result may not reflect reality".[76] But to justify removing remedial disparity, the
English courts face difficult theoretical choices between models for the
Community[77] and views of international obligation. If, on the one hand, they
view the Community merely as the product of international treaties, according to orthodox theory, the rights and remedies thereby created are quite
separate, and therefore are legitimately quite different, from those of domestic law. If on the other hand, they view the Community as an embryonic federation programmed to become an actual federation with a coherent and
unitary legal order,[78] unjustified disparity compromises the programme.
Furthermore, if they do regard the Community merely as the product of international treaties, their attempts to remove remedial disparity between
Community and domestic English law call into question[79] the dualist
separation of international and domestic law in orthodox theory. When the
English courts consider the ECJ's test for state liability as a possible model,
they face theoretical issues that require careful attention in a process of cross-
fertilisation because they crucially affect its desirability and prospects.

[72] *Supra* n. 3, 99H–100B, especially at 101C–D; Case C–213/89 *R.* v. *Transport Secretary, ex parte Factortame Ltd. (No. 2)* [1991] 1 AC 603.
[73] *M.* v. *Home Office, supra* n. 3, 448F.
[74] *Ibid.*, 463E.
[75] *Supra* n. 3, 177E.
[76] *Supra* n. 6, 89. The insertion is my own.
[77] See T. C. Hartley, "The European Court, Judicial Objectivity and the Constitution of the European Union" (1996) 112 *LQR* 95, especially at 109.
[78] See, e.g., W. van Gerven, "Bridging the Gap between Community and National Laws", *supra* n. 3, 699 ff.; *id.*, "Toward a Coherent Constitutional System within the European Union" (1996) 2 *EPL* 81; *id.*, "Bridging the Unbridgeable: Community and National Tort Laws after *Francovich* and *Brasserie*" (1996) 45 *ICLQ* 507 at 537 ff.
[79] See also *Hamble Fisheries, supra* n. 48, 724F ff.; Birkinshaw, *supra* n. 38, 65–70.

Unexplained dissatisfaction with remedial disparity is insufficient.

Institutional and procedural competence

In a long line of English cases—*Dorset Yacht Co., Anns* and *X (Minors)* v. *Bedfordshire County Council*[80]—English courts have restricted the liability of public authorities in negligence by reference to the non-justiciability of policy decisions. Lord Browne-Wilkinson, in the *Bedfordshire County Council* case, summarises the general outcome. He asks "[i]s the negligence relied upon negligence in the exercise of a statutory discretion involving policy considerations" and adds "if so the claim will pro tanto fail as being non-justiciable".[81] Craig presents the judicial concern about justiciability as a reason for the English courts to borrow from the ECJ's test in *Brasserie du Pêcheur*. He argues that the ECJ's requirement that the breach of law be sufficiently serious is capable of accommodating the concerns of English courts not to adjudicate upon matters unsuited to judicial resolution.[82]

Craig describes justiciability as a common concern, explicit in the decisions of the English courts and implicit in the jurisprudence of the ECJ.[83] Consideration of its converse, however, would have suggested differences. Whereas justiciability refers to the kind of issue suited to judicial resolution, its converse—the institutional and procedural competence of a court—refers to the qualities of a court suited to resolve a particular issue. The institutional and procedural characteristics of the ECJ and of the national administrative courts applying Community law on the Continent differ substantially from those[84] of English courts. The ECJ does, for example, benefit from the independent conclusions of the Advocate General. Furthermore, in *Faccini Dori*, the court itself, quite unlike an English court, canvassed the views of the Commission and all Member States before it decided not to attribute horizontal direct effect to directives.[85] Because of institutional and procedural differences, the ECJ's test for liability is of questionable suitability to English courts deciding cases in purely English law.

In a process of cross-fertilisation, the question of judicial competence—whether courts are competent to deal with a doctrinal innovation—is addressed. Differences in competence require attention and, if significant, necessitate doctrinal adaptation or appropriate institutional and procedural reforms. If disparity between liability in Community law and that in purely

[80] See *supra* n. 71.
[81] *Supra* n. 71, 740EF.
[82] *Supra* n. 6, 89–94.
[83] *Ibid.*, 93.
[84] See, e.g., Loughlin, *supra* n. 53; Allison, *supra* n. 53; J. A. G. Griffith, "Judicial Decision-making in Public Law" [1985] *PL* 564. See generally, Allison, *supra* n. 16, chaps. 7–10.
[85] See *Faccini Dori, supra* n. 65, 5H–6A.
[86] See generally the references *supra* n. 53.

English law does undermine the required coherence of the European Union's legal order, any significant differences in competence are additional reasons for the reform of English judicial institutions and procedures.[86] After *Francovich*,[87] Craig referred to the possible opening of Pandora's box.[88] In the classical myth, at the bottom of her box lay hope with which to ameliorate the emergent problems. To end remedial disparity in the area of liability, that hope would have to be vindicated by reforms which render what is justiciable in European law similarly justiciable in purely English law.

CONCLUSION

The considerations relevant to cross-fertilisation, ranging from the cultural to the procedural, are extensive. They can seldom receive comprehensive treatment in any one analysis, such as Craig's, subject to constraints of time and space. But, if generally neglected in European public law—whether in the case of proportionality, the public–private divide or the principle of state liability—the distinction between cross-fertilisation and transplantation is blurred. Then, the "incoming tide"[89] of Community law swells into a tidal wave that threatens domestic law.

---

[87] See *supra* n. 56.
[88] See *supra* n. 57.
[89] Lord Denning in *Bulmer* v. *Bollinger* [1974] Ch. 401 at 418F.

13

Epilogue: Recent Developments in the Law relating to State Liability in Damages

TAKIS TRIDIMAS

THE AFTERMATH OF FRANCOVICH

One of the themes of the law pertaining to state liability in damages which was identified in this volume as giving rise to particular problems is the interaction between Community law and national law in defining the right to reparation.[1] In three recent cases the Court had the opportunity to consider, on references by Italian courts, issues pertaining to the conditions imposed by national law on the right to reparation. Following the judgment in *Francovich*, by a Legislative Degree adopted on 27 January 1992, Italy took steps to implement Directive 80/987[2] and provide compensation to those who suffered loss as a result of its belated implementation. The Legislative Degree provided that actions for reparation must be brought within a period of one year from the date of its entry into force. Also, it applied retroactively to claims for reparation the implementing measures and the limitations imposed therein on the liability of the guarantee institutions to meet outstanding wage claims of employees of insolvent employers. Both aspects of the Legislative Degree were challenged on grounds of incompatibility with Community law.

TIME LIMIT

The time limit of one year was challenged in *Palmisani v INPS*.[3] It will be remembered that according to *Francovich* and *Brasserie du Pêcheur*,[4] the

---

[1] *Supra*, esp. Chapters 1, 5 and 7.
[2] Council Directive 80/987 on the approximation of the laws of the Member States relating to the protection of employees in the event of the insolvency of their employer, OJ 1908 L 283, p. 23. The Directive has been amended by Directive 87/164, OJ 1987 L 66, p. 11.
[3] Case C-261/95 *Palmisani v Istituto Nazionale della Previdenza Sociale (INPS)*, judgment of 10 July 1997.
[4] *Supra*, p. 27.

conditions governing the right to reparation must not be less favourable than those relating to similar domestic claims (the requirement of non-discrimination or equivalence) and must not be such as to make it virtually impossible or excessively difficult to obtain reparation (the requirement of effective protection). In *Palmisani* the Court had no difficulty in finding that the one year time limit satisfied the requirement of effective protection. It was a reasonable period within which persons harmed by the belated transposition could protect their rights. The requirement of equivalence was more contentious. The national court referred for the purposes of comparison to time limits applicable to other claims. Thus, in implementation of Directive 80/987, the Legislative Degree provided a prescription period of one year for benefits payable under the Directive, running from the date of submission of the application for the benefit to the Guarantee Fund. The Court held that applications for payments provided by the Directive and those made under the compensation scheme for its belated transposition differ as to their objective. The former aim to provide employees with specific guarantees of payment of unpaid remuneration in the event of the insolvency of their employer. The latter, by contrast, seek to make good the loss sustained by the beneficiaries of the Directive as a result of its belated transposition. The Court also noted that reparation cannot always be ensured by retroactive and proper application in full of the measures implementing the directive. Given the different nature of the claims, it was not necessary to undertake a comparison of the time limits applicable to them. For the same reason, the Court rejected a comparison with the time limit applicable under Italian law for obtaining social security benefits.[5]

The national court also referred to the limitation period applicable under ordinary law to claims for non-contractual liability. This is set by the Italian Civil Code to five years. The Court held that compensation for the belated implementation of a directive and the ordinary system of non-contractual liability pursued essentially the same objective, namely to effect reparation of the loss sustained as a result of unlawful conduct. They were therefore comparable. The Court did not possess all the information necessary to determine whether an action for damages brought by an individual pursuant to the Italian Civil Code could be directed against public authorities and left it to the national court to undertake that examination. The Court stated that if the ordinary system of non-contractual liability were to prove incapable of serving as a basis for an action against public authorities and the national court were unable to undertake any other relevant comparison between the time limit in issue and the conditions relating to similar claims of a domestic nature, the conclusion would have to be drawn that the one year time limit was not precluded by Community law.[6]

[5] *Palmisani*, op.cit., n. 2, paras 33–37.
[6] Op.cit., paras 38–39.

The judgment in *Palmisani* is somewhat inconclusive and leaves ample discretion to the national court. The Court of Justice is prepared to grant national courts more latitude with regard to the requirement of equivalence than with regard to the requirement of minimum protection. This is understandable since the question whether the conditions governing the exercise of a Community claim offer the requisite degree of protection is a matter for the Court to decide. By contrast, the requirement of equivalence requires a comparison to be made with the rules applicable to similar domestic claims and national courts are better placed to determine whether such actions exist under national law. This policy of deference followed by the Court of Justice undoubtedly has advantages. As already stated, the case law seeks to strike a balance between effective protection of Community rights and procedural autonomy of the national legal systems. A drawback of this approach is that it may lead to discrepancies in the degree of protection available to Community rights even within the same Member State, depending on the court seized of the claim. In appropriate cases, the Court may find that it has to offer more guidance on the issue of comparability of claims.

RETROACTIVE APPLICATION OF IMPLEMENTING MEASURES

Article 4(2) of Directive 80/987 allows Member States to limit the liability of the guarantee institutions to payment of outstanding claims for certain periods of the employment relationship and grants to Member States a number of options for determining those periods. In implementation of the Directive, the Legislative Degree took advantage of Article 4(2) and applied the same limitation of liability retrospectively to the compensation payable to employees who suffered loss from the belated transposition of the Directive. The Legislative Degree also provided for an upper limit on payments by guarantee institutions pursuant to Article 4(3) of the Directive[7] and applied the same limitation to reparation.

In *Maso v INPS*[8] and *Bonifaci v INPS*,[9] the question was referred whether a Member State is entitled to apply retroactively to claims of reparation belatedly adopted implementing measures, including the limitations provided for in Article 4(2). The Court held that retroactive application in full of the measures implementing the Directive to employees who have suffered loss as a result of belated transposition enables in principle the harmful consequences of the breach to be remedied, provided that the Directive

[7] Article 4(3) allows Member States to set a ceiling on payments by guarantee institutions in order to avoid the payment of sums going beyond the social objective of the Directive.

[8] Case C-373/95 *Maso, Graziana and Others v Istituto Nazionale della Previdenza Sociale (INPS) and Italian Republic*, judgment of 10 July 1997.

[9] Joined Cases C-94 and C-95/95 *Bonifaci, Berto and Others v Istituto Nazionale della Previdenza Sociale (INPS)*, judgment of 10 July 1997.

has been transposed properly.[10] Such application, should have the effect of guaranteeing to those employees the rights from which they would have benefited if the Directive had been transposed within the prescribed period. With regard to Directive 80/987, retroactive application of implementing measures necessarily implies that a limitation of the guarantee institution's liability may also be applied, in accordance with Article 4(2), where the Member State has in fact exercised that option when transposing the Directive into national law. The Court however added a *caveat*. It stated that it is for the national court to ensure that reparation for the loss sustained is adequate. Retroactive and proper application in full of the measures implementing the directive will suffice unless the beneficiaries establish the existence of complementary loss sustained on account of the fact that they were unable to benefit at the appropriate time from the financial advantages guaranteed by the Directive. In such a case, the complementary loss must also be made good.[11]

In principle, therefore retroactive application of implementing measures suffices to ensure reparation. It follows that, where a directive grants several options to Member States, a Member State is not estopped from exercising the most favourable option under the directive *vis-à-vis* those who have suffered as a result of belated implementation. The Court however pointed out that reparation is not always wholly ensured by retroactive application of implementing measures even where such measures transpose the directive fully into national law. The purpose of reparation is to ensure that the person who has suffered loss as a result of non-implementation is put in the same position that he would have been had the directive been implemented fully in time. A number of questions remain unanswered. For example, it is not clear what complementary losses can be said to have been sustained "on account of the fact"[12] that the employees were unable to benefit at the appropriate time from the financial advantages guaranteed by the Directive. Although the Court did not discuss further the issue of causation of consequential losses, it is not safe

---

[10] In *Maso* and *Bonifaci* the Court found that the Legislative Degree fell short of implementing the Directive properly. It calculated the period of employment for the outstanding wage claims of which guarantee institutions were responsible by reference to the date of declaration of insolvency rather than the date of the onset of insolvency, namely, the date when a request was made for the opening of insolvency proceedings. Given that the judgment declaring insolvency may be delivered long after the request to open proceedings, the effect of the Legislative Degree was that payment of outstanding wage claims might not be guaranteed for any period of employment. That would be contrary to the objectives of the Directive.

[11] *Maso*, op.cit., paras 39-42; *Bonifaci*, op.cit., paras 51-54. In *Maso* the Court also held that any rules against aggregation of claims contained in the implementing legislation may also be applied provided that they do not affect the rights conferred by the Directive. The Legislative Degree prohibited aggregation of outstanding wage claims and of claims to reparation with the *indennità di mobilità* (job seekers allowance) granted by Italian law. The Court found that the prohibition of aggregation was incompatible with the Directive because the *indennità di mobilità* was provided in the three months following the termination of employment and did not arise from the employment relationship.

[12] See *Maso*, op.cit., para 41; *Bonifaci*, op.cit., para 53.

to conclude that it is governed solely by national law. It is not realistic to expect the Court to give detailed guidance on such issues in a general and abstract manner. The case law can be expected to develop incrementally in response to specific questions asked by national courts.

It seems that a Member State may not apply to those who have suffered loss as a result of belated implementation a less favourable regime than that provided by the implementing measures. It is not permissible for example to provide a lower ceiling for compensation than that provided for payments by the guarantee institutions to meet outstanding wage claims in the future. Those who suffer loss as a result of belated implementation must be brought in the same position that they would have been if the Member State had adopted the directive in time as it chose to adopt it belatedly.

FACTORTAME: THE RESPONSE OF THE DIVISIONAL COURT

Following the judgment of the Court of Justice in *Brasserie du Pêcheur and Factortame,* the Divisional Court delivered its long awaited judgment in *R v Secretary of State for Transport ex parte Factortame Ltd* on 31 July 1997.[13] The issues before the Divisional Court were whether the breach of the United Kingdom was sufficiently serious and whether the applicants were entitled to exemplary damages.

With regard to the seriousness of the violation, the Divisional Court found that the United Kingdom had acted in good faith. At the time when the Merchant Shipping Act was implemented, the Government reasonably believed on the basis of the legal advice which it had obtained that the rules enacted to prevent quota hopping did not constitute a breach of Community law. It held however that each of the conditions of registration imposed by the Act, namely, nationality, domicile and residence, constituted a sufficiently serious breach of the Treaty. It reached that conclusion on the basis of the following factors:

- intended effect of the domicile and residence conditions was to discriminate on grounds of nationality. On the facts therefore there was little to choose between direct and indirect discrimination.
- The Government was aware that the imposition of the conditions would necessarily injure the applicants since the conditions were intended to ensure that the applicants would no longer fish against the British quota.
- The effect of introducing the registration requirements by primary legislation was to make it impossible for the applicants to obtain interim relief without the intervention of the Court of Justice. The Divisional Court

---

[13] The Divisional Court was composed of Hobhouse LJ and Collins and Moses JJ, The Times, 11 September 1997. The account given in the text is based on an unrevised transcript of the judgment.

noted that the applicants were deprived of the opportunity to prevent damage being caused to them. The situation was aggravated because, at least arguably, the measures adopted infringed the principles of proportionality and legitimate expectations. Other methods could have been chosen which would have enabled applications for interim relief to be considered on their merits by the national court. Given that the applicants were forbidden from continuing business activities which they lawfully carried out until the implementation of the Act, they should have been afforded a reasonable opportunity to take measures to avoid serious damage to their interests.

• The attitude of the Commission before the Act was adopted, which it made known to the United Kingdom Government, was hostile to the proposed legislation.

The Divisional Court noted that those factors coupled with the fundamental importance of the principle breached, namely the prohibition of discrimination on grounds of nationality, amounted to a manifest and grave disregard of the limits of the UK's discretion and gave rise to liability in damages.

The following points may be made with regard to the reasoning of the Divisional Court. It is notable that each of the conditions of registration was found to be a serious breach.[14] The rationale of this finding was that all conditions were intended to pursue the same objective, namely to prohibit vessels controlled by Spanish interests to fish against British quotas. The Court noted that, even if registration of vessels had been made subject only to a residence requirement, although the discrimination would have been indirect, it would nevertheless be the intended rather than an incidental effect of the requirement. In the circumstances, therefore, there was no difference between direct and indirect discrimination. The Court was particularly critical of the requirement of domicile. It pointed out that given the strict meaning of domicile in English law, that requirement would be particularly difficult for a foreign national to satisfy and was equally if not more discriminatory than the requirement of nationality. The Divisional Court criticised the Government for not making clear to the Commission and the Court of Justice the stringency of the requirement of domicile.

The Divisional Court rejected the thrust of the Government's defence which was that liability would arise only if it was shown that it acted without legitimate justification. The Government argued essentially that it committed an error of law which was excusable because it had acted on good faith on the basis of legal advice. The Divisional Court rejected that contention stating that, under *Brasserie*, the fact that an error is excusable does not automatically relieve a State of liability. In the circumstances, the

---

[14] It will be remembered that in *Brasserie and Factortame* the Court of Justice held that the requirement of nationality was a serious breach but was more equivocal about the requirements of domicile and residence. *Supra*, p. 22.

reliance on legal advice could not carry any great weight since there was a substantial argument to the contrary and the Government could never have been sure that its view was correct.

Notably, the Divisional Court held that, in assessing whether a breach is serious, account may be taken of the importance of the principle infringed. It pointed out that the prohibition of discrimination on grounds of nationality was one of the fundamental principles of the Treaty. Although the importance of the rule breached was not referred to as a relevant factor by the Court of Justice in *Brasserie and Factortame*,[15] the Divisional Court held that the enumeration of relevant factors in *Brasserie* was not intended to be exhaustive. Two points may be made in relation to this finding. First, it must be borne in mind that the fact that the rule breached is a fundamental one does not necessarily mean that the infringement is manifest. In the circumstances, it seems that the material factor was the Government's insistence to continue to apply the registration requirements even though it became progressively clear that they would be found incompatible with the Treaty.[16] Indeed, one may sympathise with the Government's initial position that any discrimination on grounds of nationality arising from the requirements of registration were a natural consequence of the system of national quotas. Secondly, the importance of the rule breached as a factor of the seriousness of the breach calls for a note of caution. If the basis of state liability in damages is the primacy of Community law, in principle, breach of any rule of Community law by the national legislature may give rise to liability provided that it is intended to confer rights on individuals. The basis of liability is that the rule breached emanates from a hierarchically superior legal order rather than the intrinsic importance of the rule. Liability therefore may not be denied on the ground that the rule breached is not sufficiently "important".

It is of particular interest that in establishing the rules governing state liability, the Divisional Court relied not only on *Brasserie and Factortame* but also on the case law under Article 215(2). The factors influencing liability of Community institutions referred to by Van Gerven AG in *Mulder II* proved particularly influential.[17] In his Opinion, Van Gerven AG referred to the following factors: the importance of the principle of Community law infringed; the fact that the disregard of the principle affected a limited and clearly

---

[15] *Supra*, p. 21, n. 44.

[16] See the judgments in Case C-3/87 *R v Ministry of Agriculture, Fisheries and Food ex parte Agegate* [1989] ECR 4459 and Case C-216/87 *R v Ministry of Agriculture, Fisheries and Food ex parte Jaderow* [1989] ECR 4509 and the interim order in Case C-246/89 *R Commission v United Kingdom* [1989] ECR 3125. The Divisional Court held, in the light of *Brasserie and Factortame*, that the failure of the Government to comply with the Order of the President of the Court in that case by suspending immediately the nationality requirement amounted to a serious breach.

[17] Joined Cases C-104/89 and C-37/90 *Mulder v Council and Commission* [1992] ECR I-3061, at p. 3104.

defined group of commercial operators;[18] the fact that the damage alleged by the applicant went beyond the bounds of economic risks inherent in the operators' activities in the sector concerned; and the fact that the principle in question was infringed without sufficient justification. The Divisional Court found that all those conditions were satisfied on the facts.

All in all, the Divisional Court found that the breach was serious for two reasons: first, because of the manifest character of the breach, which was established by the importance of the rule breached and the circumstances in which the breach occurred, and secondly, because its adverse effects on the applicants' interests were grave. In discussing the manifest and grave test however the Divisional Court considered that the term "grave" does not refer exclusively to the consequences of the breach. It held that, where a breach is effected deliberately and with knowledge that what is being done is unlawful, such breach can properly be described as manifest and grave even if its consequences, taken overall, are not grave.

The judgment of the Divisional Court suggests that a reasonable and bona fide interpretation on the part of a Member State of the limits of its discretionary powers may not suffice to avoid liability. There must be in addition sufficient objective grounds which justify the breach and which, in the circumstances, were lacking.

The Divisional Court attributed particular importance to the views of the Commission as the guardian of Community interest stating that where there is doubt about the legality of any proposed legislation, a failure by a Member State to seek the views of the Commission or, if it receives them, to follow them is likely to lead to any breach being regarded as inexcusable and so manifest. It is doubtful however whether the failure to follow the Commission's opinion should carry the grave consequences suggested by the Divisional Court. Although undoubtedly its views are material, the Commission has no power to provide authentic interpretations of Community law and failure by a Member State to follow its views does not necessarily mean that any breach found subsequently will be inexcusable.

On the issue of exemplary damages, the Divisional Court rejected the arguments of the applicants. It will be remembered that in *Brasserie and Factortame* the Court held that exemplary damages could be awarded pursuant to a claim founded on Community law if they could be awarded for a similar claim founded on domestic law.[19] The Divisional Court took the view that the award of exemplary damages is an inappropriate remedy for the breach of Community law. It pointed out that such damages are punitive rather than compensatory in nature. Referring to *Rookes v Barnard*[20]

---

[18] The relevance of this condition is doubtful given that in its judgment in *Mulder* the Court did not refer to it. Also, the Advocate General qualified it substantially, see *Mulder II*, op.it., pp. 3110–3111.

[19] *Supra*, p.28, n. 70.

[20] [1964] AC 1129.

and *A.B. v South West Water Services Ltd*,[21] it held that exemplary damages may be awarded for oppressive, arbitrary or unconstitutional action by the servants of the government or where statute expressly provides so. The Divisional Court understood liability for breach of Community law as a breach of statutory duty.[22] It followed that exemplary damages could not be awarded since the European Communities Act 1972 did not provide so. The applicants argued that the breach of statutory duty was similar to the tort of misfeasance in public office for which exemplary damages could be awarded. The Court however rejected the analogy pointing out that misfeasance was dependent on knowledge by the defendant that he is breaking the law or at least that he is reckless. By contrast, an action in damages for breach of Community law does not depend on subjective factors nor was there on the facts a case of misfeasance on the part of the United Kingdom.

There is no failing that the Divisional Court was disposed unfavourably towards the award of exemplary damages for breach of Community law. One may sympathise with that view. The Court referred to a number of problems of the law of punitive damages, especially where a large number of individuals are affected by the unlawful conduct of the defendant. Pointing out that the concept of exemplary damages is peculiar to common law, it saw the remedy as a source of divergence in the enforcement of Community law in the various Member States.

CONCLUDING REMARKS

The above cases show that the establishment of Member State liability in damages is by no means the end of the story but marks the beginning of a new chapter in the field of enforcement of Community rights in the national jurisdictions. One may not hold oneself a hostage to fortune by saying that it will be a long chapter and one which will not be easy to write. One of its most distinct characteristics is that it is not written solely by the Court of Justice but is co-authored by the national courts. The greater the inroads Community law makes on remedies, the more it has to rely on national courts for the construction of a coherent system of remedies for the protection of Community rights. The success of the law of remedies, and the ensuing process of internalization of Community law, depends more than any other area of Community law on the successful cooperation of national courts and the Court of Justice.

---

[21] [1993] QB 507.
[22] On this aspect of the judgment, see *supra* Chapters 6 and 7.

Index